SIMPLY DIVINE

A Witch's Book of Divination will help you to realize that your own intuition is the best magical tool of all. Discover how to work with the Law of Correspondences and the language of symbols to interpret a wide range of intriguing and accurate means of divining the future. Personally contact the inner source of harmony that will make your readings come out more clearly and allow you to divine more correctly and precisely.

Simple, practical, useful—here are nine distinctive and unique methods of divination especially designed for use by Wiccans. Classical methods and fresh insights combine to produce powerful, new ways to unlock the deep wisdom of the subconscious. Uncover the hidden influences in your life and reclaim your power of free will. Maximize your chances for personal success and happiness through the ability to see the unseen connections between the inner worlds of imagination and spirit to the material world of shape and form.

Firmly rooted in traditional Wiccan symbolism, here are proven techniques to awaken your intuition and to further train your own clairvoyant powers. Practical exercises, clear instructions, and highly effective methods make these once secret arts of divination eminently learnable—and fun.

Learn how to develop your innate psychic faculties—your ability to see the unseen—as taught by a Wiccan priestess to her own students. Quickly master simple forms of divination such as the Talking Stones, the Witch's Drum, and the Druid's Wand. Go on to explore the more advanced techniques such as the Sword Trance, the Omen Walk or the powerful Dance of the Lame God. *A Witch's Book of Divination* is a comprehensive collection of magical practices drawn from both ancient and modern sources.

ABOUT THE AUTHOR

Callia Underhill's experience in the Craft spans ten years. She is High Priestess of a Traditional Wiccan coven in upstate New York that uses Irish and Arthurian symbolism in its rituals and teachings. She is a member of the Builders of the Adytum; the Order of Bards, Ovates, and Druids; and has studied with the Servants of the Light.

TO WRITE TO THE AUTHOR

If you wish to contact the author or would like more information about this book, please write to:

Callia Underhill
c/o Llewellyn Worldwide
P.O. Box 64383, Dept. K054-X,
St. Paul, MN 55164-0383, U.S.A.

Please enclose a self-addressed, stamped envelope for reply,
or $1.00 to cover costs.
If outside the U.S.A., enclose international postal reply coupon.

Llewellyn Worldwide will forward your request. We cannot guarantee that every letter written to the author can be answered, but all will be forwarded.

FREE CATALOG FROM LLEWELLYN

For more than ninety years Llewellyn has brought its readers knowledge in the fields of metaphysics and human potential. Learn about the newest books in spiritual guidance, natural healing, astrology, occult philosophy, and more. Enjoy book reviews, New Age articles, a calendar of events, plus current advertised products and services. To get your free copy of *Llewellyn's New Worlds*, send your name and address to:

Llewellyn's New Worlds of Mind and Spirit
P.O. Box 64383, Dept. K054-X,
St. Paul, MN 55164-0383, U.S.A.

Llewellyn's Modern Witchcraft Series

A WITCH'S BOOK OF
DIVINATION

CALLIA UNDERHILL

1996
Llewellyn Publications
P.O. Box 64383
St. Paul, MN 55164-0383

Cover design and illustration: Maria Mazzara
Interior illustrations: Anne Marie Garrison
Interior editing, layout, and design: Amy Rost

FIRST EDITION
First Printing, 1996

Library of Congress Cataloging-in-Publication Data

Underhill, Callia, 1967–
    A witch's book of divination / Callia Underhill. — 1st ed.
        p.   cm. — (Llewellyn's modern witchcraft series)
    Includes bibliographical references.
    ISBN 1-56718-054-X (pbk.)
    1. Divination.   I. Title.   II. Series
  BF1751.U53 1996
  133.3'34—dc20   96-27231
                                                CIP

Llewellyn Publications
A Division of Llewellyn Worldwide, Ltd.
P.O. Box 64383
St. Paul, Minnesota 55164-0383

LLEWELLYN'S MODERN WITCHCRAFT SERIES

"Witchcraft" is a word derived from an older word, Wicca or Wicce. The older word means "to bend" or "wise." Thus, those who practiced Wicca were those who followed the path of the Wise. Those who practiced the craft of Wicca were able to bend reality to their desires—they could do magic.

Today, Witchcraft is different from what is was eons ago. Witchcraft is no longer robes and secret rites. During the Aquarian Age—the New Age—the mystical secrets of the past are being made public. The result is a set of spiritual and magical systems with which anyone can feel comfortable. Modern Witchcraft—Wicca—may be the path for you!

Llewellyn's Modern Witchcraft Series of books will not only present the secrets of the Craft of the Wise so that anyone can use them, but will also share successful techniques that are working for Witches throughout the world. This will include philosophies and techniques that at one time were considered foreign to "the Craft," but are now being incorporated by modern Wiccans into their beliefs and procedures.

However, the core of Wicca will stay the same—that is the nature of Witchcraft. All of the books in this series will be practical and easy to use. They will all show a love of nature and a love of the Goddess as well as respect for the Masculine Force. You will find that this series of books is deeply rooted in spirituality, peacefulness and love.

These books will focus on Wicca and Wiccans today, not what was done a hundred, a thousand, or ten thousand years ago. They will help you to expand your horizons and achieve your goals. We invite you to follow this series and look toward the future of what some have called the fastest growing religion in the world, a religion that is personal, non-judgmental and non-institutional, natural, and magical, that brings forth the experience of the sacredness of ALL life. Witchcraft is called "the Old Religion" and it is found present in the oldest myths and artifacts of humanity. This series will help you see what it will develop into tomorrow.

DEDICATION

To L.A. and L.S.

TABLE OF CONTENTS

Illustrations and Tables   ix

Preface   xi

Part I: Introduction, Theory, and Exercises

Chapter One   Introduction   3

Chapter Two   Theory   9

Chapter Three   Exercises   17

Part II: Divination and Diagrams

Chapter Four   Herne's Head   31

Chapter Five   The House of the Goddess   61

Chapter Six   The Witch's Drum   75

Part III: Sticks and Stones

Chapter Seven   A Witch's Geomancy   101

Chapter Eight   Talking Stones   155

Chapter Nine   The Druid's Wand   183

Part IV: Trance Oracles and Divination

Chapter Ten   The Dance of the Lame God   201

Chapter Eleven   The Sword Trance   213

Chapter Twelve   The Omen Walk   227

Appendix   Basic Circle Casting   245
                     and Banishing

Glossary of Terms and Names   253

Bibliography and Suggested Reading   259

Index   265

ILLUSTRATIONS

Figure 4a   A completed Herne's Head. A lip
             around the flat surface will keep your
             stones on the face of the diagram
             when cast.   33

Figure 4b   Diagram for the Herne's Head tool.   35

Figure 4c   Suggested colors for the diagram.   37

Figure 5a   A completed House of the Goddess.   63

Figure 5b   Diagram for the floor of the House
             of the Goddess.   64

Figure 6a   An example of a Witch's Drum
             (with symbols).   77

Figure 6b   Diagram for the Witch's Drum.   79

Figure 6c   Cut the apple horizontally to reveal the
             five seeds forming the five-pointed star.   85

Figure 7   A Witch's geomancy chart.   106

Figure 9a   The Druid's Wand.   187

Figure 9b   Using the Druid's Wand.   189

TABLES

Table 7a   Assigning the Question
             to a Planet   107

Table 7b   The Planetary Intelligences
             and Their Sigils   108

Table 7c   The Geomancy Figures   113

Table 9   The Coelbren of the Bards   186

Table 12a   The Elder Futhark   234–235

Table 12b   The Celtic Ogham Alphabet   236–237

PREFACE

The seed idea for this book took root in the fertile soil of many years of divination use and experience in the context of a Wiccan Circle. I am an initiated High Priestess of an Irish faerie coven tracing its lineage back to Gerald Gardner, although we do not adhere strictly to Gardnerian tradition and practice. The mission, if you will, of this coven (which is now a clan, encompassing several off-shoot covens) has been to teach. Members were and are required to go through several degrees and years worth of notes, exercises, papers, and tests to ultimately reach the High Priesthood. Part of this teaching includes, not surprisingly, divination exercises and techniques.

Divination is performed primarily with familiar and traditional implements: Tarot cards, runes, crystal balls, et cetera. Every year at Samhain we practice scrying with crystal balls, mirrors, or bowls of water. One of the particular gifts of the Witch is being able to see beyond the veil of the mundane. Samhain, as the Witch's Grand Sabbat, is the time when this veil is thinnest, making it the ideal time of year to practice divination.

In addition, part of our regular Circle practice usually includes each person in turn choosing a Tarot card or a rune, then interpreting the card in light of that person's knowledge. We do this in order to gain some insight into our spiritual work for the period of time until the Circle meets again. Students find this very useful and meaningful, and part of the exercise is to encourage them to become familiar with various meanings in different types of divination. For the commercial decks of cards—modern inventions that include well-written and researched booklets—this is easy. Even extensive interpretations of the Norse runes have been given in a number of good books. However, for other more intricate and extensive systems, such as Tarot, geomancy, and astrology, this has proved much more difficult. For a while, we worked on a five-part series of lessons for a relatively easy system of Tarot interpretation based on fundamental esoteric principles. However this too proved a complicated task for some to first memorize, then master. Even in scrying, the most basic of all divination practices, people often had trouble interpreting the symbols they saw (or struggled to see).

In all these cases, I realized, the problem was that people were having trouble relating to the symbols and attaching meaning to them. After all, the whole premise of divination is that the subconscious mind links specific meanings to certain symbols that are recognized by the conscious mind. In ancient divination systems, these symbols are usually taken from Nature and/or a spiritual environment. Thus was born the idea to create or revitalize systems of divination for Wiccans and Pagans, using symbols from these paths.

I began the long task of conceptualizing and revitalizing the nine systems you will encounter in this book, and writing them all down in a coherent format. Most of these systems are based on traditional sources. Putting them together for modern use and choosing appropriate symbology was time-consuming, but enjoyable, work. Some of the systems are of my own creation, and putting these together was a fascinating exercise in inspiration. The hardest part by far, however, was writing out the processes for making the tools for someone else to follow. It's a bit like that old grade school exercise of writing down the steps involved in tying your shoe or making a peanut butter and jelly sandwich—there are lots of things we do unconsciously and take for granted.

With a little perspiration, a lot of inspiration, and some professional help from the great editors at Llewellyn, these nine systems are being presented to you, the reader, with bright blessings, in the hope that you, too, will enjoy doing your divination work in the context of the path that you have chosen to follow.

No, these systems are not *purely* ancient, though they are based on traditional and ancient sources. The systems had to be adapted for modern times, but they were adapted by a person who has more than ten years experience (not to mention previous lifetimes) in living, breathing, learning, and teaching the Wiccan/Pagan path to others. That person (me) also has a sincere wish that others who have been called to follow the dynamic and unquenchable light of the ancient Craft of the Wise may benefit from the spiritual heritage that was handed down to her, and the rewards of the spiritual work that were allowed her by the Gods.

The reader may notice that not all of the symbology is taken solely from the Craft tradition. In fact, some of it is extrapolated from the astrological or esoteric principles underlying the practice of a particular system. Please don't be put off by this. As Witches, Pagans, and other workers of magic in these modern times, we have a rich treasure trove of ancestral knowledge from which to draw, the threads of which are interwoven in a rich, magical cloak of wisdom that is ours to wear. Witches, magicians, shamans, and priests throughout the ages have all shared at least one thing—the long vision to see beyond the veil of material illusion and through the dark mirror of ignorance to the illuminated realms of the Divine.

Use these systems in Circle, either individually or as a group. Use them privately to answer your questions or the questions of others. Use them as a system of meditation to gain deeper insights into the inter-related workings of Craft symbology.

Most of all, I hope that you use them to develop the Witch's long vision, and to bring back gifts of wisdom to enrich your life and the lives of others.

Yours in the Light,

Callia Underhill
Autumn Equinox, 1996

PART I

INTRODUCTION, THEORY, AND EXERCISES

CHAPTER ONE

INTRODUCTION

"Cross my palm with silver, and I will tell you your future in my crystal ball," charms the old gypsy as she beckons you beyond her curtain. "Love, money, success—all these things I can see within my crystal, and I will show them to you."

Is this the first image that comes to your mind when you hear the word "divination"? Perhaps you see, instead, the exotic picture of a Voodoo priest, shaking his magical gourd to the hypnotic beat of drums and throwing the yellowed bones of some long-dead animal to foretell the destiny of his accursed patient. Maybe you think of Cassandra, the lover of Apollo, who was granted the gift of prophecy only to be scorned and ignored by humankind, or the great Cumaen Sybil, whose inhalations of magical smoke invoked in her the Voice of Prophecy. No one remembers his name, but everyone who has taken eighth-grade history (or watched a movie about the fall of Caesar) knows of the anonymous soothsayer who warned the emperor of Rome about his unlucky day. What about Nostradamus, the most famous and perhaps most widely published of seers, who predicted, amongst other things, the rise of Hitler 400 years before World War II? Merlin, the Witch of Endor, the Three Wise Men—the list goes on and on. Famous, colorful, magical legends and persons of supernatural perception have held our attention and fantasy over the ages.

Seer, prophet, oracle, soothsayer, augur, crystal gazer, fortune teller, sybil, vaticinator, haruspex—all you have to do is glance through the thesaurus to see how many different names our language has for those who can see beyond the veil of material existence. Every culture has and had them, and they were either revered and respected as spiritual assets, or despised and feared, like the toothless and filthy old hag that is the prevailing stereotype of "fortune tellers" today.

There is another group of people who share this unfortunate picture painted of them by society; they constitute perhaps the most famous of creatures who are reputed to hold the key to hidden and forbidden realms—Witches. In their sovereignty over the powers of divination may lay much to explain why they (or we) have also been despised and feared for so many long years now.

THE ROLE OF DIVINATION

Exactly what role does divination play in the life of a Witch, particularly in the life of the modern practitioner of Wicca? Whether some of our ancestors actually participated in anything like the atrocities of which they were accused or not, the Wiccan religion today has evolved to the point where its devotees hold self-development and responsibility in high regard. Where does the practice of divination fit into this? Because our healing and spell work take place on the astral plane, and our particular veneration for the Moon leads us to naturally walk hand in hand with the psychic realms, could we say that the terms "Witch" and "diviner" are mutually exclusive? Does a Witch necessarily divine, and does practicing divination automatically make someone a Witch? People who dowse for water are commonly called "water witches," and the word "witch" itself conjures up (no pun intended) the image of someone who has extraordinary access to hidden knowledge and power. If we take into account the popular theory that the etymological derivation of the word "Wicca" comes from the Anglo-Saxon root word meaning "wise," we confirm the idea that Witches are somehow able to contact deeper sources of knowledge than the average person. Is this still true for modern Wiccans, many of whom have only recently come to the Craft for their inspiration?

Let's consider the importance of the role of divination in the Wiccan religion. While some Wiccans may not include it as a part of their religious or celebratory practice, almost all people involved or

interested in the Craft also practice or are interested in some form of
divination. Why is this so? Go back to our image of the loathsome
gypsy hag. This image is easily stepped up to become "She with
Whom We Are All Familiar," the nightmare of schoolchildren and
small dogs named Toto. With black dress and flowing robe, wart nose
and green skin, she flies on her broom across the yellow moon, or
stirs her bubbling cauldron, cackling wickedly to her black cat familiar. Just who is this? I've been involved in Wicca for more than ten
years now, and I have yet to see one of my Craft brothers or sisters
show up to a Sabbat meeting in this get-up. However, any Wiccan
worth his or her salt should be able to answer this question. She is, of
course, Hecate, Cerridwen, Nocticula, Cailleach, the Morrigan. She
is the Dark Goddess, Queen of All Witcheries. This, shall we say,
"bastardized" image of this ancient Goddess was transferred to her
followers by a public that had become fearful of her powers for whatever reason.

The Goddess herself, however, is not affected by this, as hers is an
archetypal power, and some parts of this image still give us a true picture of her. (The green skin is lamentable, but let's reclaim that too, as
a symbol of her hidden aspect of fertility.)

Let's look at the tools this Goddess carries—the broom that shut-
tles her from one world to the next (doubling as her magic wand, no
doubt); her familiar, who provides her with an animal body in which
to move about in the physical world; and her cauldron, which, of
course, shows that she is the guardian and keeper of the Great
Seething Cauldron of Life and Wisdom itself. The Dark Goddess of
the Moon is the original seer, the archetypal scryer of the astral
mists. We are doing her work when we divine, we are acting within
her sphere. Remember that in the Charge of the Goddess she says
she "will teach to you things that are as yet unknown...."

WHAT METHOD OF DIVINATION?

The gypsy has Tarot cards, the Chinese philosopher has coins and
yarrow sticks, and the priest of Odin has rune stones. What method of
divination would be best for the Witch to use?

You might say that the natural mode of divination for Witches would be scrying, either in a crystal ball, bowl of water, or a black mirror. After all, wasn't it the stepmother character in the Snow White story (portrayed, of course, as an evil witch) who asked "Mirror, mirror, on the wall..." for glimpses into the darkness of the forest? It is true that scrying, defined as gazing into a reflective surface until the waking consciousness is put into a trance state, thereby opening up the psychic faculties, comes under the direct presidency of the Moon. (Qabalistically, the Moon, lunar goddesses, the astral plane, and psychism are all relegated to the same sphere, Yesod). In fact, every year at Samhain, our coven takes advantage of the thinning of the veils between the worlds of the seen and the unseen that occurs at that time to practice our scrying techniques.

You might say that trance work is the best method of divination for the Witch to use. Speculation has been made that reports, or "confessions," of Witches flying to the Sabbat were really their remembrances of their nocturnal outings onto the astral plane (possibly drug induced by the infamous flying ointment). Trance is easily induced by dancing in circles (the hypnotic beat and dizziness produced effectively separates one from the physical plane), and in this book you will read about one such method of divination traditionally used by Witches, the Dance of the Lame God. Because an important part of Wicca is the celebration of Nature and connection with her spiritual aspects, one might say that Witches would best divine using objects they find in the natural environment. In this book you will find several methods, both traditional and new, in which stones, seeds, and sticks are systematically thrown in order to interpret the patterns in which they fall.

In the end, one might have to conclude that there is no single method of divination that is better than all the others for Witches to use in their readings. The fact is that Witches have a bewilderingly long list of methods from which to choose, from aleuromancy (divination by flour) to haruspicy (the examination of entrails) to xylomancy (the aforementioned divination by sticks and twigs). The deciding factor will be which set of mechanics the particular person works with best. Every method of divination in the world is based on a few elementary principles that always remain constant. These are covered in depth in Chapter Two. They are intended to give you the key to understanding the process of divination, so that you may thereby be the master of it.

INTERNAL AND EXTERNAL DIVINATION

Primarily, all forms of divination fall into two basic categories: external or internal. External methods of divination rely on sets of tools or representations of symbols that are manipulated by the divining force of the reader. Internal methods of divination rely on a set of symbols rising in the mind of the reader, contacted in clairvoyant and/or trance states.

Forms of external divination include Tarot, for you must have a deck of cards; astrology, with its charts and ephemerides; and rune casting, with its sticks and stones. If you prefer this method of divination, you will find in this book several systems that may serve you, such as Herne's Head, the House of the Goddess, the Witch's Drum, or Talking Stones. All of these involve a stone, set of stones, or seeds thrown onto a particular diagram and interpreted according to where they fall. These are all systems for which you will be able to make your own set of tools, so that they can become extraordinarily personalized and become your "divination companions," so to speak.

Examples of internal divination include water or crystal scrying, psychometry, and trance-induced prophecy. If you are good at visualization and/or internal dialogue, you may prefer to dig up answers to unknown questions with systems such as the Sword Trance or the Omen Walk. If you're really good at trance work, and you think you've had enough experience with it, you might try the Dance of the Lame God.

Also included in this book are two systems that can be used for divining in a meditation context, thereby combining the aspects of both external and internal methods of divination. By using the Druid's Wand to measure the distance between the moon and a certain star, you will be given an answer in one of the Druidic Triads (the philosophical writings of the ancient Celtic wise men and women) to ponder. You may be familiar with geomancy, a magical system of divination that can be described as the I Ching of the West. This system, developed by ancient magicians, has been reinterpreted within the context of Wiccan symbolism, so that contemplation of the patterns and figures received by the casting of a stone can be specifically meaningful for modern Witches.

Regardless of whether you prefer methods of external or internal divination, the actual divination process depends, as we have seen, on the patterning or setting in order of a particular set of symbols by the divining power of the reader, and the reader's further interpretation of these symbols into a comprehensive narrative. While it is true that many readers have one deck of cards or a favorite set of stones that they use for all their work and let no one else touch, a really expert diviner could tell your future with any old bag of rocks, your hairpins, a letter someone had written to you, or the remains of your dinner. It is the divining power within Witches that allows them to "see."

So, just what is this divining power, and how does one access it? The answer to this question will be covered in the next two chapters, so that you will have at your fingertips nine systems of divination to suit your fancy, but you will not fall victim to the superstition of their power. You will understand how divination works, and therefore know that *you* are the magic tool, not the stones or the sticks. You will know that you are the Witch, that you are in control of your universe, and that you have the power of the Queen of All Witcheries within you.

CHAPTER TWO

THEORY

In the old days, there were those who were said to possess "the Gift" or "the Sight." (Incidentally, they were not always spoken of or treated with respect.) However, this power, "the Second Sight," is not a special talent or domain of a certain select few. It is in all people, latent or manifested in differing degrees.

Some people, particularly in the days of old when people lived closer to Nature and their senses were not subject to overstimulation by the fast pace of today's living, had these powers develop naturally. This is referred to as psychism and is thought in some cases to be passed on genetically. Those who seemed to possess this "special" power would naturally fascinate their communities. The seer represented access to a realm ordinarily forbidden and refused to the normal person. Indeed, the first Witches may have been simply those who exhibited this power more strongly than others, having the ability to talk with animals, discern the hidden causes of illness, or commune with Nature spirits in order to relieve drought and famine. Their "powers" could have been used to help or could just as easily be used to harm if that Witch did not subscribe to a particularly high ethic. It is easy to see how these people could be greatly revered for their healing talents, or greatly feared for the advantage they had in being able to "see" hidden things.

Due to the evolution of humanity, marching necessarily along the spiral path of the Goddess, this trait would now be considered something of an anachronism. In some cases, if the possessor of these

powers was not able to control the intrusion of the unseen into every-
day life, it would be considered a pathology. However, this power is
just waiting to be developed in modern people as intuition that can be
controlled and used for good by the modern Witch or Pagan.

However, divination is not exclusively the territory of the Witch
(ceremonial magicians are, stereotypically, famous for trying to wrest
information from the freshly raised spirits of the dead), even though it
has usually been connected, in mystical language and hushed tones,
with the general practice of "sorcery," "witchcraft," and (lower your
voice to a whisper now) "the black arts."

There is much more to the art of divination than crystal ball gazing, and there is much more to the science of divination than nefari-
ous conjurations. First of all, although there are so many different
forms of divination practice, the general theory behind all of them—
the hows and whys of the way they work—is the same. It is also relatively simple. It is a logical, reasonable, and learnable procedure,
based on contacting that latent power within ourselves, then becoming familiar with the Law of Correspondences and the language of
symbols. Divining power is not something to be gained, but something to be developed. The language of symbols is something that is
easily learned and developed as well.

Basically, the whole process of divination can be easily explained
and understood by the old magical aphorism, "As above, so below; as
below, so above." Those who recognize this phrase as a stock item of
ceremonial magic might ask, "What does that have to do with Wicca?
I'm reading this book because it said it deals with divination for
Witches!" Even though our wise ancestors of old perhaps knew nothing of the specific precepts of magical practice as we know it nowadays
(maybe they didn't, maybe they did), they received their intuition, as
we still do today, from the book of Nature, the world of the Goddess'
creation. This is most easily seen, for example, when we contemplate
something the ancients have built, such as Stonehenge or the Egyptian pyramids, and ask ourselves: "How did they do that with no modern tools?" It is also seen when we are amazed at their ability to know
which herbs and natural plants yielded exactly the right medicine to
heal their sick, or how ancient astronomers could construct calendars

almost as accurate as the one we have today with all of our scientific knowledge. Ancient humans weren't really any wiser than we, but their consciousnesses were such that they could intuit more from the world around them (including the more subtle non-material worlds thought of as "above" us). Modern humanity now lives in a state much more mired down in physical existence; we are denser now, both physically and psychically, and the fine-tuning of our physical and super-physical senses are dulled by the overstimulation of modern life.

Since, in the days of the ancients, people lived much closer to Nature, they were also more closely in tune with Nature's counterpart in the human psyche—the subconscious mind. It is not a random happenstance that the Goddess of the Moon (the sovereign Nature) is referred to as "the Queen of All Witcheries." It is by contacting her that connection with, and therefore knowledge of and influence over, all beings is accomplished.

THE LANGUAGE OF SYMBOL

The language of the subconscious mind—the "words" it understands—is the language of symbol. Symbols are also the basic language of divination. Many of the ancient methods of divination consisted of methods whereby patterns were observed in Nature (the flight of birds or the marks on the entrails of a sacrificial animal) and matched to a corresponding set of predetermined interpretations or meanings. This practice is generally referred to as augury (though this term is sometimes used specifically in reference to the flight of birds). The subconscious mind works by "linking" certain ideas in the mind with other ideas through the device of symbols. So, if the augur (the person who was divining) saw, for example, that birds in flight formed a circle, and to him, a circle represented home, hearth, and abundance, then his or her prediction would be one of gain and happiness.

Here we can see where the practice of divination by augury might have eventually become misinterpreted as superstition and "hocus-pocus." Because the fundamental principle behind it is not understood, one could say, "Well, just because somebody sees a circle in the sky, and his house also happens to be shaped like a circle, that doesn't mean that there's any connection between the two. It could be merely a coincidence, nothing more. It's pure hogwash that one has anything to say about the other."

The point here is that they *are* connected, and in a Witch's universe, there are no such things as coincidences. This is because, as we discussed earlier, a Witch learns to "see" connections that are perhaps hidden from everyone else. Even though many people may not like to say it in these days when the word has negative connotations, Witches deal literally with the occult (from the Latin word for "hidden") side of things. Because the subconscious mind, and with it, Nature (and our Great Goddess), works by linking things together, it (and she) produces an inner unity amongst all beings. All Witches, or modern practitioners of Wicca, know in their hearts that All is One; they work with the principle that all the Goddess' creation exists in a living, breathing cosmic web of interconnections and interdependencies. To the Witch, what is above is as what is below, and what is below is as what is above.

So, the first step in learning to divine properly is to get in touch with and trust our subconscious minds. Wiccans are perhaps better acquainted with working with the energies of the subconscious, as we already hold the power of the Moon in veneration. We can also, perhaps, be helped by remembering part of the Charge of the Goddess: "If that which thou seeketh thou findeth not within thee, then thou shalt never find it without thee." If we rearrange the words of this sentence to read "That which thou findeth within thee, thou wilt also find without thee," we get a pretty good, simple explanation of the magician's creed "As above, so below." What we are talking about here is the **macrocosm** and the **microcosm**, which will help us to get a grasp on one of the three main aspects of the divining power—the Law of Correspondences.

Let's look at a picture of the planets revolving around the sun in our enormous solar system, then look at a picture of something on the extreme opposite of the size spectrum: electrons revolving around the nucleus of an atom. The principles underlying each system are the same (gravity, rotation, revolution), so what is true of the macrocosm will be true of the microcosm, though on a different scale. In fact, all the planets (at least the seven planets known to the ancients) can be found within our bodies, corresponding to the chakras.

An even better way to think of this magical maxim might be "As within, so without; as without, so within." If we look "without" of ourselves, we see an order in the Universe, which can be found within that Universe as a recurring theme, thereby linking things by correspondence. So, here we have two concepts upon which a sound approach to divination should be based: order and correspondence.

ORDER AND CORRESPONDENCE

What do we need to know about order? Some of us (I might even venture to say many of us) have a slight problem when it comes to this concept. If, when I mentioned the word "order," you had horrifying visions of "to do" lists and monthly bank statements all neatly balanced and chronologically filed away, or if you had to fight the urge to run screaming from the room, you might qualify for membership in this club. The concept of order has somehow picked up a connotation of patriarchy, control, and stultifying linear thought processes that are distasteful to many Wiccans. Order seems to smack of the nine-to-five world, desk jobs, neckties, and anything else that would threaten to drain away the glorious flow of creativity that is the gift of the Mother.

As lovers of Nature, we want to run free with the wild wind; to laugh, cry, and sing with the joy of the rushing waters; and to feel the limitless life energy flow through us. We think of the Goddess as free, boundless, chaotic, wild, and, in her greatest aspect, the Abyss beyond all Light and Creation—the Unknowable in her Uncreated Glory. The thought of order, routine, and rules seems to dampen this spirit. It is unfortunate, however, that this has come to be so, for the bare truth is that the Goddess' great cosmos and everything in it must be based on the concept of order to exist. Order—beautiful, pristine, perfect order—has become confused with stagnation, avarice, and inertia. Order is the pure simplicity of abstract mathematical formulas, the drum song that beats out the swirling plan of rhythm to which the Dancer of the Universe whirls.

We might even associate order more with the God, and in the next chapter we will explore the role of the God in his Mercurial aspect in connection with order. Certainly, our lovely Goddess of the Moon, and our generous Mother Earth both operate within the order of their cycles. If their rotations and revolutions are governed by order, then the tiny universes that compose our bodies and consciousnesses must be also. The Creator is always present in the Created. The cycles of the moon, sun, and seasons; the perpetual orbits of the planets; the alternation of night and day, life and death; and the progression of youth to decay, all keep their time on the spinning Wheel of Fortune, the Wheel of Life, the Sacred Circle upon which all our Craft is founded.

This, too, is why all acts of love and joy are rituals of the Goddess. Dancing, music, merrymaking, and lovemaking are all based on rhythm. Without perfect order and harmony (another extremely important concept we will come to next), our bodies would fall apart. We could not think or speak because these acts are dependent on the stringing together of thoughts and words in a specific order. We would have no music, no chants, no dancing, no eating of sumptuous feasts. It stands to reason that the better order something is in, the better it works. In my years of experience as a Tarot reader, I've seen the same phenomenon borne out again and again: the better order one's own personal consciousness is in, the better the cards are laid out and interpreted by that person. Here we might remember the old Tarot reader's adage "Ask a vague question, get a vague answer." We might extend this idea to say "Have a vague personal consciousness, get a vague answer."

This is the real problem when a divination comes out mushy and unreadable. It's not usually that the cards will not "speak to you," it's that the lines of mental and psychic force along which they align themselves are crossed and confused. The best card readings that I've ever done were always for the High Priestess under whom I originally trained. She is also a Hermetic magician and Qabalist. When she shuffled the cards, and I laid them out, they fell like clockwork into an order so crystal clear that I could see straight through to the bottom of the matter at hand.

Now, of course I'm not recommending that you go out and join a Hermetic school before attempting to learn divination. However, I will present to you in the next chapter some meditations and exercises to help you, the diviner, contact the source of inner harmony that will make your readings come out clearer and allow you to divine more correctly and precisely.

HARMONY

This brings us to our last point in this chapter: the necessary blossoming of harmony. I mentioned before that you will need to contact the source of harmony within yourself in order to become a good diviner. The harmony that we are talking about is that precise conjunction of order and correspondence. In the next chapter we will be working with these concepts and relating them to some appropriate cards from the Tarot. For our purposes correspondence is represented by the High Priestess, and order is represented by the Magician.

This third concept, harmony, is perhaps best illustrated in the Lovers card, where subconsciousness and self-consciousness, female and male, Moon and Sun, are in perfect balance. The angel in this card, therefore, is harmony, which is the joining together of God and Goddess in perfect love—the Great Rite from which is born the Child of Light and Promise. When this Child is born within you, that is, when your subconscious and self-conscious minds are working together to correlate and set in order the various components related to your divination system, then you will hear the Voice of Prophecy speak for you as truly as did the fume-inhaling prophetesses of Delphi.

CHAPTER THREE

EXERCISES

In this chapter, we will discuss some preliminary exercises you might perform in order to prepare for your divination practices. Does this sound boring, to have to practice to divine? I mentioned at the end of the last chapter the ancient sybils who spoke the most compelling prophecy whilst in the throes of drunken ecstasy. While that may sound like much more fun, you should know that these Priestesses of the Sacred Flame were first trained in maintaining the order of their own inner worlds before the Voice would speak through them.

The following exercises will train you, too, to put your inner world in order. (I'm sorry, but they do not include instructions on how to attain drunken ecstasy.) You might also want to pick out a method of divination now from the following chapters and begin to work with its symbols. If you wish to use your system seriously, it is absolutely necessary that you know the divination system inside and out before beginning to use it.

What we are dealing with here is an issue of trust—trust between your self-conscious and subconscious minds. If you have even the slightest bit of self-doubt, or if your confidence in your knowledge of the symbols and their meanings lags even a little bit, this sends a signal to your subconscious mind that you don't quite know what you're doing. In turn, your reading will come out muddled and unclear. This doesn't mean that you must memorize all the meanings and interpretations verbatim (although doing this might take you a long way toward success in your divinations), but you should know them enough to recognize them, and to have an immediate emotional reaction to them when they come up. This is especially true of the more advanced systems in this book, such as the Omen Walk, because you will not be able to conveniently refer to your interpretations without breaking your trance state. Indeed, your eventual goal is to know the symbols so well in your heart and mind that you actually transcend the need for predetermined interpretations of them. This is where truly psychic revelations in divination come into play.

If you don't feel like specializing right now, that's okay, because the following exercises will help you with any kind of divination at any time. You can continue doing these exercises, if you like, after your preliminary training period is done, for they will always help you, no matter how advanced you become. You might even choose to use them before each of your divination sessions, if circumstances permit. For now, begin by picking out one of the techniques in this book and reading the chapter through once, twice, five, or even ten times, until you feel you are conversant in the symbols. At the same time, also begin to think about the Law of Correspondences. As an added bonus, you'll find that working with the Law of Correspondences will help your magical studies in any other arena; it will bring you closer to the Goddess as you begin to see the interwoven strands of her Web of Creation in every aspect of your daily life.

In performing these exercises to sharpen up your divination skills, you will be instructed to use the Tarot cards (in itself an exemplary divination system) that represent the aspects of the Goddess and God related directly to our work here. We use the Tarot cards because concentration on their symbolism is the quickest way to integrate their powers into your Witch's bag of tricks. It is best to use the Rider-Waite deck or the Builders of the Adytum deck (which you will have to color yourself according to the instructions that come with them) for meditation purposes, as they are the most symbolically potent. The Tarot of the Old Path deck or some other deck related to the Craft would work well also. However, if you have another deck at hand that you consider "your" deck, then by all means use it. Just make sure that is it somewhat traditional in its depiction of the figures. (Although there are many beautiful and creative decks out on the market, I'm afraid that working with the High Priestess in the form of a Hollywood actress, a plant, or some character from Charles Dickens will not afford you much progress.)

So, to familiarize yourself with the Goddess' power of correspondence, let's continue with the exercise of the High Priestess, where we will see her in her role of Goddess of the Moon.

EXERCISE OF THE HIGH PRIESTESS

The best way to work with the Tarot cards to develop divination powers is a surprisingly easy one. Simply take out the High Priestess from your Tarot deck, set it before you, and let your gaze wander over it, familiarizing yourself with its symbols for several minutes. This is nothing new; it is a technique used by esoteric schools to train their students, and it will work for you in the same way. However, the exercise should be treated like a meditation, and you will want to adopt an attitude of contemplation while doing it.

Sit quietly in a chair where you won't be disturbed, with some method of timing that won't startle you out of your meditative state. (A sand egg timer works well.) You may also wish to light a candle and incense to help you focus. Use a blue, violet, or silver candle, and a scent that is appropriately lunar, such as jasmine, benzoin, or violet. Perfumes and incenses are the particular domain of the Moon Goddess, by the way, because the molecules of their smoke and aroma diffuse out evenly into the environment until there is roughly an equal amount per square area, thereby uniting—"corresponding"—all the points of space within the room.

Before beginning the exercise, it is important for you to be completely relaxed. Release all the tension in your muscles, either by alternately tensing and releasing them, or just by concentrating on them—starting with your toes and continuing all the way up to your head. Then begin taking long, deep breaths, and continue breathing slowly and rhythmically all the way through the time that you are looking at your card. All you want to do is look at the card, notice its symbols, and let them sink into your subconscious mind. Do this for five minutes or so.

After the time is up, begin to imagine yourself as the High Priestess. Feel yourself sitting upon her cubic throne, swaddled in her white and blue robes, with the lunar crown upon your head. What you are trying to achieve here is a connecting with the unifying power of the Moon Goddess. Feel the tides of all creation flowing through you, and then feel her peace and serenity as she sits silently balanced between the two pillars of opposing polarity. Make sure you continue to breathe deeply while you are doing this, and don't go much beyond five minutes.

Spend at least a week on this exercise, doing it once a day, at a time of day that is restful and peaceful for you. Throughout the rest of the day you might want to continue your work by trying to feel the connections between things that you encounter in your daily surroundings. Recognizing hidden relationships that may have previously escaped you will help you make more intuitive analyses of divination spreads or casts.

EXERCISE OF THE MAGICIAN

This exercise is intended to help you get in touch with Mercury, the god of the mind. This is the Horned Lord in his aspect of Lord of the Winds (since air corresponds to thoughts and mental states). In other pantheons, he is Odin, Merlin, Lugh Lamphada, and Thoth. While the power of the Moon Goddess will gain your admittance to the fluid world of the psychic, Mercury will be your guide there.

This exercise is much like the previous one. You should use a yellow candle and an incense associated with Mercury. Cinnamon, nutmeg, or lavender work well. Look at the Magician card for five minutes or so, then mentally assume the position of the Magician. Visualize yourself standing in a lush garden of lilies and roses. You wear the white inner robe and red outer robe of the Magician. In your right hand you hold a magic wand. Raise it above your head and over your right shoulder. With your left hand, point your index finger at the table in front of you, on which are laid the tools of the Magician and of the Magic Circle: a wand that matches the one you hold in your right hand, a silver cup, a gleaming sword, and a golden pentacle.

Visualize that these tools are jumbled up on the table. They are leaning on each other, the cup is tumbled over—a general mess. Next, point your finger at them, and by doing so, you automatically arrange them in the right order, as pictured on the card with which you are working.

For this exercise, take five minutes or so per day for a week, like the first exercise.

The important part of this exercise is that you follow up with it during the day. You should try to extend your practice into the practical, mundane world. You want to look for hidden relationships between things in the world that you might have overlooked before. The power of Mercury is the power of ordered, concentrated thought, so concentrate on things. Before with the High Priestess, you wanted to *feel* the connections between things; now you want to *see* connections. As a real test of your powers, try to find the connections between things that seem ludicrously incongruous—such as bananas and car engines, or keyholes and bathroom sinks. The connections are there, and you will realize what they are if you practice this exercise long enough. Keep in mind that no event or object will ever reveal its significance to you when considered alone. It will only become clear and significant when compared to its surroundings or surrounding circumstances. This is particularly important in the case of divination.

All this will strengthen your ability to eventually link together the symbols of your chosen system, so that you may properly "tell the story" that the cards, bones, or stones are trying to tell you. In the next exercise, you will learn to hear the Voice of Nature, which is the Voice of inspiration, of prophecy, and also the Voice of Truth. Isn't that why we consult our oracles—to find Truth where before it was unknown?

EXERCISE OF THE LOVERS

In order for our subconscious minds to aid us in divination, they have to be able to correlate symbols with essences, ideas, or empirical thoughts. As we have already discussed, the Moon, representing our subconscious mind, is the connecting power, while our self-conscious minds interpret the symbols to be meaningful. This latter concept is represented by Mercury. The essential, empirical thought we could term our superconscious mind or Higher Self, and assign this concept to spirit.

We can illustrate this by looking to the Lovers card for help. In classic versions of the card, there is a man and woman together, with a grand, winged angel, or spirit of light, hovering over them. Here we see the psyche at work in perfect harmony: the man (the self-conscious mind) looks to the woman (the subconscious mind) for meaning and guidance. The woman, however, is not the source of this wisdom herself. She looks up to the angel, toward spirit, toward the realm of deity to inspire her so that she may enable the man to speak correctly. Now, of course, these symbols do not really have anything to do with actual men and women. We each have all three of these aspects within us. The more in harmony your own internal spirit is, the more in order, or correct, your divination will be.

The first part of this exercise is to look at your Lovers card for about five minutes, like before, but this time using a white candle and an uplifting incense like frankincense, rose, or sandalwood. Instead of assuming the position of the card, you are going to synthesize the skills you gained with the first two cards and work with them in practical application.

First, do your five minutes or so on the Lovers card. Then, in whatever degree you are able, go outside. Whether you live in the country or the city, take a walk through the woods, around a couple of blocks, or in a park. Look at the world as a large tapestry woven by the Goddess, and with both of your newfound powers, observe each thread in the tapestry and how, together, they make the picture you see of your surroundings. Look for connections between things and people. Look for colors, shapes, and sounds that correlate. Look for letters spelled out in tree branches and ancient symbols drawn in the constructs of modern civilization.

For example, say you notice the blue of a bird sitting in a tree. Let that lead you to the next incident of blue—say, a blue house, then on to a blue car, and so on. See if you can make up a story about all these blue things. Follow a common thread running between them all. This may seem silly, but you will be amazed at what you will find if you apply yourself diligently. I remember an experience I had on the New York Thruway while riding along in a car. For the first time, I realized the very tangible connection between divination symbols and the world. I saw, amongst the barren winter trees, a dilapidated barn that from the side view was shaped like the rune figure Ur. It dawned on me then that symbols and the letters of alphabets, especially magical ones, arose for our ancestors' observation of the subtle interconnection and patterns of energy of various elements in their environment. The hidden side of life—the mystical and magical—is not so far removed from us, but right beside us and around us at all times, waiting for us to open our eyes and see.

After a few sessions of your walking and looking, you will begin to see these patterns in the Universe, in the living, breathing, flowing, changing tapestry of life. You will begin to know things, see things that other people do not see. In that moment, you will begin to truly learn the art and science of divination. All you have to do is *look*.

HEARING THE VOICE OF PROPHECY

Many times while studying divination, would-be readers will ask questions like "Well, how do I know what is the truth of a querent's situation, and what I may be making up? I have such a fertile imagination. Couldn't it all be in my head?" These are legitimate questions, and a true pitfall for the serious student of divination. That is why the serious student must be concerned with listening for the objective Voice of Wisdom within. The previous exercise with the Lovers will help you achieve this, although there is more you can do to bring this power into your life, where it will give you more benefit than just helping you to divine. It will bring you closer to the realm of the Gods themselves, particularly the Great Goddess. For in order to hear the Voice, you must enter her domain, which is the still and silent abode of space, earth, and night-time sky—and also the inner space of stillness from which we gain peace, rest, and inspiration.

We must enter this silent space and try to hear the Voice of the Goddess whispering in the winds of Nature. Fleet-footed Mercury is smart, quick, and clever, but he can also chatter on endlessly in our minds if we let him, bombarding our neurons with idea after idea, word after word. To hear the Voice, we have to go beyond words and thought to the very source of All. While this is a lofty goal and one that we will not (and probably should not try to) achieve every moment of the day and night, it is something on which to work. This is the "alpha state" of brain activity, the state of deep meditation where the fountain source of Creation springs up. It is Ceridwen's Cauldron, the Silver Cup, and Holy Well that renews us and regenerates us.

Mercury works through the senses. The senses are his tool. His five fingers are, so to speak, the means by which the Goddess touches her world. These give him his material—sights, smells, and images to think, and consequently, to chatter about.

To achieve the inner stillness, we must shut off the senses from their exterior influences and outside impulses. This is why, incidentally, we gain insight and inspiration while we sleep, and why we talk about "sleeping on" some decision or problem. However, by learning to control this function and work with it during the day, we will gain great benefit from it, as well as being able to turn it on at will while divining.

The teachings of the Druids, from which some of our Wiccan practices distantly derive, incorporated this technique in their divinations. It was called *imbas forosna* and involved being enclosed in a dark place for some period of time, then being released into bright light. The seer was supposed to emerge from this sensory deprivation experience with "occult" information about the matter or question at hand. This sensory deprivation symbolized being submerged in the Cauldron of Knowledge, the Mother's Womb, and the state of sleep. The bright light represented our old friend Mercury. The answer was found in the well of the subconscious mind and brought forth into the light of self-consciousness, where it would be interpreted and understood.

So the exercise connected to our divination powers is to confine yourself in a dark place (such as a closet or small bathroom with no windows). Seat yourself comfortably and relax, stilling your mind as you did in the High Priestess exercise. Retreat within yourself, and try to remove yourself from the report of your senses. You can't see, touch, taste, or smell anything, and you gradually go deeper and deeper within yourself to a place where your sixth sense is the prevailing function. If you like, you can even devise a pathworking exercise where you go to a soundless chamber or dark cave. When there, still your mind, and if any words come into it, let them pass by unnoticed. Don't try to sweep them out of your mind, just let them pass without actually "listening" to them. When you have spent your five minutes in your "state" (or however long you have determined your session will last) step out into light (if you are doing a pathworking, make sure you retreat from your cave back to your normal waking space first) either by setting up a bright lamp outside the door beforehand, or by going outside into sunlight. If you had any symbols or ideas arise in your mind while in the dark, see if you can articulate and interpret them when in the light. This is what will be happening within you while you are divining—a constant weaving back and forth between the dark and light as you derive meaning from symbols and try to put it into words your querant will understand. I, as a reader, even have trouble speaking if I've gone really deep for an interpretation, and have probably sounded like a babbling idiot to my querant.

Also, make sure you practice. Orchestrate the procedure in whatever way is convenient to you. Just make sure the general principle remains the same. You could also try laying on the floor or a bed with a blanket covering you (but make sure you can breathe). Again, don't concentrate on this exercise for too long. Ten to fifteen minutes is long enough for the first time. You want to maintain control over your powers, not emerge from your session a discombobulated mess. The more advanced you become in these matters, the more time you can spend on these exercises, and the deeper you can go. However, it is necessary to work up to this point slowly, so as not to burn yourself out.

In the chapters that follow, you will begin reading about nine different systems of divination for Witches. However, before sending you off into this adventure, I must talk a little bit about the inevitable dark side of divination—its own particular dangers and pitfalls.

A WORD OF CAUTION

With all due respect to our good friends at the psychic call-in lines, I believe most of us involved on the Pagan path are taught, and realize, the importance of the virtues of self-reliance and responsibility. By the Law of Three we know that what we send out comes back to us three-fold. We are therefore the authors, so to speak, of our own books—the books of our lives. Our lives and environments are nothing but what we make them. Thus, divination is something that should help us understand ourselves and how we interact with our world and vast cosmos, rather than making us slaves of fate or destiny.

You must always keep in mind that divination readings show us *patterns*. They show the cause of things (the past) that are happening in the present, and the result of them as well (the future), if the patterns remains as they are. We, as humans, have, above all, *free will*. Just the fact that we are interested and willing to look into the underlying patterns that affect our daily lives means that we also have the capacity to take control of them. That is why most readings are said to only look ahead for a space of several months. The future grows from the seeds sown in the present, and so lays shrouded on the horizon in the midst of possibility, waiting to be shaped by the changes we make today.

Divination should not be used as a crutch, telling you what new car to buy, or whether or not you should get out of bed on any given day. You have your own reasoning intelligence to tell you that. The powers of divination are a gift from the Gods to help us see light in times of darkness, and should never be abused or misused. The best approach is to treat divination as a religious rite, for so it is.

Life on Earth is difficult, with all of its choices and decisions. It is meant to be difficult so that we can grow to be strong and wise. It is easy to see how a tool such as divination, which helps us to make more intelligent choices in difficult circumstances, could become addictive or relied upon too much. People who become addicted to divination are in danger of losing their will, or rather, giving up their will in exchange for easy answers. We must be careful not to allow the systems to tell us what to do, nor should we get in the habit of running to them for help every time the faucet breaks or someone says something we don't like. Many readers, in fact, find their systems won't "speak" to them when approached too often, and/or in a frivolous manner. Here the wisdom of the Gods speaks for itself. The highest use of divination is in the exploration of spiritual questions, or of the nature of your own inner being. In this instance, you will find they speak most candidly and eloquently, albeit not as plainly as one might wish.

Divination should never be used to harm other people or find out things about them that may potentially be used to harm them, nor should it be used to satisfy idle curiosity. Remember that the Gods, as we understand them, are living, conscious intelligences who have other conscious intelligences working under their auspices. No misuse of power escapes them unnoticed.

It is also necessary to remember that when we deal with divination, we are dealing with spiritual forces. Therefore, purification of body and mind is of the utmost importance. The subconscious mind is the source of much wonder and miracle, but it is also the source of madness and lunacy when it is working out of its sphere and order. We know that the Moon Goddess unites all things, and if you suddenly had all people's thoughts, feelings, and impulses inside your head, you would go more than a little batty. This is the realm of the Greek God Pan, whose name in Greek means "all," and who causes panic and madness when he is invoked frivolously. Your Mercury function, the God functioning as the Magician within you, acts as a stopgate for these energies.

So, as Semele was burned to ashes when she looked upon Zeus in his full glory, it's better not to take the risk of this power shorting out your unprepared circuits. To this end, you might want to perform a short purification ritual before your divination sessions. I realize that this may be a little cumbersome for those times when you are asked to do a quick reading "off-the-cuff," and so you may want to devise a brief version of a purification ritual for those times. Alternatively, you could do a quick, inner version of the "Stilling of the Mind" exercise we previously discussed, to try to hear the Voice, and ask that its purity guide you to speak the Truth. While the previous exercises with the Tarot cards are entirely safe (even protective in some measure), and the Voice of Inspiration a wholly beneficent force, when you really begin to read well, you may also begin touching upon the realm of the psychic—the astral plane. Unfortunately, just because things inhabit the astral plane does not necessarily mean that they are beneficient. So you want to make sure that you are not leaving yourself open to psychic disturbances. Purification is always a good idea.

With that said, please advance now to the following chapters, and enjoy them. Wicca is a religion rich with beautiful and transformative symbols. As our special deity is the Goddess of the Moon herself, we can do naught but come to understand her better through our divination work. As for the sets of symbols you will encounter in this book, they have been carefully developed to reflect the legends, mystery, and magic of the Craft of the Wise. So the thoughts and feelings of love, devotion, and joy that are associated with our religious practice can be drawn upon to help you to "read the hidden book of the Universe." It is my sincere wish that you may begin to better understand yourself and your place in the interwoven Universe that springs forth from the union of our Golden Lord and Our Bright Lady—a Universe that they have created for us in perfect love and perfect trust.

PART II

DIVINATION AND DIAGRAMS

CHAPTER FOUR

HERNE'S HEAD

The first divination system we are exploring is a relatively simple one. It involves casting two stones onto a diagram of the god Herne, the figure of Herne, himself, comprising many different symbols. This form of divination is good for both predicting the outcome of events as well as obtaining advice about what course of action you should take regarding a particular problem. Before we look at the symbols composing the diagram, you should know a little bit about the god Herne.

Herne is a name for the Horned Lord. A variation of the name Herne is Cerne, which is equivalent to the name Cernunnos or Kernunnos. The root "cern" or "corn" comes from Latin and means horn, as can be seen from the words for horn in the Latin-based languages: "Il Corno" in Italian, "La Corne" in French, and "El Cuerno" in Spanish. Some English words with this root are "cornucopia," "unicorn," and "cornet." Some authors have speculated that the name Cernunnos is actually a Latinized form of Cernowain, or Cerno-Owain, which can be translated as "the Horned Owen." There is a character named Owain in the Mabinogion. He appears as a powerful Otherworld figure, something along the archetype of the hero or perfect warrior. So we see that Herne is basically a horned god figure from the faery realms.

Herne is a pan-European deity, meaning that he was worshiped throughout many countries in many forms. While in the British Isles he was commonly portrayed with stag horns, he was also often depicted with bull horns, and in Craft mythology, he is present in both forms. (As you will see, this system of divination uses the bull-horned aspect of the

Horned God. This is because the bull aspect is associated with the dark half of the Year Wheel, and with wisdom more than power.)

Herne is also associated with the Wild Hunt. There are Celtic legends that speak of a spectral horned man, known as the Master of the Hunt, who led a pack of wild ghostly dogs across the English countryside. When the Hunt passed through the land, the howling dogs and the hunting horn of the Master were said to be heard for miles around. To this day in the countryside of the British Isles, and most notably near the Windsor Forest area, one can find people that will swear by the most solemn oath they know that they have heard, or less frequently, seen, the Wild Hunt and its Master.

There are also some legends in which a hero from the Celtic tradition met with, fought, and slew the Master of the Wild Hunt. Paralleling this theme, in the Mabinogion, Arthur and Owain are opponents in a chess match. The Master of the Hunt was also called the rider of the storm, and was associated with winds and thunder, riding his coal-black steed through the skies on stormy nights. This associates Herne with the element air.

Herne as the Horned God is also ruler of the Underworld, the Guide of Souls. So in some respects, he is like a Celtic Hermes, Greek Mercury, or Egyptian Hermanubis figures. This "Mercury aspect" of Herne also relates him to the element of air. Since air is the element related to the discipline of divination, Herne is a suitable figure to use.

THE NECESSARY TOOLS

For this form of divination, you will need two stones and the diagram of Herne's head (shown in figure 4a). The two stones should be fairly flat, but rounded, and about one-half inch in diameter. You may collect your stones at a special time, such as a Sabbat or a full moon, or at a special place, such as the beach or a favorite woodland spot.

When you have your stones, mark a circle on both sides of one of them, and mark an "X" on both sides of the other. The "O" and "X" basically stand for positive and negative, and you will see how these principles come into play as you read the interpretations of how each falls in the diagram. The "O" stone is called the **Light Stone**. The "X" stone is called the **Shadow Stone**.

You must also prepare a diagram of Herne's head, as shown on page 35 (figure 4b). Because your stones will be about half an inch in diameter, the ideal size of the diagram is about one and a half feet by two feet. (However, if you find smaller or larger stones, your diagram could be proportionally smaller or larger). I recommend painting the diagram on a flat, wood board. You can paint the different symbols different colors (suggestions are given, but feel free to improvise) or just use one color. Oil paints (though they can take up to a week or two to completely dry) and indelible marker both work well. When the diagram is completed on the board, you can use other slats of wood to form a "lip" around the edges of the board. This lip ensures that the stones stay within bounds when cast.

You might also obtain a large piece of white posterboard on which to draw the diagram, using one color or many according to your preference. If you are going to go the posterboard route, leave at least a two-inch rim along the sides of the diagram. When you are finished with the diagram, cut, fold, and secure the edge to form a one-inch lip all around the posterboard. Posterboard is of heavy enough stock that the rim pieces will stay in place.

Ready-made trays or boxes (such as a flat display tray available in jewelry supply catalogs) can also be used. Just make sure the bottom of the box or tray is plain and takes paint.

Figure 4a: A completed Herne's Head. A lip around the flat surface will keep your stones on the face of the diagram when cast.

THE DIAGRAM AND ITS SYMBOLS

Don't worry about how artistic your completed diagram looks. Most of the symbols are not complicated, and are easy to draw. If you lack confidence in your artistic talents, draw your diagram in pencil on the board or posterboard. This way you can make sure you are pleased with your results before you start to ink it in or color it.

You will see that the diagram (figure 4b) incorporates many traditional Craft and Pagan symbols. The **mistletoe** represents divine inspiration. The **three rays** descending from the mistletoe circle represent the Celtic holy word "Awen," signifying divine guidance and inspiration. The middle ray of Awen also forms the stem of a chalice, and the half-circle on Herne's forehead is actually the upturned **bowl of the chalice**. The **eight-pointed star** is the "third eye," which is related to the pituitary gland and the moon, and thus placed in the chalice, a lunar symbol. The **horns** and twelve **zodiac symbols** need no explanation.

Herne's eyebrows are in the shape of a **bird** in flight. The **eyes** are in the shape of nuts, and refer to the nuts of wisdom in the Celtic tradition. The **four triangles** are symbols of the four elements. On Herne's face we have fire (pointing upward) and water (pointing downward). Outside of Herne's face is air (the upward pointing triangle that you can remember by seeing the letter "A" within it) and earth (the other downward pointing triangle). The **sword** points upwards into the chalice, signifying the Great Rite, the Union of God and Goddess. The **sword shaft** and **crossbar** are Herne's nose, while the **hilt circle** and **crescent** are Herne's mouth.

The **sun** and **moon** are masculine and feminine symbols, respectively. The **apple** is the fruit of the Summerlands. The **spiral maze** is a traditional symbol of death and rebirth.

The **serpent** is traditionally an Underworld symbol, and ancient depictions of the Horned One often show him with snakes. Here the serpent denotes restriction, which is a concept associated with the planet Saturn in astrology. Time is also a concept associated with Saturn. Therefore, when a stone falls on the serpent's head or coils, it will be possible to judge a time element for the question.

Figure 4b: Diagram for the Herne's Head tool.

Suggested Colors for the Diagram

In my opinion, a colored diagram looks more pleasing than a diagram done all in one color; however, the choice is yours. On the opposite page are some suggested colors for the diagram (figure 4c).

The background of the board or posterboard should probably be left its natural wood color (in the case of the board) or white (in the case of the posterboard). You might also choose to paint the background of the board some neutral color such as white or a light gray.

CONSECRATION OF YOUR TOOLS

When you have completed your diagram, and have made ready your stones, you are going to have to consecrate them, as you would any other magical tool. Throughout the book we will keep to a varying form of Consecration by the Elements. You will need the following:

- Your completed stones and Herne's Head.
- A small table to use as an altar.
- A white candle on the south side of the altar.
- A small bowl of water on the west side of the altar.
- A small dish of salt on the north side of the altar.
- Incense (a stick of incense is fine) and something to burn it in (a bowl of soil or sand) on the east side of the altar.

The two stones should be in the center of the altar, and Herne's Head beside the altar to the east.

You should perform the ritual on the night of the full moon, the time of the month when your psychic awareness and powers will be at their height. Take a short bath before the ritual, making sure you are calm and relaxed. If you have a robe that you wear for magical work, you may wear it. You can also perform the ritual skyclad if you wish.

After your bath, proceed to the altar. Light the candle, and from it start the incense burning. You may wish to cast a Circle for the consecration ritual, using your own method or the procedure given in the Appendix, but this is not strictly necessary. First start with the

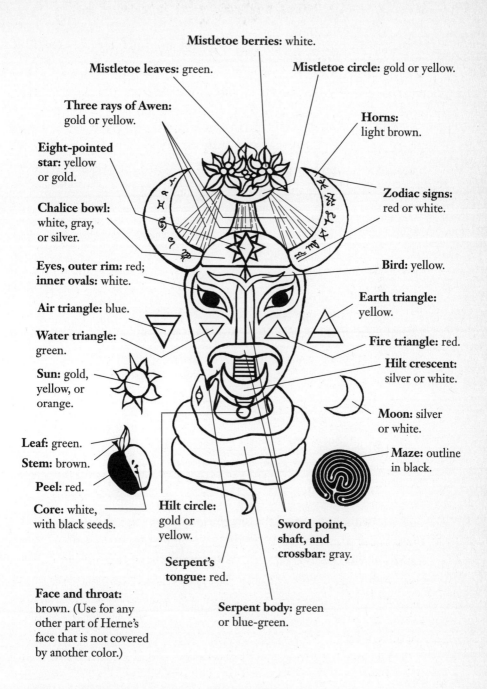

Mistletoe berries: white.

Mistletoe leaves: green.

Mistletoe circle: gold or yellow.

Three rays of Awen: gold or yellow.

Horns: light brown.

Eight-pointed star: yellow or gold.

Zodiac signs: red or white.

Chalice bowl: white, gray, or silver.

Bird: yellow.

Eyes, outer rim: red; **inner ovals:** white.

Earth triangle: yellow.

Air triangle: blue.

Fire triangle: red.

Water triangle: green.

Hilt crescent: silver or white.

Sun: gold, yellow, or orange.

Moon: silver or white.

Leaf: green.

Maze: outline in black.

Stem: brown.

Peel: red.

Core: white, with black seeds.

Hilt circle: gold or yellow.

Sword point, shaft, and crossbar: gray.

Serpent's tongue: red.

Face and throat: brown. (Use for any other part of Herne's face that is not covered by another color.)

Serpent body: green or blue-green.

Figure 4c: Suggested colors for the diagram.

Light Stone. Take it up, and pass it through the smoke of the burning incense, and say:

I consecrate thee by the element air.

Pass the stone through the flame of the candle and say:

I consecrate thee by the element fire.

Anoint the stone with a drop of the water from the bowl and say:

I consecrate thee by the element water.

Place a bit of salt on the stone and say:

I consecrate thee by the element earth.

Next, repeat the above procedure with the Shadow Stone.

When both stones are consecrated by the elements, you will finish their consecration by blessing them with the element of spirit. Hold them both aloft above the altar, and chant the following incantation:

Stone of Shadow, Stone of Light,
Thou art blessed by Spirit's might!
Guide my path by day and night,
That I may live my life aright!

Place the stones back in the center of the altar. Take up Herne's Head and perform the same elemental consecration on it as you did the stones, finishing with earth. Be careful not to ruin your diagram. Do not pass it too close over the candle flame, and only a bit of water dabbed on the corner of the diagram is necessary. When you have consecrated Herne's Head by the four elements, hold it above the altar to give it the final blessing with the following incantation:

Hallowed Head of Holy Herne,
Within Thee sacred Spirit burns!
Guide my Path by Day and Night,
That I may live my life aright!

When you are through, put out the incense and candle, and clean up. Put Herne's Head and your stones away in a safe place for future use.

ASKING A QUESTION OF HERNE'S HEAD

As I mentioned previously, this form of divination is good for both ascertaining the future outcome of a situation and obtaining advice as to what course of action you should take regarding a problem. A cursory examination of the interpretations of each symbol will show that this is so.

Obviously you will have some question in mind when you approach Herne's Head. You should not ask frivolous questions, or questions to which you already know the answers. Set up Herne's Head so that the sword in the diagram is pointing east, the direction associated with air, and thus Herne. Take up the Light and Shadow Stones together, and chant the following incantation:

Head of Herne, Head of Herne,
Swiftly speak that I may learn
The problem's source,
The future's course,
The path to take,
The choice to make!

Cast the two stones onto Herne's Head, and note where they fall. Turn to the following rules, symbols, and interpretations section to learn what Herne has to say about your question.

THE SYMBOLS AND THEIR INTERPRETATIONS

Both stones will be used to answer the question, and you should turn to the interpretation for each and combine them to receive your answer. Observe the following rules:

- The Light Stone shows the positive side of the answer, and the Shadow Stone shows the negative side of the answer.
- If only one stone falls on a symbol, Herne has only answered your question in part. Some part of the future is cloudy, or an option in a decision-making process is not yet fully formed.

- If neither stone falls upon a symbol, or if either stone bounces completely outside of the entire diagram and falls to the floor, Herne will not answer your question at this time. Wait at least twenty-four hours before asking any question of Herne.

- If a stone touches two or more symbols (as might happen with, for example, the bird and sword shaft, or the serpent's tongue and hilt crescent or hilt circle), you must read the interpretations for both or all of them to fully understand Herne's message.

- If the message of the two stones seems contradictory, the future is not yet solidified, and Herne cannot answer your question. Wait at least twenty-four hours before asking the question again (though you may ask other, unrelated questions immediately, if you desire).

Interpretations for each symbol include both the Light Stone and the Shadow Stone. Starting from the top of the diagram and roughly working downward, the symbols are interpreted as follows:

The Mistletoe

Light — You are under the protection of divine guidance. Trust your intuition and all will work out well. Could indicate a vision or other psychic experience that makes the whole situation seem crystal clear. The end of the problem or situation is nearer at hand than you think. There will be success, enlightenment, and joy. A good omen for the outcome of any situation.

Shadow — Destiny or karmic influences are leading you along on your present course, but you are struggling against the inevitable outcome of the situation, and thus only prolonging your troubles. You are choosing the "pleasurable" and not the "good," and are concerned with your own material or sensual desires, not your spiritual development. The future outcome will not seem favorable to you at the conclusion of affairs, but will be very beneficial for you in the long run.

The Left Ray of Awen

Light — Too often you are giving someone the benefit of the doubt. You need to be a little more stern with other people, or they will walk all over you. Develop a "no-nonsense" attitude toward the situation, and it will give you a sense of security. You are budgeting your time properly and do not need to make any changes in your schedule. You are on the proper course, but if you lack confidence, consult a mother figure, particularly an older woman. She will be able to shed some additional light on the situation. The future will give you a sense of material security.

Shadow — You are not giving enough time for the situation to fully develop yet and are being impatient. You may be too hard on other people involved. They will be more easily persuaded by sweetness than bitterness. Inertia in the situation will be overcome with hard work, not laziness. Consider giving more effort to the situation, or else the future tides will turn further against you. If the problem you ask about is a recurring one in your life, think over your past relationship and dealings with your mother or other women, and see how this might be causing you to act in certain ways.

The Middle Ray of Awen

Even though this forms the stem of the chalice, it is interpreted as the middle ray.

Light — An excellent omen for success in the situation. You are taking a balanced approach to the situation, and divine guidance is flowing through you to bring about a successful conclusion to the matter at hand. Keep up your resolve, don't go to extremes, and you will enjoy success.

Shadow — Still a good omen for success, but you are preventing yourself from achieving that success. You have some inner blockages or a subconscious will to fail in the situation. You are your own worst enemy. There really are no outside obstacles to your success, only inner ones. You will have to adjust your attitude and behaviors to the situation in order to succeed. Try to spend some time in meditation thinking about what it is that is preventing you from achieving your heart's desire.

The Right Ray of Awen

Light — In order for things to work out properly, you must devote a great deal of energy and attention to the matter at hand. Adopt a compassionate and sympathetic attitude toward others involved for the best success. A father figure should be sought for advice; he has the answer or information you need. Generally, a good sign of success in any endeavor, as long as your energy level keeps up. A father figure is instrumental in a favorable outcome.

Shadow — You are spreading yourself too thin; you have too many projects and concerns to deal with right now, and the result is that you are exhausting yourself and not getting anywhere with anything. You must get your priorities straight before you can handle the situation that demands your attention most. Consider taking a day off from your daily affairs to rest and prioritize your life. If you do not, the disorder in your life will cause the situation to work out against you. If the problem you ask about is a recurring one in your life, think over your past relationship and dealings with your father or other men, and see how this might be causing you to act in certain ways.

The Chalice Bowl

Light — There will be joy, success, love and a happy conclusion in the matter you inquire about. Can indicate happiness in the home, with family, or with a significant other—perhaps even the birth of a child. If you have a decision to make, follow your heart and not your head. If you can't make up your mind, ask the advice of a loving woman. Can also indicate quick recovery from illness.

Shadow — There is unhappiness in love or problems with family, possibly arguments or problems with children. The future will not fulfill your desire. Your emotional state or attitude toward the situation is clouding your judgement in making a decision. Try not to react so emotionally to the situation. Don't take everything so personally. A woman may be causing you problems. To turn her around, speak lovingly to her and express concern for her well-being. If the query has to do with illness, the patient will recover, but not quickly.

The Eight-Pointed Star

Light — Opening of psychic awareness (perhaps telepathy or clair-voyance) and the proper use of magical powers. Follow your intu-itions, hunches, and gut reactions; they will prove correct and lead you on to success. Invoke the Moon Goddess of the tradition you follow and ask her to help you in your situation.

Shadow — Your inner self is presently off balance. Do not trust your hunches and intuitions, because you will be in danger of mak-ing a poor decision. Try to reason out the situation instead. Can indicate the misuse of psychic or magical ability. In any magical work that you are thinking of undertaking, be careful not to inter-fere with the will of another person and not harm another person. It is time to close down your psychic faculties and involve yourself in mundane affairs in order to gain a clearer perspective on the sit-uation or decision to be made. This will bring you a better chance of success.

The Left Horn

This is really a symbol of the waning moon. If a stone half touches a zodiac sign, and half touches an empty space in the horn, read only the interpretations pertaining to the zodiac sign. If a stone does not touch any of the zodiac signs, but is still within the horn, it should be interpreted as follows.

Light — The tides of the inner plane are working against you, and any decision made at this time will not meet with success. Delay any decisions for a lunar month (twenty-eight days) if possible.

Shadow — A bad omen. Do not take any action or make any deci-sions whatsoever for at least a lunar month (twenty-eight months).

Spend some time in meditation, relax, sleep late, and keep calm. Reserve your strength, because there is a battle ahead for you if you want to achieve success.

Aries

Light — You must be aggressive and energetic, acting with force and confidence, if you are to achieve success. If you have a decision to make, choose the option that will allow you to be the most active and energetic.

Shadow — Beware of making an impulsive and foolhardy decision. You are too impatient. Give the situation more time to develop. Your own big ego is causing your problems. Give in to another, or else arguments will result.

Taurus

Light — You must be persistent in order to reach your goal. As the Charge of the Goddess tells us: "Keep pure your highest ideal. Strive ever towards it. Let naught stop you nor turn you aside." Proceed cautiously and deliberately, planning every step toward your goal. Can indicate financial security as long as you make conservative investments, and save and spend wisely. A loyal friend or loved one will help you make a decision. In making decisions, take the most practical option.

Shadow — You are being stubborn and resentful. If someone has angered you, try to forgive that person, as your negative thoughts are affecting your own life and keeping you from success. You are not being very charitable or compassionate towards another person. Give freely and generosity will be returned to you three times over. Your haphazard, "hit-or-miss" approach to your goal will not bring the success you desire. In decisions, be conservative, and take the option that will bring you the most financial and emotional security.

Gemini

Light — You will have no problem making the correct decision, as long as you follow your reasoning mind. You have a good intellect, and are aware of all of the factors involved in your decision. Be versatile, however, as the situation may quickly change in the near future. Brothers, sisters, or other relatives may be able to give you good advice; consult them. A good omen for things relating to communication, school, letters, books, and all things having to do with the mind. In decisions, choose the option that will allow you to most explore your intellectual ideas and allow you to communicate with others. A short trip will prove beneficial and clear your mind.

Shadow — You are not aware of all the factors necessary to make a decision. You have only superficially examined the situation. Calm down; you are too nervous and scattered. You have too many things going on in your life right now. Can sometimes indicate misunderstandings or problems with communication, perhaps with siblings or relatives. Choose your words carefully either in speaking or in writing. You may want to consider whether it is best to keep silent and quiet, but alert in the matter. Can also indicate that you should be careful while driving or that your car will need some minor repairs.

Cancer

Light — You already intuitively know what your decision must be. Proceed in a sensitive and caring way. A mother or mother figure will be instrumental in carrying out your plans. An excellent omen of success for questions concerning the home, family, and real estate. You will attain emotional security in these areas. In decisions, choose the option that will allow you to protect your own interests most.

Shadow — Your own negative moods are keeping you from success. You must gain confidence in yourself and your ability to handle the situation. You are presenting a tough exterior, but may be crying inside. Vent your emotions, and you will gain a clearer perspective, but be careful not to smother loved ones with your emotions. You are approaching the subject too directly. An indirect, subtle, even sneaky approach will work best for you.

Leo

Light — An excellent omen for success in matters dealing with pleasure, hobbies, creativity, children, and romance. This is a good time to take calculated risks and act with resolution. Enjoy yourself and share your good fortune with others. In decisions, choose the option that will most allow you to enjoy yourself. A good time to choose the pleasurable over the good, since the pleasurable is the good in this situation. Think big!

Shadow — You are concentrating too much on pleasure now, and not enough on work. Hunker down, work diligently, and keep yourself out of the limelight. Now is not the time to seek recognition for yourself or your actions. Can indicate problems with children or with a romantic partner. The problems have been caused by your own aristocratic and dramatic attitudes. Get off of your perch, and things will improve. The future will be bright as long as you lay low and don't press the situation at present.

Virgo

Light — An excellent omen for success in your daily work environment, as long as you are industrious and pay attention to details. If the query regards health, the patient will improve. Be charitable towards others, or involve yourself in some volunteer work. In decisions, you must analyze the situation carefully and critically. Be discriminating in your choice, and choose the option that will allow you to work diligently toward your goal and allow you to involve yourself in details.

Shadow — You may not achieve success because you are too much of a perfectionist—too critical with others. You must learn to be more flexible, so others will not avoid you so much. Your attitudes may have earned you the dislike of your co-workers or employees. Choose a more modest goal for the present, and work towards perfection in smaller steps. If you do not, you may still achieve your goal, but probably at a price that you would rather not pay. If the question regards someone's health, the patient will not recover within the near future.

The Right Horn

As with the left horn, this is a lunar symbol—that of the waxing moon. Again, as with the left horn, if a stone half touches a zodiac sign, and half touches an empty space in the horn, read only the interpretations pertaining to the zodiac sign. If a stone does not touch any of the zodiac signs, but is still within the horn, it should be interpreted as follows.

Light — The tides of the inner planes are working with you, propelling you along. Any decision made at this time will encounter little difficulty. Proceed with your plans, but remain flexible, since the situation may change (for better or worse) with a lunar month (twenty-eight days).

Shadow — The tides of the inner planes are with you as you implement your plans to achieve your goal. However, you may encounter some difficulties on the road to your success. The situation may change for the worse within twenty-eight days, but you should overcome it and make good progress.

Libra

Light — A good omen for romance, marriages, and all types of partnerships. If there is a lawsuit or other controversy in the offing, you can expect a favorable outcome as long as you remain gracious and diplomatic. Though you may be indecisive, try to be impartial in your decision making and not allow extraneous emotions to interfere. Use your intellect and reasoning mind. Choose the option that will allow you to be social or make peace with others.

Shadow — A sign that you are discontent with a decision you have made through poor judgement. Don't be afraid to admit your mistakes and retrace your steps. If you are having problems in a partnership (either romantic or business), try not to be so flirtatious or forward. Balance should be your watchword here.

Scorpio

Light — An excellent omen for undertaking all types of magical and occult work. Perhaps all you need is a simple spell to push you over the edge to success. Also a good omen for sexual relationships, but be careful that your relationship is not just revolving around sex; there must be emotional support as well. There may be the possibility of inheriting some money or property. Secrets and hidden things will come to light. A complete change of the situation for the better is in the near future.

Shadow — Be careful of undertaking any magical work at this time. It could backfire on you if your motives are not pure. Relationships that are based only on sex will crumble, since they have no emotional foundation. In rare instances, may indicate the death of a loved one. A dark secret is either being kept by you or from you. It is probably better left undisclosed and undiscovered, else there will be a change for the worse in the situation.

Sagittarius

Light — An excellent omen for pursuing higher education; studies of philosophy, wisdom, and religion; and making long journeys (both physically and mentally). If a lawsuit is in the offing, there will be a favorable outcome for you. If you are having difficulties with a problem, you should consult a professional for advice. An excellent time to expand your horizons and explore new things. In making a decision, choose the option that will allow you to experience something new.

Shadow — You may be spreading yourself too thin, experiencing too many new things at once. Cut out the extraneous things in your life and spend more time on your main concerns and your decision will be clear. Beware of putting your foot in your mouth; someone may take a good-natured remark the wrong way. A legal judgement may not be in your favor.

Capricorn

Light — An excellent omen for improving your career situation, or setting your sights on some honor or achievement. Superiors will take note of you and help establish a good reputation for you. A very good omen for success in any situation as long as you proceed cautiously and prudently, and respect other people. In making decisions, choose the most conventional or conservative option.

Shadow — You are too rigid in your ambitions, and this may cause you to fail. Remain more flexible. Consider whether you are really motivated by a desire to achieve success or a desire to avoid failure. If the latter, you will not enjoy your success when you achieve it, because you will always be defending it. Enjoy the chase, not the prize. Be generous with your heart and purse, or else your miserliness will come back to haunt you three times over. A bad time to ask for a raise or favors from superiors.

Aquarius

Light — A wonderful omen for all matters concerning friends and professional or charitable groups. May indicate that you will encounter new magical friends that will assist you in your development or reaching your goal. In making decisions, consider your own opinions first, and don't be so quick to take advice from others. Remain independent. Choose the option that will allow you to enjoy a sense of freedom, or the choice that is most progressive, original, and unpredictable. Have fun being yourself, without regard of what others think.

Shadow — An unpredictable situation is causing you problems and will continue to do so. Could it be that you have gotten yourself into this mess because of your own "know-it-all" attitude? Don't be intractable—retrace your steps if you must. If emotions are involved, remain impersonal and aloof, for this is the only way you are going to come out of the situation emotionally unscathed.

Pisces

Light — Since you are highly impressionable at this time, the only way you are going to achieve success in this situation is through some careful self-introspection. Analyze the strengths and weaknesses of your personality, and see how your behaviors have created the present situation. How are you limiting yourself? Write down every option that you have and weigh them carefully with pros and cons. Capitalize on the strengths, and eradicate the weaknesses of both your personality and the situation. You have an intuitive understanding of what decision you must make. Follow your heart, for it is guided by your higher self.

Shadow — You have not given enough attention to the situation. You have been mentally wandering and have not clearly defined your goals. You are vague and not sure what you want out of the situation. It is likely that you have been unassertive, allowing others to take advantage of you. This is keeping you from success, and the near future will bear this out. Define your ideals, and work toward them with energy and drive, or failure will be almost certain.

The Bird

Light — You will soon receive a welcome message that you have been successful in your endeavors, or that someone is willing to help you achieve your goal. Beneficial news through letters, conversations, and like communications. Look to where the other stone falls to see what the message might involve.

Shadow — An unfavorable message or communication will be received, probably indicating trouble or failure in some endeavor. Someone may be spreading gossip about you, harming your reputation. Look to the other stone for more information on how to turn the situation around to your favor.

The Right Eye

Light — Success is in sight. It would be almost impossible to make a wrong decision given the choices that you have.

Shadow — Success is still in sight despite your foolish actions in the past. However, you must exercise discretion in making a decision. For advice, consult someone you consider wise.

The Left Eye

Light — Success is almost in sight. However, you are going to have to sacrifice something in order to attain what you want. The value of what you sacrifice should be equal to the value of what you want. In decision making, you have already made some bad decisions. Don't make another one. There is danger of doing so now.

Shadow — Success will be almost impossible to attain, no matter how hard you work at it. Re-evaluate your goals and make sure you have the necessary talent and nerve to achieve them. At the present time, you may find that you do not. For advice, consult someone you consider wise.

The Air Triangle

Light —Your thoughts are clear, and you can be confident that your decisions will be correct, whatever they may be. However, be sure to act quickly and on your own convictions—independently. You don't have much time left to seize what you want. Good fortune and success will soon be on their way; you may even receive a message concerning the good fortune before it actually occurs. Can signify optimism and joy.

Shadow — No decision should be made at this time, since the situation will change by the time of the next solstice or equinox. By that time, the decision may have made itself for you. After all, you are probably being fickle—you don't really even know what you want out of the situation. Keep your tongue silent about your plans. Talkativeness only lessens your chances of attaining what you want. Any slyness or dishonesty in achieving what you want will come back to haunt you three times over. You will have to clear your head of negative thoughts, and remain balanced and silent if you are to achieve success. Even then, it may be partial success.

The Earth Triangle

Light — You cannot fail if you continue on your course of action with resolution, endurance, thoroughness, and confidence. If you are making a decision, choose the most practical of the options for the best results in the long run.

Shadow — You will not succeed if you continue on this course of inertia, laziness, and unreliability. You may think you are working very hard toward your goal, but are you taking the most direct route to it? Are you working toward your heart's desire, or just laboring at something else while merely wishing that your heart's desire will fall in your lap? Re-evaluate your priorities, or you may become a workaholic with nothing to show for your pains but a materialistic nature. If you are making a decision, another option that you are not aware of will soon present itself. Delay your decision until you know what it is.

The Fire Triangle

Light — Success is almost certain as long as you remain forceful, enthusiastic, and excited about your goal. Move on with your plans now, while the Lady of Fortune is smiling on you. You will be able to get much accomplished. Have courage and jump into the fray. Your energy will carry you to your goal. If you are thinking of making a decision, your best option is the one that will allow you to be most creative and active.

Shadow — Your foolhardy and impulsive actions are leading you down the path to failure. Your irritability, impatience, and restlessness are clouding your judgement. Therefore, you should delay any important decisions at this time. If they are life-changing decisions, you should wait until the next equinox or solstice before considering making a choice at all.

The Water Triangle

Light — A friend or loved one whose advice you value should be sought out. He or she will be instrumental in helping you achieve your goal. If you are encountering difficulties attaining what you desire, try to be more modest, respectful, and cordial to the other people involved. It will work wonders. In making a decision, choose the option that makes you feel safe, calm, and secure.

Shadow — Your unsympathetic nature will not bring you success. Remember that whatever goal you choose, it can only be attained with the help of other people. Meditate on the fact that all good things come from the Gods, but that the Gods use other people as instruments to deliver good fortune to you. You may be conforming to the expectations of others, and may be acting in ways that other people expect you to act. Consider whether this is really in your best interests. Your emotions are clouding your judgement. If you are able to separate the emotional element from what you are considering, you can confidently make a decision. If you cannot separate your feelings from the situation, delay the decision until you can.

The Sword Point

Light — A sure sign of success, victory, and conquest as long as you work hard, and do not let any obstacles slow you down. In family situations, sometimes it can mean the birth of a male child. If you are in trouble, invoke the Horned Lord for protection. However, if you are in trouble with the law, or have done something illegal, the Sword of Justice will catch up with you.

Shadow — Defeat. A competitor will be victorious, because he or she is working harder than you are. In family or romantic situations, it can indicate arguments and dissension on the horizon, particularly where male egos are involved.

The Sword Shaft

Light — Success is still attainable, though the road to it may be filled with tears and pain. Nonetheless, the situation will provide you with a lesson that you desperately need to learn. If your query concerns a decision, do not make one at this time if at all possible. The situation needs more time to develop. You do not have all the necessary facts.

Shadow — Fate is against you. You will not be able to achieve what you desire because of some past wrongdoing. Abandon the situation, or you will only earn tears and sorrow. If you are making a decision, none of the options are viable. Choose the lesser of the two evils if a choice must be made.

The Sword Crossbar

Light — The obstacles that you are encountering are surmountable. You can still attain what you desire. Steel your nerve, have confidence in yourself, and proceed on course. If you need to make a decision, consider whether the options are mutually exclusive. You may be able to do both. If not, choose the more difficult of the options, since you will be able to surmount any obstacles, and the rewards will be greater.

Shadow — There is an obstacle in your path that you will not be able to overcome. The only thing you can hope for is that it will disappear of its own accord. No amount of effort will get rid of it. A friend or loved one may be disloyal, or there may be tension in your personal relationships. If you are about to make a decision, stop dead in your tracks, abandon the situation, and start over again. You need to re-evaluate your priorities.

The Hilt Circle

Light — You are in firm control of the situation. Others will obey you, though you may have to be persistent with them. You will soon reach the fullness of success. You will be able to turn any decision toward your advantage so choose any option, keeping in mind that the one that appeals to your mind and not your heart is probably best in the long run.

Shadow — You lack control over the situation. You have been too mild and unaggressive. You need to grasp the sword firmly with both hands and charge toward your goal. You may destroy what you most desire by doing so, but if you do destroy it, you can rest assured that it was not worth having. If you are indecisive, do not make a decision just to get it over with. Be patient. Your knowledge of the situation, as yet, is incomplete.

The Hilt Crescent

Light — A message regarding a competitor or rival will soon come to you. Having received this message, you will gain the advantage. There will be victory after strife, and pleasure gained through hard work. If your query concerns a decision, make one quickly before the situation changes. Go with your emotions and gut reactions in choosing.

Shadow — A competitor or rival has the advantage over you. The only way you will be victorious is by listening to the inner voice of intuition. Do not make any decisions at this time, for in a lunar month (twenty-eight days) the situation will have altered so much as to make it worthless.

The Hilt Base

Light —You are just starting out on this new endeavor, or at least, are just starting to make progress. Proceed with discretion and discrimination. Your judgement is good, but it is too early to say whether you will ultimately achieve success. If you are considering a decision, move forward with your plans. You have little to lose at this point.

Shadow — You have made a false start, because your foundation or plans were faulty. Retrace your steps and start over. Pay attention to every detail of the situation. Plan every step or failure will be certain. If you are considering a decision, you may still move forward with your plans, but be aware that your judgement is clouded. Best to ask another, preferably someone that has achieved success in this area, for a second opinion as to your course of action.

The Sun

Light — An excellent omen for every question. You will attain material happiness and success. Whatever the endeavor, it will succeed. You cannot fail in making the right decision. If you are still wary, trust your head and not your heart. Also, if you have recently lost something, if the stone falls upon one of the rays of the sun, it will indicate the direction in which the lost object can be found. The uppermost point is north, the bottom south, the right east, the left west. The other rays are the quarter points. Go to the place where you last remember having or seeing the object, and look in the direction indicated.

Shadow — Since the sun is such a powerful symbol, success can still be attained, but the future is cloudy and uncertain. Don't put too much hope in what you are trying to achieve because it may not work out to your advantage. The best you can do is to think things through every step of the way, evaluate every option, and make informed, reasoned choices. You can still have fun along the way, even if the situation does not work out.

The Moon

Light — Trust your instincts about the future, and you will achieve success. If you are making a decision, trust your intuition and emotions, and you will not go wrong. If you cannot make a decision based on the information you have, you should try crystal gazing; an important symbol will be revealed to you, since your psychic abilities are stronger at this time. A woman may be able to give you advice.

Shadow — There will be some deception and unforeseen perils or secret enemies in the near future, making success unlikely. No risks should be taken at this time, and no decisions should be made. Everything is in a state of flux, and many changes will occur within a lunar month (twenty-eight days).

The Apple Stem and Leaf

Light — You are on the road to success. If the question concerns love, you are misguided. There is someone else in your life that has taken a fancy to you, but you are either ignoring them, or are too busy concentrating on other things to take any notice. Be flexible. He or she may be just what you are looking for. In making a decision, choose the option that will allow you to be most productive.

Shadow —Your plans will soon crumble to the ground. You are hanging on to outworn customs, ideas, or relationships that you should have outgrown a long time ago. You've eaten the apple, now throw away the stem. In making a decision, choose the option that will allow you to progress in your life. Don't stay where you are. You need to experience new things and new environments.

The Apple Seeds

Light — Spiritually, you are on the right path. You have inborn, natural magical powers, but they require training and discipline to bring them to full fruition. In material endeavors, you will be starting a new project that will bear you wondrous fruits. Proceed as planned. If you are making a decision, choose the option that most conforms to your core beliefs and ideals.

Shadow — Your disenchantment with your spirituality is affecting all other parts of your life. Consider studying other traditions, exploring new ideas. What you have been concentrating on may have been convenient, but may not have been the best path for you. Don't be afraid to start all over again, as you have gained valuable experience. Think of it as a rebirth. In material endeavors, your idea and plans were good, but not implemented well. They will not bear fruit. Re-plant, choosing a different crop if necessary. In rare instances, it can indicate that someone is working magic against you.

The Apple Flesh

Light — Success; love; the complete fruition of your plans. Follow your heart if you need to make a decision.

Shadow — Failure. The situation will not work out to your advantage. Do not follow your heart if you need to make a decision. Stick with the most practical, reasonable option.

The Spiral Maze of Death and Rebirth

Light — Though things may seem confusing right now, you are on the right track. Success may be just around the corner, so do not give up! It can sometimes indicate that a completely new attitude must be adopted toward the situation before you achieve success. Sleep is known as "the little death," so "sleep on it" if you have a choice to make. The answer may come to you in a dream, or you may wake up intuitively knowing what course of action you must take. If you have a dream that you believe is significant, take note of any women that appear in the dream. If you recognize them, ask their advice after you have awakened. If you do not know them, recall what actions they took or performed during your dream. It will be an omen of what you should do.

Shadow — You are running around in circles. You don't know what you want, and consequently, are not working towards anything. You need to clearly define your goals, or you will continue in this pattern of inertia. Do not make any decisions at this time. Every option will end in failure.

The Serpent's Tongue

Light — The only way that you will be able to succeed is by using sweet and subtle speech to persuade others that your view of the situation is correct. You already know the wisest course of action to take if you are making a decision. You just lack confidence to follow it through. Ask the advice of a person you consider wise, and he or she will re-affirm what you need to do.

Shadow — A friend has turned against you, or someone is spreading false information about you. Beware of making a decision at this time since someone has lied to you, hoping to influence your choice. Find out who this culprit is, but try to do so without confronting that person. If the culprit discovers that you know he or she has falsely represented the situation to you, the situation may turn further against you.

The Serpent's Head and Upper Coil

Light — What the Shadow Stone indicates will occur within one month.

Shadow — What the Light Stone indicates will occur within two months.

If the other stone does not fall on any symbol, Herne is telling you that the question will cease to be important within the indicated time period.

The Serpent's Second Coil

Light — What the Shadow Stone indicates will occur within two months.

Shadow — What the Light Stone indicates will occur within four months.

If the other stone does not fall on any symbol, Herne is telling you that the question will cease to be important within the indicated time period.

The Serpent's Third Coil and Tail

Light — What the Shadow Stone indicates will occur within three months.

Shadow — What the Light Stone indicates will occur within six months.

If the other stone does not fall on any symbol, Herne is telling you that the question will cease to be important within the indicated time period.

Herne's Throat

Light — Ask the same question, and throw the stones again.

Shadow —Herne will not answer your question. Do not ask it again. Either you already know the answer conclusively, or Herne has judged that it will be better for you to proceed without direction from him.

CONCLUSION

As a final note, I wish to mention that, should you be an advanced student and fairly conversant with the symbols given in this form of divination, a very profitable undertaking may be to meditate on each symbol and derive your own meanings for them. May Herne always speak true to you!

CHAPTER FIVE

THE HOUSE OF THE GODDESS

Our second form of divination, the House of the Goddess, also makes use of symbols in a structured diagram form. It is a small box painted with symbols on the bottom. There are twenty-eight sections containing one symbol each.

Many cultures had a way of dividing the zodiac into twenty-eight sections. Each section had a particular name and specific energy attributions varying with each culture. The twenty-eight sections were often referred to as the twenty-eight **lunar mansions**. When the moon was in a certain section of the sky, some activities were deemed favorable and others deemed unfavorable. Certain sections were beneficial and others were considered evil. So this form of divination is to be used when an answer to a question is desired immediately, and is also used to decide whether it is favorable or unfavorable to take a particular course of action at a given time.

GATHERING YOUR TOOLS

There are only two tools required for the House of the Goddess. One is a flat moonstone from one-fourth to one-half inch in diameter. You can procure one at most occult stores, gem shops, or even a science specialty store. You will be consecrating and blessing it for your divination use, so you need not worry about "foreign" influences lingering on it.

The other tool is the House of the Goddess itself, a wood box with a removable lid. The twenty-eight symbols and sections are drawn on the "floor" of the house. Traditionally, magical tools (including divination tools) are more potent if made by the person who is to use them. If you can handle a ruler, black marker, hammer and nails, you should be able to construct this tool from scratch.

Because the diagram is divided into twenty-eight squares, each one inch by one inch, the bottom of your House should be at least seven by four inches. Your lid should also be this size or a little bit larger so it covers the entire top of the box (the lid will not be attached to the finished box, however). The sides should be high enough to allow the moonstone room to move freely inside the box; two to three inches seems to be ample height.

Your hardware store will usually cut down any pieces of wood to the correct size for you. You may also sometimes find pieces of the correct size in larger craft or hobby stores. These stores might also offer suggestions on the best way to affix the sides of the box to the bottom (small nails, wood glue, et cetera).

The diagram can be drawn on the wood with pencil, then blacked in with a fine-tipped black marker of indelible ink, or with paint. I recommend drawing the diagram on the floor before putting on the sides, just so your drawing hand has room to move comfortably.

The lid for your House of the Goddess should be inscribed with a lunar symbol. Using a drawing compass, you should be able to draw a lunar symbol such as this one:

Color this lunar symbol in whatever color(s) you prefer, or add any other personally significant symbols.

If you desire, you can finish all the pieces of wood with a lacquer finish to give your House of the Goddess a polished look.

The dimensions for your box could be larger or smaller than those described above. However, you do need a box with a bottom big enough for you to easily draw and read the diagram and symbols on it.

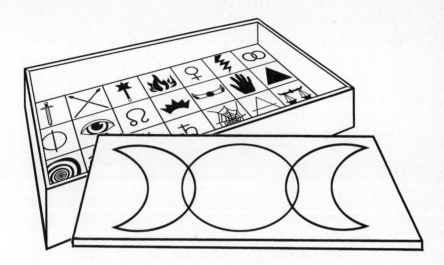

Figure 5a: A completed House of the Goddess.

Alternative Boxes

Instead of constructing your own box for the House of the Goddess, you could purchase a plain, ready-made box with a lid. The material could really be anything, but preferably something organic, such as wood or cardboard. Please note, however, that buying a box is not as good as putting one together for yourself.

THE DIAGRAM AND ITS SYMBOLS

As mentioned before, the diagram for the House of the Goddess consists of twenty-eight symbols representing the twenty-eight lunar mansions. The symbols are arranged in a grid, each horizontal line of the grid having seven squares and symbols (see figure 5b, page 64). Starting in the diagram's upper-left-hand corner and going across, the symbols are:

    1. A sword (pointing downward).

    2. Two crossed spears.

    3. A labrys (a double-sided axe with curved blades).

Figure 5b: Diagram for the floor of the House of the Goddess.

4. A flame of fire.

5. The astrological symbol of Venus.

6. A lightning bolt.

7. Two interlocked circles.

8. A circle with a vertical line through it.

9. An eye.

10. The astrological symbol of Leo.

11. A crown.

12. A winged disk.

13. A hand.

14. An equilateral triangle.

15. A whirlpool spiral.

16. The astrological symbol of Scorpio.

17. Two parallel lines.

18. The astrological symbol of Saturn (or a sickle or scythe).

19. A spider web.

20. The symbol of the element air (a triangle with a horizontal line through it).

21. A balance of scales.

22. A knife dripping blood.

23. A serpent.

24. A tower.

25. A grid of lines.

26. A star atop a mountain.

27. A waning moon (horns pointing to the right).

28. An equal-armed cross atop a sphere.

When you draw this diagram on your House of the Goddess, you can color in the symbols with paints or other colored markers, choosing whatever colors appeal to you. You do not need to include the numbers in the squares of your drawing.

CONSECRATION RITUAL FOR THE HOUSE OF THE GODDESS

The best time to perform this ritual is, of course, the night of the full moon. Failing that, you may perform it on one of the eight Sabbats. As a last resort, any time during the period of the waxing moon (from new moon until full moon) will do.

For this ritual, you will need the following items:

- A small table facing north to serve as an altar.
- A stick of incense (or granulated incense and a piece of charcoal upon which to burn it) set on the east side of the altar.
- A white candle set on the south side of the altar.
- A bowl of water set on the west side of the altar.
- A small dish of salt or soil set on the north side of the altar.
- Your completed House of the Goddess, and your moonstone.

Before you begin the ritual, you should sit in front of the altar for several minutes to still your mind and meditate on the purpose of the ritual. When you feel composed, light the candle, and from the candle set your incense going. Take a bath in water sprinkled with salt, relax your body and calm your mind. After your bath, you may robe or remain skyclad as you wish. Proceed to your working area. Light the candle and from it start the incense going. You may wish to cast a Circle for the consecration ritual, using your own method or the procedure given in the Appendix, but this is not strictly necessary.

Take up the moonstone, and hold it in your hand for a couple of minutes until it becomes warm and imbued with your essence. Pass it through the smoke of the burning incense, then pass it through the flame of the candle, anoint it with the water from the bowl, and rub a few grains of salt onto its surface. When this is done, hold the moonstone aloft over the altar, and speak the following incantation over it three times:

Eye of the Goddess, Seeing Stone,
Hear the spell I now intone!
By Maid and Mother and ancient Crone,
Show the Truth when thou art thrown!

Place the moonstone back on the altar and take up your completed House of the Goddess, with its lid. Again, pass the whole thing through the smoke of the incense, the flame of the candle (quickly, so as not to burn down the House of the Goddess), anoint a corner with a bit of water, and rub a bit of salt on one of the corners. Hold it over the altar, and repeat the following incantation over it three times.

Mirror of Heaven, Queen of the Sky,
By charmèd spell I call thee nigh!
Indwell this House that's made for thee
Wrought with love, by rune and tree.

When you are finished, take the moonstone, place it in the House, replace the lid, and hold it up over the altar one last time. Repeat the following incantation once:

Silver Moon, my night-time Sun,
End ye well, what I've begun!

You are now finished with the consecration ritual. Put out the candle flame, and leave the incense to burn until it goes out of its own accord. Then clean up. Keep your moonstone in the House, and keep the House wrapped up in white silk or linen when not in use.

DIVINATION BY THE
HOUSE OF THE GODDESS

As mentioned previously, this form of divination is to be used only when you need a quick answer to a question or when you need to know whether a certain time is favorable for a specific undertaking. While you will get accurate answers, you will not get long, drawn-out readings. That's both the advantage and disadvantage of this divination system.

To consult the Goddess you must have a question. This form of divination can either give you a quick "yes or no" answer, or it can tell you whether a time is favorable for something. Therefore, either frame your question so that all it needs is a "yes or no" response or frame it in terms of "Is it favorable for me to do [such and such] at [specifying a time or time period]?" In this way, it can be used to help make a decision whether to act or remain passive in a certain situation.

Take the House of the Goddess out of its wrapping, hold it in your hands, and ask your question aloud or inwardly three times. Then repeat aloud the following incantation (a traditional formula for invoking the Goddess) three times:

ANA ISA EE-A
[pronounced: anna-eeza-ee-ah]

When you have done this, shake the moonstone in the House of the Goddess firmly, but gently, three times (making sure you hold it so that the lid is firmly in place). Place the House on a level surface, and gently lift off the lid. You will find your answer where the moonstone falls. If the moonstone touches more than one square, read every square it touches in order to find out your answer, unless it is a yes-or-no question. In that case, the stone must be within one square, and you will have to shake the House again if it is not.

If you are reading for another person, allow that person to hold the House to ask the question, but you should be the one to recite the charm and shake the box to find out the answer.

LIST OF INTERPRETATIONS

The interpretations of each of the squares and symbols is as follows. The first interpretations given are to answer "yes or no" type questions, while the remainder of the interpretation has to do with favorability or unfavorability of times for specific undertakings.

Sword (1)

No. Favorable for occult practices, the job or career, competitive business deals, matters dealing with authority figures. Unfavorable for everything else.

Two Crossed Spears (2)

No. Favorable for confronting enemies, discovering hidden secrets, and overcoming illness. Unfavorable for everything else, but particularly unfavorable for journeys by or over water, sudden love affairs, and political actions.

Labrys (3)

No. Favorable for all things relating to work, particularly practical scientific or mathematical work, or work dealing with the outdoors. Also favorable for things that require strong determination in achieving some practical (non-emotional) ambition. Unfavorable for everything else, but particularly bad for travel, love, and marriage.

Flame of Fire (4)

Yes. Favorable for passion and sensuality, work and trade. Also favorable for marriage or a committed relationship, but is an indication that there will be some conflicts. Also good for overcoming obstacles, but you will have to use energy, wit, and subtlety to do so. Unfavorable for everything else, but particularly for things dealing with land or buildings.

Astrological Symbol of Venus (5)

Yes. Favorable for artistic and poetic endeavors, love, friendship, travel, health, and change of residence. Also good for matters that may require you to persuade another person of your point of view. Unfavorable for everything else, but particularly bad for work and business, humanitarian endeavors, and anything that involves large entities or a group of people.

Lightning Bolt (6)

No. Favorable for matters where you require spiritual protection, or for confronting enemies or finding out secrets. Unfavorable for everything else, but particularly unfavorable for health (slows down recovery) or matters dealing with land. Business and financial matters are not favored as there may be some deception involved.

Two Interlocked Circles (7)

Yes. Favorable for love, friendship, health, family, and money. Basically favorable for almost everything, with few exceptions. It is unfavorable for seeking revenge and matters dealing with lawsuits or courts.

Circle with a Vertical Line (8)

Yes. Particularly favorable for family matters, emotional relationships, love, and friendship. Also favorable for travel. Unfavorable for everything else, and may indicate that you are now paying for an ill-thought-out past action.

Eye (9)

Yes. Very good for questions involving love and romance. It will cause disappointments in all other areas (indicating painful separations and disunity), and is extremely unfavorable for questions involving travel.

Astrological Symbol of Leo (10)

Yes. Favorable for love, spiritual matters, and business success, but only if you exert yourself and have ambition. Unfavorable for travel, health, and changes of residence.

Crown (11)

Yes. Favorable for almost everything, including business deals, money, marriage, and travel, but only if these are planned out carefully. Unfavorable, however, for health and confronting enemies or hiding secrets from others. Unfavorable for taking risks.

Winged Disk (12)

No. Favorable for things dealing with the mind such as study, books, and school. Also favorable for sending letters and other communications. Unfavorable for everything else, particularly emotional matters, where the heart may tend to get the head in trouble by making wrong decisions.

Hand (13)

Yes. Generally good for financial or business matters, though the benefits of the matter at hand will be fleeting. Also good for travel. Unfavorable for everything else, but particularly for health problems (especially ones connected to dietary factors), or endeavors where you have to take the initiative. Whether favorable or unfavorable, always an indication that secret influences are at work in the situation.

Equilateral Triangle (14)

No. Favorable for all occult practices (particularly divination) or matters where mental analysis is required. Unfavorable for everything else, but especially for journeys, emotional attachments (particularly when these are new relationships), and making decisions.

Whirlpool Spiral (15)

No. Unfavorable for almost everything, though it is favorable for scheming, secret plans, and plotting against enemies if that's what you're up to (remember the Law of Three). Also indicates protection if you are in the midst of some catastrophe.

Astrological Symbol of Scorpio (16)

No. Favorable for financial risks (though it may indicate greed) and escaping retribution for mistakes in the past. Unfavorable for everything else, and particularly poor for love, travel, and health.

Two Parallel Lines (17)

Yes. Favorable for emotional relationships, marriage, matters where the person has great responsibility, and things dealing with the occupation or advancement to a higher position. Also good for questions regarding travel or changes of residence. Unfavorable for all other things.

Astrological Symbol of Saturn (18)

No. Unfavorable for almost everything (especially when the matter deals with the family or a family member) except conflicts, conspiracy, and exposing scandals or enemies. Lawsuits and justice are also favorable.

Spider Web (19)

No. Disastrous for almost everything, so nothing new should be undertaken at this time, and no new actions should be initiated. The only thing favored when the moonstone falls here might be ferreting out the secrets and secret plans that others may be plotting against you.

Symbol of the Element Air (20)

Yes. Favorable for communications, writings, and long-term relationships (though with an indication that one of the partners will be domineering, so this should be considered before making a serious commitment). Also good for business and trade, though there is an indication of some loss before gain is made. Unfavorable for other things, but especially changes of residence and travel (though this can sometimes indicate a forced change of residence through whatever circumstances).

Balance of Scales (21)

Yes. Favorable for questions dealing with health, travel, and earnings. It also favors military personnel or military matters. Unfavorable for other things, especially sexual relationships.

Knife Dripping Blood (22)

No. Unfavorable for almost everything, except confrontations with enemies and bringing evil-doers to justice. Particularly unfavorable with regard to romantic or family relationships.

Serpent (23)

No. Favorable for achieving success in the career through interventions of friends and loved ones, but usually indicating some conflicts along the way. Favorable for matters of deep spirituality and health. Unfavorable for everything else, especially business deals and romance. Relationships started or intensified now will end in tears and separation.

Tower (24)

Yes. Favorable for almost everything, as long as prudence and caution are carefully exercised. Unfavorable for travel, however.

Grid of Lines (25)

No. Favorable for health and overcoming enemies. Also favorable for any question dealing with scientific or experimental things. Unfavorable for everything else, especially love, family, and pregnancy.

Star Atop a Mountain (26)

Yes. Favorable for love, friendships, business contracts, charitable works, health, and politics (including "office politics"). Unfavorable for everything else, especially travel.

Waning Moon (27)

No. Favorable for very little except saving money and close, committed relationships. Not good for business contacts, loaning money, matters connected with land, or letters and communication (there will be delays and frustrations with these).

Equal-armed Cross Atop a Sphere (28)

Yes. Very favorable for questions regarding money, travel (but beware of losing your luggage), spiritual matters, and romantic relationships. Generally favorable for everything except health matters.

CONCLUSION

Though the system is a somewhat simple one, the House of the Goddess can't be beat when you need a quick answer to a pressing problem and don't have time to perform a divination with a more complex system. After the "rush" to have an answer has passed, you may profitably engage in another, more complex form of divination in order to ascertain why the House of the Goddess gave you the answer that it did.

CHAPTER SIX

THE WITCH'S DRUM

Our third and last form of divination using a diagram—the Witch's Drum—is one encountered in more traditional forms of the Craft. However, one need not be from a family in which the Craft "has been handed down for generations" in order to learn and use it. After all, drums and Witches and Pagans seem to go together like ducks and water—as attendance at any one of the large Pagan festivals will prove to you. Drummers at such festivals have no problem drumming all night long. Also, many Craft and Pagan groups and solitaries use drums and drumming in their rituals, though this may be more common in shamanic traditions. Thus, this is a form of divination that should definitely be in your magical repertoire.

Few authors heretofore have mentioned divination with drums. Paul Huson, in his book *Mastering Witchcraft*, mentions it as a traditional form of divination amongst Witches, and gives a diagram similar to the one found in this chapter. However, his book does not give the keys to interpretation, except for some sketchy comments.

Traditionally, devil's apple seeds were cast upon a drum bearing an eight-pointed star (formed by two interlaced squares) and the cast interpreted according to where they fell on the diagram and according to the diviner's own rules. In my presentation of this form of divination, I stick to the traditional diagram. However, you are going to use apple seeds instead of devil's apple seeds. Witches have long seen apples as a rather "Otherworldly" fruit. Besides the fact that apples were the sacred crop of Avalon (which many see as a variation on the

Pagan Summerlands), when one cuts an apple open on its side, a five-pointed star is revealed. This is the Witch's Pentagram, making the apple and its seeds an excellent tool to use with this form of divination.

Apples have also been considered the "fruit of knowledge." This mainly comes from Christian tradition. Although scholars are not certain what kind of fruit grew on the Tree of Knowledge in the Garden of Eden, some aver that it was apples. Others disagree. (Fortunately, as Witches and Pagans, we can let this debate rage on without us.)

THE DRUM

If you are going to be a strict traditionalist in this form of divination, you are going to have to acquire a drum if you do not have one. Any type of drum will do. For instance, if you practice your religion in the Celtic tradition, you may want to acquire a traditional *bodhran* drum.

The drum should be large enough to hold the circle of the diagram, which can be drawn from seven to thirteen inches in diameter. Since you will be casting apple seeds on its surface, you will want to leave at least a two-inch edge around the diagram. If you drew the diagram to the very edge of the drum, it is likely that none of the seeds would ever fall in the outer triangles; once they hit there, they would be likely to pop off the drum to the ground. This would definitely skew the results of your divination. So, the smallest possible diagram would be one of seven inches on a nine-inch drum. The largest possible diagram would be thirteen inches, so this could be painted on any drum that is fifteen inches or larger in diameter.

Many Witches and Pagans, as we have mentioned, use drums in their rituals or at festivals or simply to "jam" with others who enjoy drumming. There is no reason why you can't use your Witch's Drum for both divination and drumming if you want.

Alternatives to the Drum

A drum is not strictly necessary as it can be rather expensive. You can use other objects. For example, you could buy a plain, undecorated tambourine in a music shop, turn it over, and paint the diagram on its inside (the side that you do not hit). Since the inside of the tambourine already has a "lip" around it, you can paint the diagram as far to the edge as you can manage. So, with this option, you can choose any tambourine from seven to thirteen inches. You can also consider staining the two different semi-circles different colors, if you wish, as with the drum option.

Alternatively, you can paint or draw the diagram on a square of wood, or even a square of white posterboard. The only requirement is that your wood or paper be large enough to contain the diagram circle (again seven to thirteen inches). If using a square board, you may also want to fashion a lip around the edges using slats of wood. As with the drum and tambourine, you may want to color each semi-circle a different color for the God and Goddess, although this is not strictly necessary.

Figure 6a: An example of a Witch's Drum (with symbols).

The Diagram

When you have chosen your drum and decided on the proper size diagram for it, simply paint the diagram (see figure 6b) on the drum, using paint or a black or dark stain. You may also want to stain the left half of the circle and the right half of the circle different colors suitable to the diagram's imagery. For instance, you could stain the God half red and the Goddess half blue, or gray and green. The choice is up to you. Just make sure that this additional staining does not obliterate the lines of the squares in the diagram, because these are important in the divination system.

Looking at the diagram given on the opposite page, you will note that there are words and numbers on it. When you draw the diagram on your chosen tool, these will not be included. They are only given as aids in learning the diagram, and they will be referred in the section on interpretation. All you need to draw on your chosen medium is the circle, the squares, and the dividing line down the center. You may also want to draw a small symbol at the top of the diagram on your tool so that you will know where the top is. This is the point marked "Hallows" on the diagram. Any simple symbol will do—a pentagram, a circle, an "X," whatever you choose.

Hallows is the top of the diagram, since this is considered the beginning of the Witch's Year. Going clockwise around the diagram, you will note that the rest of the Witch's Sabbats are given in order. In some traditions, the God is considered to rule that half of the year beginning with Hallows and ending with Beltane. The God rules this half of the year as the Lord of Death, and his reign begins with the Feast of the Dead, Hallows. The Goddess rules the half of the year beginning with Beltane and ending with Hallows. She reigns as the Lady of Life.

Each Sabbat has particular ideas associated with it, and these ideas will form the basis of your interpretations for the apple seeds that fall in those areas. You will also note that there are eight stars at the edge of the diagram. The stars need not be included on your drum. They are merely indications that, whenever a seed falls in one, the interpretation remains the same. In one sense, these areas represent the inner

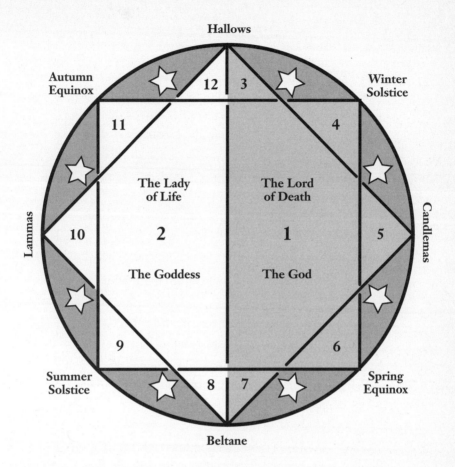

Figure 6b: Diagram for the Witch's Drum.

planes as "places that are not places, times that are not times." For this reason, they are outside of the eight-pointed star, which is a symbol of the Year-Wheel and Time.

The diagram can be decorated or left plain as it is, as you see fit. There is certainly wide latitude for those with artistic abilities. For instance, you may want to paint or draw a symbol of each Sabbat in the triangles they represent. You could draw symbols of the God or Goddess in those areas that represent them (as shown in figure 6a, page 77).

Again, this is not strictly necessary, but if you have an artistic flair, some ideas are given below, keyed to the name of the space and its number:

1. **Lord of Death:** A drawing of the God, a sun with black rays (the sun at midnight, a symbol of the Lord of Death and Rebirth), a crown (symbolizing rulership of the Underworld), the symbol of Taurus (the Horned Lord), or the symbol of Mars.

2. **Lady of Life:** A drawing of the Goddess, a crescent moon, a triple moon showing the waxing and waning crescents flanking the full moon, a rose, the symbol of Venus.

3. **Hallows** (the Lord taking up his reign): A sickle, a sword, a serpent.

4. **Winter Solstice:** A rayed sun (signifying the birth of the Sun God), a fire (for the Yule log), a mistletoe sprig with berries.

5. **Candlemas:** A torch (for the Feast of Lights), a candle, a scourge (as a symbol of purification).

6. **Spring Equinox:** An eight-spoked wheel (a symbol of the zodiac, since the Spring Equinox begins the zodiacal year), an equal-armed cross (signifying the balance of forces), a bird (as harbinger of spring).

7. **Beltane** (the Lord relinquishing his reign): A dolmen (as a phallic symbol of the God), a spear, an arrow, a flower.

8. **Beltane** (the Lady taking up her reign): A chalice, a wreath of leaves, or any other feminine symbol of fertility or fecundity.

9. **Summer Solstice:** A rayed sun (signifying the sun at the height of its strength), an oak tree, or an acorn (both associated with the sun).

10. **Lammas:** A sheaf of wheat (for the beginning of the harvest), an apple, an ear of corn.

11. **Autumn Equinox:** A bunch of grapes (signifying the celebrations at the end of the harvest), a drinking horn.

12. **Hallows** (the Lady relinquishing her reign): A cauldron, a spiral, or any other feminine death/rebirth symbol.

Empty spaces shown at edge of diagram (figure 6b marks these with stars) can be left blank, or you can add pentagrams or eight-spoked wheels as symbols of spirit.

If your tool is large enough, you can also write in the names of the Sabbats around the edges of the diagram. As you can see, there is much room for creativity here in making your Witch's Drum. Make it embody your own creative spirit, but never mind if you have no artistic talent, or do not want to mark your drum with symbols. It is more traditional to leave the diagram empty.

CONSECRATING THE WITCH'S DRUM

Once you have fashioned your drum or other tool in the manner most pleasing to you, it will be time to consecrate it. You will not be consecrating the apple seeds that you will use in the divination, as a new apple and new apple seeds are used for each question put to the Witch's Drum. (This is explained later in this chapter.)

If you have an altar, use it. If not, set up a table in a room where you will be undisturbed. The time for the consecration should be the night of the full moon or one of the eight Sabbats. Have on your altar the following materials:

- An incense burner with some incense on the eastern edge.
- A white candle on the southern edge.
- A chalice or bowl of rain water on the western edge.
- A dish of salt on the northern edge.

Your drum or other tool should be on the floor next to the altar.

Take a bath in water sprinkled with salt, relax your body and calm your mind. After your bath, you may robe or remain skyclad as you wish. Proceed to your working area. Light the candle and from it start the incense going. You may wish to cast a Circle for the consecration ritual, using your own method or the procedure given in the Appendix, but this is not strictly necessary.

When all is set, take up the drum and pass it over the smoke of the incense three times and say each time:

By Powers of Air, I conjure thee
To reveal all things as named by me!

Next pass the drum three times over the candle flame and say each time:

By Powers of Fire, I conjure thee
To answer questions asked by me!

Anoint the drum three times with a bit of rain water from the chalice or bowl (any part of the drum will do; you need not anoint the diagram and risk smudging it), each time saying:

By Powers of Water, I conjure thee
To guide my Path judiciously!

Rub a bit of the salt onto the drum three times, saying:

By Powers of Earth, I conjure thee
To show the future's course to me!

When you are finished, hold the drum above your head and recite the final incantation (just once):

I conjure thee by Hallows Night
To show the path to Inner Sight!
I conjure thee by Winter's Fire
To show me all that I desire!
I conjure thee by Crowns of Light
To show me Truth by day or night!
I conjure thee by rains of Spring
To show me what the future brings!
I conjure thee by Beltane rounds,
To show the future in thy bounds!
I conjure thee by Summer's peak
To show the answers that I seek!

I conjure thee by Lammastide
To show me where thy wisdom bides!
I conjure thee by Autumn dew,
Forevermore to answer true!

When you are finished, replace the drum by the side of the altar and say:

By smoke, by flame, by salt, by cup,
Peace! Hail! The Charm's wound up!

This concludes the consecration ritual. Banish the Circle, if you have cast one, or put out the incense and extinguish the candle.

Types of Questions to Ask of the Witch's Drum

The Witch's Drum is not a very comprehensive form of divination. It is really used to receive an augury of the success of some particular venture or option. Thus, the best types of questions to ask should be phrased: "Will I be successful if I do...?" or "What will happen if I do...?" or "What will be the outcome of...?"

Questions phrased like "Should I do...?" are not very good for this type of divination since it is easy to become confused in interpreting the fall of the seeds. For instance, if one asked "Should I break up with my boyfriend?" and a positive augury is received, does it mean that you should break up with your boyfriend (as if the drum were answering "yes"), or does it mean that you should not break up with your boyfriend because a rosy future lies ahead?

Likewise, questions framed as choices are difficult to answer by the Witch's Drum. If one asked "Should I take the new job or stay in my present position?" and a positive augury is received, you would not know which course of action will be more successful. It is much better to ask "Should I take the new position?" or "Will I be happy if I take the new position?"

THE APPLE SEEDS

Each time you want to perform a divination with the Witch's Drum, you will have to pick an apple from a tree (or buy one if you don't have access to an apple tree). Any type of apple is fine. If you are going to ask several questions at one sitting, you need to have as many apples as you have questions. If you have only one question, you need one apple. If you have three questions, you need three apples, and so on.

THE DIVINATION

To start the divination, place your drum before you, with the Hallows point uppermost. You should also have a piece of paper and a pen or pencil with you. Take up your chosen apple, and concentrate on your question, mentally repeating it to yourself as long as you wish. When you feel that your question has "entered the apple," hold it above your head and say the following:

Apple Flesh,
And Apple Seed,
You have Wisdom,
I have need!
By Lord and Lady,
Star and Wheel,
Aid me now
And Truth reveal!

Next, lay the apple on its side (with its top and bottom facing your left and right), and cut it in half with a sharp knife. If you have cut it properly, you will see five seeds forming a five-pointed star in the flesh of the apple (figure 6c). Take out these five seeds with your fingernail or the tip of the knife.

Figure 6c: Cut the apple horizontally to reveal the five seeds forming the five-pointed star.

These are the five seeds that you will use to cast on your drum. They represent spirit and the four elements—fire, water, air, and earth. After you have taken out the seeds, eat the flesh of the apple half from which you took them, internalizing the wisdom and knowledge of the fruit. Save the other half of the apple until the end of the divination.

After you have dried the seeds on a cloth or towel (they can be a bit sticky, and you don't want any apple juices marring your diagram), hold them in both hands, again thinking of your question and mentally repeating it to yourself for as long as you wish.

When you are ready, throw the seeds one at a time onto the diagram. The first seed that you throw is the **spirit seed**. Immediately after it has fallen, note its position on your paper. Then proceed to throw the next seed, the **fire seed**. Record its position. Throw the next seed—the **water seed**—and record its position. Similarly, throw the next two seeds—these are the **air** and **earth seeds**—and record their positions.

While throwing the seeds, if one seed happens to knock another out of one part of the diagram and into another, note the knocked seed's new position as well, as this will be important in judging the divination.

RULES OF INTERPRETATION

The divination is basically interpreted by combining the significance of the seed (according to its element) and the meaning of the space upon which it falls. Advanced students of the Craft, with a good background in the meanings of the elements and the meanings of the Sabbats, will probably be able to judge their own divination without my preliminary assistance. Others may consult the list of interpretations below. Whichever method you choose, take note of the following rules:

- The seeds should be interpreted in the order in which they were thrown—spirit, fire, water, air, earth. The seeds are interpreted this way because this is the order in which the elements are born from spirit, the Causeless Cause and Creator of all things.

- The spirit seed will generally show the beginning of the matter or why the question has been asked. Usually, this will be some influence from the past.

- The fire seed will generally show what the near future will bring, and how the situation is shaping up in the Unseen or inner planes.

- The water seed will show the questioner's attitude toward the question or situation.

- The air seed will show something that the questioner does not expect. He or she will have to deal with this influence before the result is reached.

- The earth seed will tell the result of the situation.

- If a seed falls on a line so that it is impossible to tell if it is one section or the other, read the interpretations for both.

- If a following seed knocks a previously thrown seed into another position, whatever is represented by the following seed will affect what is represented by the previously thrown seed. The new position of the previously thrown seed will show how that influence will change. For instance, imagine you have already thrown the spirit, fire, and water seeds. You throw the air seed next, and it knocks the water seed into a different position. This shows that an unexpected influence (the nature of which is determined by where the air seed falls) will change your attitude toward the question. Your new attitude will be determined by where the water seed has been knocked.

LIST OF INTERPRETATIONS

As was noted earlier, the Witch's Drum is a simple form of divination and has simple interpretations. Therefore, while you can expect an accurate assessment of the influences in the situation, these will not be elaborate. Of course, if you have a developed clairvoyant faculty, you will be able to go more in depth, but this is true of any method of divination. For example, a man in opposition to your goal may be indicated by one of the seeds. Someone with greater psychic abilities might be able to tune in to the appearance, temperament, and occupation of the man, while the less psychic diviner must be satisfied with the simpler interpretation.

Below is the list of interpretations. They are arranged according to seed and keyed to the numbers in the diagram on page 79.

Spirit Seed: Beginning of the Matter, Foundation for Question

Section 1 — The questioner wants to know whether he or she has enough skill, motivation, and purpose to bring a situation or project to a successful conclusion. There may be a choice to be made, though the questioner is indecisive. If a woman is the questioner, the question concerns a man. Whatever the question, invoke the God for aid.

Section 2 — The questioner is concerned with what the future will bring, as the past and present seem to be changeable and fluctuating in terms of success. If the questioner is a man, the question concerns a woman. Whatever the question, invoke the Goddess for aid.

Section 3 — The questioner may have been wronged in some way by a person in a position of authority. He may be wondering whether justice will eventually be done. Alternatively, he may be asking whether to sever ties with the situation and proceed to something new.

Section 4 — The questioner has experienced a sudden loss or reversal of fortune concerning the subject matter of the question. She will want to know how this will affect the outcome of the matter. May concern women or material goods/money.

Section 5 — The questioner feels he lacks control over the situation and is at the mercy of fate. He will want to know how to gain better control of the matter at hand. The question may concern overcoming a recent negative experience, or a situation with a woman or women.

Section 6 — The question concerns bringing a situation or project to a successful or happy conclusion. The project or situation has just begun recently. The question may concern mental or intellectual satisfaction.

Section 7 — The questioner is questioning the truth of the words of others. She does not know if the words of others may be relied on and seeks confirmation. The questioner should be strongly cautioned to follow her intuition.

Section 8 — The questioner has a choice to make, but is having difficulty deciding whether he should follow the path that others expect, or whether he should follow his own heart. He is probably looking for what will result from taking one or the other courses of action.

Section 9 — The questioner has already achieved some progress in the situation, or may have successfully completed some phase of a project, or has overcome some obstacle. The question may concern an energetic man. The questioner may want to know whether some additional action is necessary to consolidate the success or may be wondering what his next step should be.

Section 10 — The questioner feels that he is not making progress in the area of the question's subject matter. A new opportunity has presented itself. He wants to know whether he should seize this new opportunity or rest on his past harvests of success. It is a question of acting on a new impulse or remaining inert.

Section 11 — The questioner has experienced many ups and downs in the situation. Sometimes enjoying happiness, other times suffering sorrows. She wants to know whether lasting success will eventually be achieved. The question may concern emotions or emotional satisfaction.

Section 12 — The questioner believes that there are some hidden influences working in the present situation, and seeks to discover what these may be and how they will affect the situation. He may feel that someone is keeping secrets from him.

Any Star — The questioner does not know why she is asking the question. It may be out of idle curiosity; perhaps she already knows the answer or the matter has already been conclusively decided.

Fire Seed: Near Future

Section 1 — An obstacle will be placed in front of the questioner's success. Achievement will seem doubtful, and the questioner may feel the situation is lost.

Section 2 — Growth, progress, and a quickening of the situation toward success.

Section 3 — The questioner will have to act quickly to consolidate past gains. He will have to leave the situation at once, or there will be disappointments in the near future.

Section 4 — The end of the situation is in the near future. Problems will be resolved in favor of the questioner, and she will be able to make a new beginning.

Section 5 — A woman will help the questioner overcome an obstacle. She is of fair complexion or an independent woman in control of her own affairs.

Section 6 — Great activity is in the near future. Other opportunities or possibilities or courses of action will present themselves. The questioner does not have enough information yet to make a decision.

Section 7 — Arguments, conflict, and dissension are in the near future. If the question regards making a choice, some unfavorable event may eliminate one of the options.

Section 8 — A turn for the better is in the near future due to the influence of a well-placed friend. A friend will give the questioner help and good advice.

Section 9 — A favorable event will bring the questioner closer to success.

Section 10 — A great change will come in the near future. The situation may change so completely that the present question will be irrelevant. Destruction will be followed by renewal.

Section 11 — There will be a sudden improvement in the situation. The end of the situation will seem near, but something is still left over to be done. The questioner should not act hastily, or he may meet with failure.

Section 12 — Tears and sorrow are in the near future. A woman ill-disposed to the questioner may prove his undoing.

Any Star — The questioner may allow the situation to work itself out because of fear of taking action. She will put herself at the mercy of circumstance, instead of guiding the situation by her own will.

Water Seed: Questioner's Attitude

Section 1 — The questioner is full of energy and ready to conquer any obstacles. He is optimistic and in control of the situation.

Section 2 — The questioner is indecisive, uncertain, but hopeful.

Section 3 — The questioner is despondent, pessimistic, and in a dark mood.

Section 4 — The questioner is frustrated and weary.

Section 5 — The questioner is in a negative frame of mind and feels that he lacks control of the situation. She may have a desire to get the situation over with as quickly as possible.

Section 6 — The questioner is excited, happy, and hopeful.

Section 7 — The questioner is in a conflicted state of mind, and does not know what he wants. He may be argumentative or angry.

Section 8 — The questioner is hopeful and expectant, though indecisive, and lacking energy. She may be relying too much on the opinions of others.

Section 9 — The questioner is joyous and happy.

Section 10 — The questioner is thankful, in good spirits, but a bit weary for having come through a difficulty.

Section 11 — The questioner knows what he must do, but may lack the resolve to carry through with his plans.

Section 12 — The questioner is serious, stern, but courageous.

Any Star — The questioner is overly emotional regarding the situation or problem, and lacks perspective.

Air Seed: Something the Questioner Does Not Expect

Section 1 — A man will intervene. If the questioner is a male, the man will be opposed to him. If female, the man is favorably disposed toward her.

Section 2 — A woman will intervene. If the questioner is female, the woman will be opposed to her. If male, the woman will be favorably disposed toward him.

Section 3 — Someone has or will deceive the questioner. She should question the motives of all involved. Something is hidden from the questioner, but in time she will find out what it is.

Section 4 — The questioner may lose money. It will turn out that his actions are ill-timed.

Section 5 — The questioner will lose control of the situation, making a new beginning or directed decision impossible.

Section 6 — A new opportunity will unexpectedly present itself. The questioner should take advantage of this new beginning.

Section 7 — The situation will come to an end sooner than the questioner thinks or has planned. She must act quickly to maintain control over the situation.

Section 8 — Unexpected good news will arrive by letter or some other means of communication. The bearer of the news is well disposed toward the questioner.

Section 9 — The questioner will soon see that success is assured.

Section 10 — There will be an increase in activity, allowing the questioner to make a leap toward success.

Section 11 — A new acquaintance will enter the questioner's life and figure prominently in the resolution of the situation. At the same time, the questioner may lose a friend.

Section 12 — Someone is working against the questioner, hoping that the questioner will not achieve his success or resolution of a problem.

Any Star — There will be a conflict ending in argument. Tempers will flare.

Earth Seed: Result

Section 1 — Unfavorable. The questioner will be unhappy.

Section 2 — Favorable. The questioner will be happy.

Section 3 — Unfavorable. Unfortunate combinations of people or things.

Section 4 — Unfavorable if the questioner is unable to release past situations and move forward. Favorable for making new starts.

Section 5 — Unfavorable. The questioner will find himself in a hopeless situation.

Section 6 — Favorable for the beginning of anything new; otherwise unfavorable, particularly for questions regarding money, business, or material goods.

Section 7 — Unfavorable. A competitor or rival wins out over the questioner.

Section 8 — Favorable resolution of all situations and problems.

Section 9 — Favorable for all questions. The questioner will achieve success.

Section 10 — Favorable, as long as the questioner acts quickly to consolidate her gains when she receives them.

Section 11 — Favorable for questions involving the emotions or money. Unfavorable for the start of new ventures and all other things.

Section 12 — Unfavorable. The questioner will not achieve success. If he does, he will be unhappy with it.

Any Star — The divination fails. No augury can be received. The diviner's judgement should not be trusted to interpret the signs correctly.

THE END OF THE DIVINATION

When you have written down all of the placements of the seeds and interpreted them, you are finished. However, you will still have the half of the apple that you were told to save at the beginning of the divination (perhaps many halves of apples if you have asked multiple questions). This half must be buried in the Earth, along with the seeds that you used during your divination. This is a small ritual of thanksgiving to honor the spirit of the apple and its wisdom, as well as to honor the tree from which the apple was picked.

SOME EXAMPLES OF DIVINATIONS

Even though the interpretations are brief and do not convey much information in and of themselves, the diviner that learns to read between the lines will be able to come up with an accurate reading. To show you what is meant by this, here are three examples of divination by the Witch's Drum.

Example One

A female questioner once asked "Should I accept the new employment position that has been offered to me?" The following were the results of the divination.

- Spirit: Section 2, Lady of Life.
- Fire: Section 3, Hallows, Lord of Death reigning.
- Water: Section 10, Lammas.
- Air: Section 4, Winter Solstice.
- Earth: Section 1, Lord of Death.

The earth seed knocked the air seed into section 5, Candlemas.

Interpretation

The spirit seed indicated that the questioner's employment situation was in a state of flux. She confirmed that she had recently changed jobs to the position that she was now in, and was wondering whether to change again so soon. The fire seed indicated that she would have to act quickly in this decision or risk disappointment. She confirmed that she had to decide within the next couple of days.

The water seed indicated that she was in good spirits and thankful for having received this new offer of employment, especially as she was encountering some difficulty with her new present employer. The air seed indicated that she might lose some money, and that her actions might be ill-timed. The earth seed indicated that accepting the new employment would be unfavorable and that she would be unhappy there.

The earth seed knocking the air seed into the Candlemas position indicated that the questioner would lose control of the situation. She was told that the cast did not advise her to make the change. She did not, and stuck with her present job, where she is still employed. It is interesting to note that she never actually declined the employment offer. She never notified the prospective employer that she was declining the position. She assumed that someone else was chosen for the position a couple of days later. So, in a sense, she did lose control of the situation, insofar as the prospective employer offered the position to someone else.

Example Two

A young male questioner asked "Will my new relationship with (a new girlfriend) last through the year?" The results were:

- Spirit: Section 9, Summer Solstice.
- Fire: A star.
- Water: Section 6, Spring Equinox.
- Air: Section 1, the Lord of Death.
- Earth: Fell on the line between section 11, Autumn Equinox, and Section 2, the Lady of Life.

Interpretation

The spirit seed indicated that the young man was basically quite happy with the present situation, as he had achieved some progress or success in the situation, or had surpassed some obstacle. He confirmed that he was quite happy at the time. He had just come out of another relationship that had broken up because he had worked odd hours at his job. His schedule did not conform to his old girlfriend's schedule; thus, they could not spend much time together. The obstacle that he had surpassed was that he had gotten his employer to switch him to a more normal working schedule.

The fire seed fell on a star. (Actually, on my own personal diagram these spaces are blank; it fell on the section between Lammas and Summer Solstice.) This indicated that the young man really wasn't looking to take any specific action in the situation. He really was not thinking of marriage or any long-term commitment at present. The water seed indicated that he was happy and hopeful about the new relationship. (He obviously was, at least to me.)

The air seed indicated that a man would intervene in the relationship, and since the questioner himself was a young man, this new person would be ill-disposed to the questioner. A rival for the young lady's affections seemed to be indicated. The earth seed fell on the line between the Autumn Equinox and the Lady of Life. Both of these are favorable to the question (the Autumn Equinox was especially favorable for this emotion-related question). Thus, it was judged that the relationship would last through the year.

As it turned out, the relationship did last through that year. (It was May when the questioner asked the question, and the relationship lasted until the following February). However, it wasn't a rival for the young lady's affections that was the unexpected man in the situation. It was the young lady's father, who did not approve of the questioner. Eventually, this drove a wedge between the questioner and his girlfriend, resulting in the break-up.

Example Three

A thirty-two-year-old woman once asked whether she should stay in her present career (which involved insurance sales) or whether she should go back to school to pursue a master's degree in hopes of getting a more challenging position in a few years. I told her that it was difficult to determine "choice questions" from the drum, and that she should ask whether it would be favorable for her to go back to school or whether it would be favorable for her to maintain her present position. She chose the former option, and framed her question thus: "Would it be favorable for me to go back to school for an M.B.A. degree?" The seeds fell as follows:

- Spirit: Section 8, Beltane, ruled by the Lady.
- Fire: Section 12, Hallows.

- Water: Section 1, the Lord of Death.
- Air: Section 2, the Lady of Life.
- Earth: Section 2, the Lady of Life.

Also, the air seed knocked the water seed into Section 7, Beltane, ruled by the Lord of Death.

Interpretation

The spirit seed fit the situation perfectly. The woman had a choice to make, but was having difficulty deciding whether to follow her heart (go to school) or follow the path that others expected her to take. This confirmed the question since insurance sales was a family business, and she thought her mother, in particular, expected her to take over the business someday.

The fire seed indicated that tears and sorrows were in the near future, and that a woman may be the questioner's undoing. The questioner confirmed that she had not broached the subject to her family, but that there would probably be some sorrow and disappointment when her family learned that she was considering leaving the business.

The water seed indicated that she was ready to meet the challenge of going back to school full time, even after being out of school for ten years. She had saved up some money, so she felt in control of the situation. Her only worry was her parents' reaction to her plan. The air seed confirmed her concern over her mother's reaction since it indicated that a woman would be opposed to her.

The earth seed indicated, however, that the result would be favorable if she went back to school to pursue the M.B.A. The air seed, knocking the water seed into Candlemas, indicated that, while the first water seed interpretation indicated confidence, her mother's reaction would undermine her resolve and put her in a conflicted state of mind.

Eventually, however, the woman did go back to a very reputable school for her M.B.A., and took a position as a financial analyst with a Wall Street investment firm after she graduated.

CONCLUSION

Divination by the Witch's Drum is both an accurate and fascinating system. It can take some time to get used to the diagram and to learn what each of the spaces means in relation to each elemental seed, but your end results will be worth all the time and effort you put into becoming familiar with the system.

PART III

STICKS AND STONES

CHAPTER SEVEN

A Witch's Geomancy

Geomancy, which literally means "divination by earth," is an ancient form of divination that answers questions through the use of sixteen figures composed of dots in a certain pattern. Most scholars agree that the practice of geomancy originally came to Europe via the Arabic culture, probably sometime during the late Middle Ages, before the Renaissance. The magician Henry Cornelius Agrippa did much to popularize the practice of geomancy during his lifetime. Other Renaissance scholars also studied the system and have left behind writings. The most notable of these is Robert Fludd and his *Tractatus de Geomantia* or "Treatise on Geomancy." In more modern times, magicians such as Aleistar Crowley, Israel Regardie, and Franz Hartmann have done much to keep geomancy alive during this century. Geomancy was also one of the divination systems included in the curriculum of the Order of the Golden Dawn.

The magical theory behind the practice of geomancy is much the same as behind other divination systems. The diviner seeks to ascertain the forces prevailing on the inner planes in order to determine how these forces will work out on the physical plane. This is one of the manifestations of the principle "As above, so below." Geomancy, in essence, seeks to bring "heaven to earth."

In one of its oldest forms, a person seeking to use geomancy would procure a box full of slightly wet sand or soil (hence the term "divination by earth"). With a stick or wand, the person would make sixteen rows of a random number of dots in the sand. These sixteen rows of dots were then used to determine four geomancy figures. These original four figures were manipulated in a certain way (which you will learn in this chapter) to arrive at eleven other figures, for a total of fifteen. The last three of these eleven figures were termed the two Witnesses and the Judge, and they contained the answer to the divination question. The whole process is loosely akin to the Eastern system of the I Ching, and indeed, geomancy might fairly be termed "the I Ching of the West."

Eventually, other methods for determining the original four figures were developed. These methods included throwing four sticks four times, throwing a die or pair of dice sixteen times, and grabbing a random number of stones or pebbles out of a bowl sixteen times. The system was even expanded to use certain principles of astrology. Twelve of the fifteen figures obtained (that is, all figures excluding the two Witnesses and the Judge) would be placed into the twelve houses of a horoscope chart. Each geomancy figure had a planet and a zodiac sign assigned to it. Thus, one could use these correspondences to set up a simplified horoscope for the question. This allows for much more detailed answers to geomancy questions.

However, such complicated procedures will not be discussed here, as they would require a book unto themselves. Instead, this chapter will stick with the most traditional form of geomancy, which considers only the two Witnesses and the Judge in ascertaining answers to questions. Should you wish to explore geomancy more in-depth after experimenting with the system set out here, you can consult the suggested reading list at the end of the book.

The sixteen geomancy figures that form the basis of this system are usually given Latin names, such as Carcer, Amissio, and Caput Draconis. Instead of using these Latin names, I have re-named each of the sixteen figures to comport with Pagan symbolism and practice, in order to make this system more accessible to Witches and Pagans. Each name that I have given also comports with the basic meaning of the figure's Latin name. For instance, I have re-named the figure "Acquisitio" as the "Cauldron." Acquisitio means gain or acquisition. The cauldron is a Pagan symbol of plenty, gain, and nourishment. So, if you want to continue your study of geomancy with other books that give the Latin names, you will have no trouble adapting to their meanings.

Also, instead of using a box of wet soil, four sticks, or any of the other more complicated methods for determining the figures to answer a question, you will be using a simple tool called the **Witch Stone**.

MAKING THE WITCH STONE

Geomancy is wonderfully simple from the standpoint that few external tools are needed. In fact, the only tool necessary is a casting object. Since geomancy is obviously related to the earth element, a simple stone, the Witch Stone, will serve this purpose. It should be a rounded, fairly flat stone about one inch in diameter. It should also have a fairly smooth surface so that you may paint or draw the necessary symbols upon it. Since this stone will become your main tool in geomancy, you may want to collect it from a special place such as a favorite outdoor relaxation spot, the seashore, or the forest. You may also want to search for it at a special time such as one of the Sabbats (particularly the Winter Sabbats of Yule and Candlemas, since winter corresponds to the earth element), a full moon night, or your birthday.

When you have found your stone, you must paint or draw two symbols on it. On one side you will draw a figure of the sun, on the other side, a figure of the moon. These can be as primitive or as artistic as you wish, from simple astrological sigils done in one color (for the sun, a circle with a dot in the center; for the moon, a crescent) or artistic drawings complete with rays, smiling faces, many colors, or whatever. If you feel that you would like to keep each symbol only one color, it would probably be most appropriate to make the sun yellow or gold, and the moon silver or white. However, the choice is yours. After all, it is your Witch Stone.

After you have decorated your Witch Stone as well as your talents allow, it will be ready for use. However, before you ask your first questions, your Witch Stone should receive some kind of blessing or consecration, as all magical tools should. The following simple ritual is given for this purpose.

CONSECRATION RITUAL
FOR THE WITCH STONE

This simple ritual will give your Witch Stone a blessing by the four elements. You will need the following materials:

- Your completed Witch Stone.
- A small table used as an altar.
- A white candle on the south side of the altar.
- A small bowl of water set on the west side of the altar.
- A small dish of salt on the north side of the altar.
- Some incense (an incense stick is fine) and something to burn it in (a bowl of soil or sand is fine) on the east side of the altar.

You should perform the ritual on the night of the full moon, the time of the month when your psychic awareness and powers will be at their height. Take a short bath before the ritual, making sure you are calm and relaxed. If you have a robe that you wear for magical work, you may wear it. You can also perform the ritual skyclad, if you wish.

After your bath, proceed to the altar. Light the candle, and from it start the incense burning. You may wish to cast a Circle for the consecration ritual, using your own method or the procedure given in the Appendix, but this is not strictly necessary. Take up the Witch Stone, and pass it through the smoke of the burning incense, and say:

I consecrate thee by the element air.

Pass the Witch Stone through the candle flame and say:

I consecrate thee by the element fire.

Anoint the Witch Stone with a drop of the water from the bowl and say:

I consecrate thee by the element water.

Place a bit of salt on the Witch Stone and say:

I consecrate thee by the element earth.

Now hold the Witch Stone above the center of the altar, and say the following incantation:

> *Stone of Destiny, Stone of Earth,*
> *Stone of Sorrow, Stone of Mirth,*
> *Stone of Moon, Stone of Sun,*
> *Stone of Plenty, Stone of None,*
> *Shall I laugh? Or shall I cry?*
> *How do the Witnesses testify?*
> *Shall I be sad? Shall I be pleased?*
> *Tell me what the Judge decrees.*

You should now place your consecrated Witch Stone in a pouch or box for safekeeping, to be taken out only when it will be used. Place this in the center of the altar. Meditate before the altar for another ten minutes. As you do so, imagine shafts of power from the incense, candle flame, water, and salt shooting out towards the Witch Stone in the center of the altar, each element giving the Witch Stone a special blessing. When you are through, put out the incense and candle, and find a special place to keep your stone, such as a pouch or a small box.

PREPARING TO CAST THE CHART

The beauty of this type of divination is that few materials are needed. You must have your Witch Stone, something with which to write, and a blank geomancy chart (see figure 7a, page 106).

Step One. As a first step you should record the divination number, the date, and the time on the chart. You may also wish to record the planetary ruler of the day and hour, if you know these.

Step Two. Next, you should write down your question in the space provided on the chart. Your question should be phrased as specifically as possible. Geomancy, as outlined here, is best used to answer questions that run like: "What will be the result of [this situation, this course of action]?" or "How will [this situation, this undertaking] turn out?"

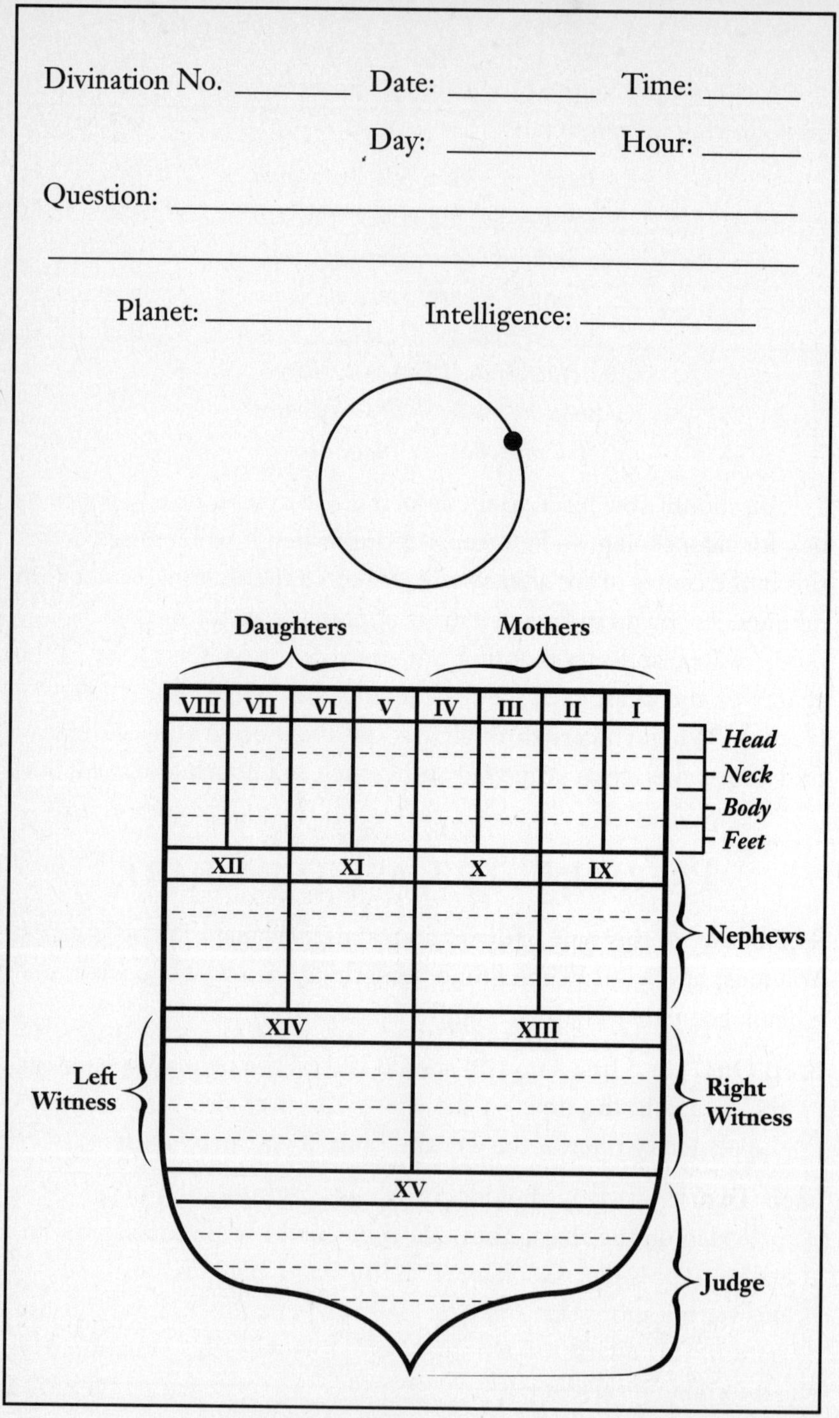

Divination No. _____ Date: _____ Time: _____

Day: _____ Hour: _____

Question: _____

_____

Planet: _____ Intelligence: _____

Figure 7: A Witch's geomancy chart.

Your question will fall into one of seven broad categories, corresponding to one of the seven planets. Look at the "Assigning Questions to a Planet" list (table 7a, below) to determine which planet covers the topic of your question. Write in the name of the planet on the chart where indicated.

ASSIGNING THE QUESTION TO A PLANET

Sun — For all questions involving joy, success, advancement, leadership, natural power, healing, light, purification, growth, and protection.

Moon — For all questions involving women, cycles, birth, generation, the home, inspiration, poetry, emotions, travel (especially by water), the sea and tides, fertility, memory, rain, intuition, psychic abilities, and secrets.

Mercury — For all questions involving communications, language, intelligence, study, books, cleverness, science, business transactions, thievery, divination, knowledge, writing, letters, neighbors, and brothers and sisters.

Venus — For all questions involving love, harmony, attraction, friendship, pleasure, sensuality, sexuality, and creativity.

Mars — For all questions involving strength, struggle, war, anger, conflict, aggression, courage, military honors, and breaking negative spells.

Jupiter — For all questions involving politics, earthly power, honor, royalty, public acclaim, responsibility, wealth, business, good fortune, and success.

Saturn — For all questions involving overcoming obstacles, limitations, binding, death, buildings, property, history, time, and protection.

Table 7a

Step Three. Next, you must reference this planet to its **planetary intelligence**, listed on page 108 (table 7b). The intelligence is the guiding entity of the planet. It is invoked so that your mind will be properly attuned to receive and correctly interpret your final answer. Write in the name of the intelligence in the space provided.

THE PLANETARY INTELLIGENCES AND THEIR SIGILS

Sigil	Intelligence	Planet
	Sorath	Sun
	Chasmodai	Moon
	Taphthartharath	Mercury
	Kedemel	Venus
	Bartzabel	Mars
	Hismael	Jupiter
	Zazel	Saturn

You will inscribe one of these sigils in the center of your air-invoking pentagram, depending on the planetary nature of your question. Refer to step five in the "Casting the Chart" section.

Table 7b

Step Four. Your next step will be to invoke the planetary intelligence ruling your question. This is done by inscribing an invoking pentagram of air in the invoking circle on the chart. Begin at the large dot at the rim of the circle, and draw the first line horizontally to the left, then continue until the pentagram is completed. The invoking pentagram of air is used because the element air corresponds to divination as a magical discipline, even though geomancy specifically refers to the earth element. No matter what your question, this is the pentagram to use.

Step Five. Your final step before beginning to cast your Witch Stone is to draw the sigil of the planetary intelligence in the center of the completed pentagram while silently invoking the intelligence by name to aid you in your divination (use any words you deem appropriate).

CASTING THE CHART

Now you are ready to cast your Witch Stone. You will be casting it a total of sixteen times, specifically in four groups of four and recording the results in the "shield" of the geomancy chart.

Take up your stone, ask your question once to yourself silently, then cast the stone. The rules are:

- If the sun face appears, record one dot.
- If the moon face appears, record two dots.

Thus, on your first cast, if the sun face appeared, you would record one dot in the top fourth of the box underneath the Roman numeral I. If the moon face appeared, you would record two dots. Repeat the casting procedure three more times, each time recording one dot or two in the second, third, and fourth section of box I, respectively. These first four casts are all recorded in the four sections of the I box, the first recording at the top, then proceeding downward. At the end of four throws, you will have a completed four-line geomancy figure.

The Mothers

Your next step is to repeat the whole procedure, casting the Witch Stone four more times, and recording your casts in box II. When this figure is finished, you will repeat the procedure of four more casts, and record your results in box III. Your final four throws will be recorded in box IV. After your have recorded your last dot or two dots in box IV you may put your Witch Stone away. The rest of the boxes will be calculated from the figures in these first four boxes (boxes I through IV).

These first four figures (I through IV) are called the **Mothers**. The top row of dots of the Mothers are called **heads**. The second row of dots of the Mothers are called **necks**. The third row of dots of the Mothers are called **bodies**. The fourth row of the dots of the Mothers are called **feet** (see figure 7a, page 106). From these you will fashion the next four figures (located boxes V through VIII), called the **Daughters**.

The Daughters

The first Daughter, figure V, is composed of the heads of the Mothers. So, examine your chart to see what the top row of box I contains. If one dot, record one dot under figure V. If two dots, record two dots under figure V. Then proceed to figure II. If the head of box II is one dot, record this also under figure V. If the head of figure II is two dots, record this under figure V. Then proceed to figure III. Whatever its top row is, record it under figure V. Then proceed to figure IV. Whatever its top row is, record it under figure V. Now you will see that you have formed figure V, the first Daughter, from the heads of the Mothers.

The second Daughter, figure VI, is composed in a similar manner. However, this time you will be looking at the necks of the Mothers. The second row of figure I will be the first row of figure VI. The second row of figure II will be the second row of figure VI. The second row of figure III will be the third row of figure VI. The second row of figure IV will be the fourth and final row of figure VI.

The third Daughter, figure VII, will be formed from the bodies of the Mothers. Thus, the third row of figure I will be the first row of figure VII. The third row of figure II will be the second row of figure VII.

The third row of figure III will be the third row of figure VII. The third row of figure IV will be the fourth and final row of figure VII.

The fourth Daughter, figure VIII, will be formed from the feet of the Mothers. Thus, the fourth row of figure I will be the first row of figure VIII. The fourth row of figure II will be the second row of figure VIII. The fourth row of figure III will be the third row of figure VIII. The fourth row of figure IV will be the fourth and final row of figure VIII.

When you have completed these operations, you will have completed figures I through VIII—the four Mothers and the four Daughters.

The Nephews

Now you will form figures IX through XII, which are called the **Nephews**. The Nephews are formed in a different way. Start with figure IX. You will see that this box in the chart is placed below figures I and II. Figure IX will thus be formed from figures I and II. Look at the top rows (the heads) of figures I and II. Add the number of dots of these heads. If the resulting sum is odd, record one dot in figure IX. If the resulting sum is even, record two dots in figure IX. Next add together the second rows (the necks) of figures I and II. If the sum is odd, record one dot in figure IX. If the sum is even, record two dots in figure IX. Next add the third rows (the bodies) of figures I and II. If the sum is odd, record one dot in figure IX. If the sum is even, record two dots in figure IX. Lastly, add together the bottom rows (the feet) of figures I and II. If the sum is even, record two dots in figure IX. You will now have completed figure IX.

The other Nephews (X, XI, and XII) are composed in a similar manner. Figure X is composed by adding together the heads, necks, bodies, and feet of figures III and IV. Figure XI is composed by adding together the heads, necks, bodies, and feet of figures V and VI. Figure XII is composed by adding together the heads, necks, bodies, and feet of figures VII and VIII. When you have completed these operations, you will have completed figures I through XII—the Mothers, Daughters, and Nephews.

The Witnesses

Your next step is to form the **Witnesses**, figures XIII and XIV. Similar to the Nephews, the Right Witness (figure XIII) is composed by adding together the heads, necks, bodies, and feet of the first two Nephews (figures IX and X). The Left Witness (figure XIV) is composed by adding together the heads, necks, bodies, and feet of the third and fourth Nephews (figures XI and XII).

The Judge

Your final step is to form the **Judge**, figure XV. It is composed by adding together the heads, necks, bodies, and feet of the two Witnesses, figures XIII and XIV.

From these three final figures, the Right Witness, the Left Witness, and the Judge, you will be able to determine the answer to your question. Refer to the chart provided on page 113 and note the names of the these three figures. Owing to the nature in which the figures are composed, there are only eight possible Judges:

- The Cauldron
- The Pentacle
- The Chalice Filled
- The Chalice Emptied
- The Coven
- The Path of the Seeker
- The Great Rite
- The Knotted Cord

If you obtain a Judge other than one of these eight, you have done your calculations incorrectly, and should check them over to see where you went wrong. Check the following lists to interpret your figures.

GENERAL EXPLANATION OF THE GEOMANCY FIGURES

You should know the basic symbolism and significance of each geomancy figure. This includes knowing the planet assigned to each figure, though you need not know much astrology to use this traditional form of geomancy. The planets are included opposite the list of the sixteen figures (table 7c) to help you remember each figure's basic significance.

THE GEOMANCY FIGURES

The Lord of Death
Mars

The Lady of Life
Venus

The Chalice Emptied
Sun

The Chalice Filled
Sun

The Pentacle
Venus

The Cauldron
Jupiter

The Censer
Mars

The Altar
Mercury

The Knotted Cord
Saturn

The Great Rite
Mercury

The Guardian
Saturn

The Gateway
Jupiter

The Underworld
Saturn and Mars

The Summerlands
Jupiter and Venus

The Path of the Seeker
Moon

The Coven
Moon

Table 7c

The Lord of Death

This figure can be likened to an upraised sword, a traditional symbol of Mars. As a weapon of the God, this figure is called the Lord of Death. To receive this figure is more good than bad. However, it also denotes rash and inconsiderate actions, so one must be on one's guard. It can also indicate a man or boy. Traditionally, this figure is bad for most situations, but good for love and war.

The Lady of Life

This figure resembles a standing woman, a fitting symbol for the Goddess, who is present in all women. As complementary to the Lord of Death as a Mars figure, the Lady of Life is a Venus figure. This is also a reference to the love affair of Venus and Mars or Aphrodite and Ares in Greco-Roman mythology. This is a good figure to receive, especially if the question relates to women. It can represent a beautiful girl or woman with a pretty face. However, one of the messages of this figure is not to be deceived by beauty, since beauty does not guarantee benevolence. Be on your guard. If it sounds too good to be true, it probably isn't true.

The Chalice Emptied

This resembles an upturned chalice spilling its contents, and is not a good figure to receive. It usually indicates fortune or good luck passing out of one's life in some way. However, some compensating aid or protection will be offered to the person receiving this figure. It can also indicate a loss of confidence, and needing to rely on other people for emotional support.

The Chalice Filled

As a complement to the Chalice Emptied, this emblem represents a chalice filled with the sacred drink. It is a wonderful figure to receive, because it indicates good fortune, protection, safeguard, confidence, and success. Trust your intuition. You will receive inner guidance.

The Pentacle

This figure obviously resembles a pentacle with its five points. The pentacle is an earth symbol. Venus rules it here because Venus rules

Taurus, the sign of fixed earth. This is a bad figure to receive since it represents Venus in a poor cosmic state, or "afflicted" as astrologers would say. It indicates loss and material things being taken away from the person who receives this figure; therefore, it is very bad for gain. However, it is good for questions relating to love or friendship.

The Cauldron

The bottom three dots of the figure represent the Cauldron. The top three dots signify its vapors. The Cauldron is a symbol of the Celtic god Dagda, who owned the Cauldron of Plenty. In comparative mythology, Dagda is seen as a Jupiter figure. Hence, Jupiter is assigned here. It is a good figure to receive, and it indicates attainment, fulfilling desires, success, receiving material things, comprehension, and a good grasp of the situation at hand. It also indicates an addition to existing possessions or money, and is excellent for profit.

The Censer

The bottom four dots represent the Censer, and the upper three dots represent the smoke of the incense arising from it. The Censer is a tool assigned to the element fire, and so the fiery planet Mars is assigned to it. It is a bad figure to receive, as it indicates a fiery temper, rashness, and acting out of passion instead of common sense. It can also indicate using sexuality for immoral or emotionally manipulative ends.

The Altar

The bottom three dots represent the base of the Altar, while the top four dots represent the top of the Altar. The Altar is the focus of the circle, the meeting place between humanity and the Gods. Meeting places and markets are traditionally assigned to Mercury, as this figure is. It is a good figure to receive, since it indicates wisdom and clear thoughts. You may proceed without too much worry, since it is good for beginning an undertaking.

The Knotted Cord

These six dots make a circle, a symbol of eternity, but also of restriction. Saturn is the planet related to restriction and limitations, and so it is assigned to this symbol. This is a bad figure to receive, as it denotes imprisonment, confinement, an inability to act, delay, and binding. Now is not the time to proceed with a new undertaking.

The Great Rite

The bottom three dots, forming an upward pointing triangle, represent the Earth Mother. The upper three dots, forming a downward pointing triangle, represent the Sky Father. Here they come together in the marriage of Heaven and Earth, the Great Rite. You will note that if you add together the figures of the Lady of Life and the Lord of Death by geomantic addition, the figure of the Great Rite will result. Goddess meets God, and so their conjoining is ruled by Mercury, which has to do with meetings and communications. This figure is more good than bad. It indicates union, coming together, agreement, marriages, relationships, allies.

The Guardian

This emblem represents a downward-pointing stone that blocks the path through the Gateway. Since it is a form of limitation it is assigned to Saturn, and is a bad figure to receive. It indicates loss, sorrow, disappointment, grief, worry, condemnation, and perversion.

The Gateway

It is quite clear that this emblem represents a doorway or gateway. The planet Jupiter is associated with long travels, and so it is assigned to this figure as the beginning of a journey. It is a good figure to receive, and indicates joy, laughing, good health, and progress. It can also indicate beauty, grace, or a pleasing manner.

The Underworld

The focus of this figure is the two dots at the bottom of the figure. It represents a path (the upper three dots) leading downward and opening to a gateway. Thus, it is symbolic of the Underworld. It is ruled by Saturn (death) and Mars (male force of the God). It is a bad figure, representing strife, contest, fighting one's way through a bad situation. It is a sign of disaster to come. It can also indicate unpleasant karmic repercussions.

The Summerlands

This figure is a path leading upwards, symbolically toward the Summerlands. It is ruled by Jupiter (the sky) and Venus (symbolic of happiness and peace). It is a good figure, indicating attainment and success. It can also represent pleasant karmic rewards.

The Path of the Seeker

This emblem represents the Path. It is ruled by the moon, since the moon is a symbol of our inner nature. The Path leads inward toward spiritual development. This figure is neither good nor bad, but generally has a bad effect on good figures. It can mean a street, path, or journey. Solitary meditation will reveal your answer.

The Coven

This figure is composed of eight dots, the most dots of any figure. Therefore, it symbolizes the coming together of people, or a coven. It is ruled by the moon, because the moon traditionally symbolizes large gatherings or the public. It is neither good nor bad; it indicates people, the public, congregations, a crowd. A friend may hold the answer to your question. Consult that person.

Often, even before consulting the meanings of the Witnesses and the Judge in the interpretation chart, one can ascertain a little bit about the answer to the question by referring to the "favorable" or "unfavorable" nature of the Witnesses and the Judge. The nature of each figure is listed below.

Favorable	Unfavorable	Neutral
Lady of Life	Lord of Death	Path of the Seeker
Chalice Filled	Chalice Emptied	Coven
Cauldron	Pentacle	
Altar	Censer	
Great Rite	Knotted Cord	
Gateway	Guardian	
Summerlands	Underworld	

Note that you should not impute the "favorability" or "unfavorability" of these geomancy signs to the things after which they are named. The Cauldron is no more a "favorable" tool in the Craft than the Pentacle; the Lord of Death is not evil or bad and so on. These are only symbolic associations made for the purposes of geomancy.

INTERPRETATION

Your first step in interpreting your geomancy chart is to make a general survey of the two Witnesses and the Judge according to their favorability. Figure XIII is called the Right Witness. Figure XIV is called the Left Witness. Figure XV is the Judge. To ascertain a general outcome for your question, use the following rules, coupled with the list of general explanations given in the last section.

1. If both Witnesses are favorable, and the Judge is favorable, the outcome will be favorable.

2. If both Witnesses are unfavorable, and the Judge is unfavorable, the outcome will be unfavorable.

3. If both Witnesses are favorable, and the Judge is unfavorable, the outcome will be as you desire it in the short run, but will work against you in the long run.

4. If both Witnesses are unfavorable, and the Judge is favorable, the outcome will be unfortunate for you in the short run, but to your advantage in the long run.

5. If the Right Witness is favorable, the Left Witness is unfavorable, and the Judge is favorable, you will make a good start, and then experience delay and frustration. The outcome will be favorable, but only partially so.

6. If the Right Witness is unfavorable, the Left Witness is favorable, and the Judge is favorable, you will encounter obstacles and delay immediately, but will make enough progress in the future to have a partially favorable outcome.

7. If the Right Witness is favorable, the Left Witness is unfavorable, and the Judge is unfavorable, your good beginning will steadily come to an unfortunate end.

8. If the Right Witness is unfavorable, the Left Witness is favorable, and the Judge is unfavorable, you will encounter obstacles and problems at the beginning of the situation. The tide will turn to your advantage for a short time, but not long enough to ensure a favorable outcome.

9. If the Right Witness is neutral, your beginning is neither good nor bad. It could go either way.

10. If the Left Witness is neutral, the ending is neither good nor bad. It could go either way.

11. If the Judge is neutral, you will not be able to determine whether the outcome is favorable or unfavorable by this general survey. You will have to consult the more lengthy interpretations of the Witnesses and the Judge.

After you make your general survey of the situation, you must consult the following list to find out the number of the interpretation you must read. When looking for your interpretation, it is best to start with the Judge, then find your Left Witness within that Judge's listings. You will then find your Right Witness. If it is a different Right Witness from the one that you have, you have made an error in your calculations somewhere and need to check your work. This is a good way to double-check on your calculations. Assuming that all is well, refer to the interpretation number, and then flip ahead to read the answer to your divination.

Judge (XV)	Left Witness (XIV)	Right Witness (XIII)	Interpretation Number
Cauldron	Coven	Cauldron	1
	Cauldron	Coven	2
	Path	Pentacle	3
	Pentacle	Path	4
	Lord of Death	Gateway	5
	Gateway	Lord of Death	6

Cauldron (continued)	Censer	Guardian	7
	Guardian	Censer	8
	Altar	Summerlands	9
	Summerlands	Altar	10
	Lady of Life	Underworld	11
	Underworld	Lady of Life	12
	Great Rite	Chalice Filled	13
	Chalice Filled	Great Rite	14
	Knotted Cord	Chalice Emptied	15
	Chalice Emptied	Knotted Cord	16
Pentacle	Coven	Pentacle	17
	Pentacle	Coven	18
	Path	Cauldron	19
	Cauldron	Path	20
	Altar	Gateway	21
	Gateway	Altar	22
	Lady of Life	Guardian	23
	Guardian	Lady of Life	24
	Lord of Death	Summerlands	25
	Summerlands	Lord of Death	26
	Censer	Underworld	27
	Underworld	Censer	28
	Knotted Cord	Chalice Filled	29
	Chalice Filled	Knotted Cord	30
	Great Rite	Chalice Emptied	31
	Chalice Emptied	Great Rite	32
Chalice Filled	Coven	Chalice Filled	33
	Chalice Filled	Coven	34
	Path	Chalice Emptied	35
	Chalice Emptied	Path	36
	Great Rite	Cauldron	37
	Cauldron	Great Rite	38
	Lady of Life	Gateway	39
	Gateway	Lady of Life	40

Chalice	Summerlands	Censer	41
Filled	Censer	Summerlands	42
(continued)	Underworld	Lord of Death	43
	Lord of Death	Underworld	44
	Pentacle	Knotted Cord	45
	Knotted Cord	Pentacle	46
	Altar	Guardian	47
	Guardian	Altar	48
Chalice	Coven	Chalice Emptied	49
Emptied	Chalice Emptied	Coven	50
	Knotted Cord	Cauldron	51
	Cauldron	Knotted Cord	52
	Censer	Gateway	53
	Gateway	Censer	54
	Lord of Death	Guardian	55
	Guardian	Lord of Death	56
	Lady of Life	Summerlands	57
	Summerlands	Lady of Life	58
	Altar	Underworld	59
	Underworld	Altar	60
	Great Rite	Pentacle	61
	Pentacle	Great Rite	62
	Path	Chalice Filled	63
	Chalice Filled	Path	64
Coven	Cauldron	Cauldron	65
	Coven	Coven	66
	Gateway	Gateway	67
	Pentacle	Pentacle	68
	Summerlands	Summerlands	69
	Guardian	Guardian	70
	Lady of Life	Lady of Life	71
	Underworld	Underworld	72
	Altar	Altar	73
	Lord of Death	Lord of Death	74

Coven	Chalice Filled	Chalice Filled	75
(continued)	Censer	Censer	76
	Chalice Emptied	Chalice Emptied	77
	Path	Path	78
	Great Rite	Great Rite	79
	Knotted Cord	Knotted Cord	80
Path of	Path	Coven	81
the Seeker	Coven	Path	82
	Cauldron	Pentacle	83
	Pentacle	Cauldron	84
	Gateway	Summerlands	85
	Summerlands	Gateway	86
	Guardian	Underworld	87
	Underworld	Guardian	88
	Lady of Life	Censer	89
	Censer	Lady of Life	90
	Lord of Death	Altar	91
	Altar	Lord of Death	92
	Great Rite	Knotted Cord	93
	Knotted Cord	Great Rite	94
	Chalice Filled	Chalice Emptied	95
	Chalice Emptied	Chalice Filled	96
Great Rite	Great Rite	Coven	97
	Coven	Great Rite	98
	Cauldron	Chalice Filled	99
	Chalice Filled	Cauldron	100
	Pentacle	Chalice Emptied	101
	Chalice Emptied	Pentacle	102
	Gateway	Underworld	103
	Underworld	Gateway	104
	Summerlands	Guardian	105
	Guardian	Summerlands	106
	Lady of Life	Lord of Death	107
	Lord of Death	Lady of Life	108

Great Rite	Censer	Altar	109
(continued)	Altar	Censer	110
	Path	Knotted Cord	111
	Knotted Cord	Path	112
Knotted	Knotted Cord	Coven	113
Cord	Coven	Knotted Cord	114
	Cauldron	Chalice Emptied	115
	Chalice Emptied	Cauldron	116
	Pentacle	Chalice Filled	117
	Chalice Filled	Pentacle	118
	Gateway	Guardian	119
	Guardian	Gateway	120
	Lady of Life	Altar	121
	Altar	Lady of Life	122
	Censer	Lord of Death	123
	Lord of Death	Censer	124
	Summerlands	Underworld	125
	Underworld	Summerlands	126
	Great Rite	Path	127
	Path	Great Rite	128

INTERPRETATION MEANINGS

In the following interpretations, the Judge is given first, the Left Witness is given next, and the Right Witness third. Make sure you read the correct interpretation.

1. *Cauldron*: Coven, Cauldron

This combination is generally good, indicating gain and acquisition through the help and good will of others. A positive atmosphere encourages proper actions and leads to greater abundance, but there are likely to be some ups and downs along the way. In order to bring about a successful outcome to the situation, it is likely that you will have to put your trust or confidence in others. When you do achieve the success that you desire, you must definitely be careful not to over-indulge yourself. Remain economical, both in purse and heart.

2. *Cauldron*: Cauldron, Coven

Mild success or a mildly favorable result will be achieved with regard to the question. You and another person (or perhaps several people) are cooperating in working toward a common goal. However, you will still have to work hard at achieving that goal. Beware of relying too much on luck, being showy, conceited, or imprudent, and all should go fairly smoothly. Occasionally, problems can result from exaggerating your emotional state and being careless in how you express yourself to others.

3. *Cauldron*: Path, Pentacle

This is not a good combination for material gain or material success. There is likely to be some loss or fluctuation in finances. You need not look very far for the reason—you have been either irresponsible or lazy. However, this combination does tend to favor the emotional and romantic life, giving ease in communicating feelings. If you are having difficulty in a personal relationship, the easiest way to set things aright is to yield to the other person's sentiments. You may have a hard lesson to learn when you receive these Witnesses and Judge; the world of material things does not necessarily bring emotional security, and you should look to your personal relationships for help, guidance, and inspiration, instead.

4. *Cauldron*: Pentacle, Path

Love is not favored when this combination is received because the emotions are inconstant—always seeking some new thing or new person to satisfy the senses. No time is given to develop a relationship. Projects involving money or material things are not favored either for much the same reason—what you are seeking will not satisfy you. Major moves and purchases should definitely be avoided. The influence of the plentiful Cauldron is generally favorable for all other things, however, so this combination indicates a partially favorable outcome for situations not involving love or money.

5. *Cauldron*: Lord of Death, Gateway

The beginning of the situation seems auspicious, happy, and well-aspected, but it will take a turn for the worse as opposition, trouble, and failure block your way. Usually, this is because of an increase in argumentativeness. However, the bad may be turned to good, and the lessons learned from hardship will increase the potential for ultimate gain. You will have a great deal of energy and courage to cope with any arising problems. Right now you need to concentrate on your actions in getting to the ultimate goal, and not on the ultimate goal itself.

6. *Cauldron*: Gateway, Lord of Death

Present misfortune, grief, unhappiness, and pain lead you to seek a better life. Strength and fortitude gained in sadder days gives you a profound appreciation for the joys of life. Better days are ahead, though you must beware that you are not betrayed by a man who does not have your interests at heart. This combination advises you to take your future into your own hands, seize available opportunities, and forge ahead. You have little to lose.

7. *Cauldron*: Censer, Guardian

You have placed yourself in a situation of trials and testing in the hopes of gaining a strongly desired prize. You will have to undergo much suffering and pain in order to win it, and there will be times when you think no more despair can be borne. You will have to battle for a favorable outcome, and perhaps become a little stern, but be forewarned—the struggle is uphill all the way, and you may not succeed, possibly even risking physical strain.

8. *Cauldron*: Guardian, Censer

This combination is generally unfavorable for every type of question. You are not likely to be pleased with the outcome of the situation. A violent emotional nature or temper has blocked your passage to a successful outcome. Unless you plan on fighting enemies or going to war, know that you are expending energy on something that is not likely to manifest.

9. *Cauldron*: Altar, Summerlands

This combination will lead to a successful resolution of every situation and bring a favorable outcome. Your success will lead you on to better things, and better friends and associates who will help you achieve future goals. These Witnesses and Judge are good for the beginning of any undertaking, but especially those involving communication, travel, relatives, education, or business.

10. *Cauldron*: Summerlands, Altar

Attainment and success will be achieved through a fortunate meeting with some person who will aid or advise you. Sometimes it means gaining the advantage in a situation through what you read in a book or newspaper, or learn from some other media. This is an excellent sign for meeting with others in a professional situation—seeking employment or a raise, for instance. This combination generally brings a favorable result for all types of questions.

11. *Cauldron*: Lady of Life, Underworld

This combination usually leads to good results and is favorable for all questions. The beginning of the matter is fraught with strife and conflict, but with the help of a woman, you will attain what you desire. Her aid may seem like a lucky break. These figures also tend to indicate social pleasures after much disharmony.

12. *Cauldron*: Underworld, Lady of Life

This combination of Witnesses and Judge typify the Legend of the Descent of the Goddess in which the Goddess went down to the Underworld to meet the Lord of Death and Rebirth. All good things seem to be withering now. Your only chance for success is in cutting your losses and ending your projects, as this combination is unfavorable. Take heart, though, as the situation will present itself again in the future in a more favorable form, where your chances of attaining your heart's desire will be greater.

13. *Cauldron*: Great Rite, Chalice Filled

This is a good combination of figures, indicating achievement and success. It is favored for all types of situations. You have a discerning intellect and good reasoning powers, and know how to take advantage of opportunities when they arise. A stroke of good fortune may put you in contact with someone who will aid you.

14. *Cauldron*: Chalice Filled, Great Rite

An excellent combination of figures, good for all types of questions. It especially favors communication and journeys. You will be successful in getting what you want. Sometimes this is achieved due to the fact that you are working in conjunction with someone else. Your energies, combined with those of your partner in the situation, will create a whole much greater than the sum of its parts.

15. *Cauldron*: Knotted Cord, Chalice Emptied

This combination usually indicates that good fortune is passing out of your life, bringing restriction, frustration, and delay. No action should be taken at this time in terms of starting new projects, as they will not turn out successfully. Do not spend too much time worrying over this, however, because the failure of the present situation will be to your benefit in the future.

16. *Cauldron*: Chalice Emptied, Knotted Cord

Delays, frustrations, and restrictions are passing out of your life, so you will be able to achieve at least some partial success in the situation at hand. This combination is only somewhat favorable, because you may have to sacrifice something dear in order to gain something greater in the long run. Better planning and organization would increase the chances of success, though the situation will still not turn out to be all that you hope.

17. *Pentacle*: Coven, Pentacle

They say too many cooks spoil the pot, and two is company but three is a crowd. Loss is indicated here because not enough resources are being given to the situation, and those that are given are being spread thin. People may be horning in where they do not belong just to benefit from the fruitful things earned by others. However, in romantic matters or situations dealing with friendship, this combination is favorable, since it indicates the introduction of a new person to your circle of friends.

18. *Pentacle*: Pentacle, Coven

The situation is in danger of becoming inharmonious due to an influx of outside influences, which include the unfavorable opinions of other people. Someone is trying to use the old "divide and conquer" trick against your own best interests. You will not win out against opposition unless you can remain charming, serene, and self-confident. Disregard what others say about the situation, especially if it seems they would be bitter if you achieved success.

19. *Pentacle*: Path, Cauldron

Partial success will be attained unless the situation deals with romance, relationships, or bringing people together in harmony. In these latter situations, greater success will be attained. If the question deals with money matters, fluctuation leading to eventual loss is indicated, unless the matters seek to bring you and another person closer together in a more harmonious relationship.

20. *Pentacle*: Cauldron, Path

Favorable for all types of questions and situations. You are on the correct path toward attaining abundance and achieving success, especially if the situation has nothing to do with monetary gain.

21. *Pentacle*: Altar, Gateway

A project or new endeavor begins well with clear objectives and solid plans. This will blossom into success, happiness, and gain. However, be careful that you do not become over-confident or indiscriminate with your newly earned good fortune.

22. *Pentacle*: Gateway, Altar

An introduction to a helpful person or new friend leads to success, gain, and happiness. Life begins to glitter around you and your bright future, but to remain happy, you will have to keep in mind that it is your personal relationships that make your life rich, and not the material things you have in your possession.

23. *Pentacle*: Lady of Life, Guardian

You will encounter blocks and difficulties when starting out on a new project or searching for a solution to your problem. However, all your work and struggle will eventually bring some profit, though it may be small in comparison to the effort spent. There will be much tending, but little growth.

24. *Pentacle*: Guardian, Lady of Life

A woman will cause you much trouble and grief, possibly through her beauty, charm, or powers of persuasion. The message here, whether the situation involves an actual woman or not, is that all that glitters is not gold, and things that look pretty on the outside may be rotten on the inside. Also, a situation that looks like it begins very auspiciously has a trouble spot somewhere. This trouble spot should be sought and rooted out, or else loss is fairly certain.

25. *Pentacle*: Lord of Death, Summerlands

A venture will start out with all engines running, and enthusiasm and energy will run high for all involved. The future looks bright and success seems certain. However, if the question involves love, romance, or friendship, there may be some loss and disappointment owing to rash decisions and impetuous actions.

26. *Pentacle*: Summerlands, Lord of Death

Relationships, including those with family and friends, are favored by these Witnesses and Judge, bringing great enjoyment and closeness. For all other types of questions, actions taken will be too forceful, giving the tendency to run into destruction if not checked. This is especially true if the question involves a young man with an impetuous nature; he may bring about loss or regret.

27. *Pentacle*: Censer, Underworld

Prepare yourself for tough times to come. The forces of the carnal nature are ruling here in these Witnesses, so the Judge will bring loss due to intemperate action. This is particularly true where romance and enemies are involved. Two wrongs make a wrong, since hate, greed, and lust engendered in the situation manifest an ever-descending spiral of degeneration. The situation is headed for rock bottom if your lower nature and baser impulses are not held in check. There is a possibility of a favorable outcome, but only if the question involves overcoming obstacles, and only if you have the courage and energy to deal with frustrations.

28. *Pentacle*: Underworld, Censer

This combination is unfavorable for every type of situation and question. Strife and conflict abound, bringing out the worst sides of the people involved. Stress and problems compound each other, making things worse.

29. *Pentacle*: Knotted Cord, Chalice Filled

This is a warning against excess. You have been enjoying the good things of life, and have taken all that has come your way. However, if you have been living beyond your means, or have taken undue advantage of someone, it will soon be time to "pay the piper." Your attitude has been one of self-importance and confidence that is based on falsehood. Your true self will soon be shown as it really is. This combination is not favorable for romantic or relationship questions. For material questions, you can avoid loss by remaining cautious and economical.

30. *Pentacle*: Chalice Filled, Knotted Cord

This combination is favorable for material endeavors, as it indicates that resources are used with enough discipline, patience, and circumspection to bring about an increase of wealth and abundance. Where the question involves romance or relationships, however, there is restriction and a feeling of being imprisoned. This may lead to depression, stagnation, and sadness.

31. *Pentacle*: Great Rite, Chalice Emptied
This indicates a period of loss and the destruction of previous wealth and security. However, help and solace will lie in the friendship and protection of another person or other people. You will still have to suffer the loss, but it won't be a total disaster.

32. *Pentacle*: Chalice Emptied, Great Rite
Some relationship, partnership, or collaboration will end in financial loss and regret. However, these Witnesses and Judge tend to favor romantic inclinations in questions dealing with the emotions. All other types of questions are answered favorably by this combination, so situations other than financial ones will work out well.

33. *Chalice Filled*: Coven, Chalice Filled
This is an excellent combination to receive, because it indicates success and favorable outcomes in all endeavors. Creative or spiritual work done by groups of people is especially favored. Not much can go wrong with this situation.

34. *Chalice Filled*: Chalice Filled, Coven
Success, happiness, attainment are indicated by these Witnesses and this Judge. There may be cause for a celebration with a group of people. Though success may be somewhat variable in the beginning, your intuition is leading you along the right track.

35. *Chalice Filled*: Path, Chalice Emptied
This combination will usually bring variable favorable results to the situation, though success will only be partial and somewhat fluctuating. However, it is a very good sign to receive if you are contemplating a journey—either physically, or inwardly and spiritually. This combination is also favorable if you inquire whether good news will be received from a particular source.

36. *Chalice Filled*: Chalice Emptied, Path

Now is the proper time to advance with your plans and ambitions. However, achievement will not come as easily as you think and you will have to put in some extra effort to succeed. New opportunities will open up, but you will have to be active in making them open up, instead of just waiting passively.

37. *Chalice Filled*: Great Rite, Cauldron

This is an excellent figure to receive. The situation will put you in a position of power and stability such that you may be able to help others. Indeed, someone may request your help or advice when these figures are received. You are ready to progress to the next stage in achieving your goals. This may entail a partnership, expansion of a business venture, or even a marriage or serious relationship. Further advancement will be the result, as well as self-fulfillment and happiness.

38. *Chalice Filled*: Cauldron, Great Rite

A partnership or joint project holds the promise of great bounty and success. This is a situation where both partners (or all partners, if there are more than two involved) bring their own talents and resources to work equally for the greater good. Financial and material gain is also indicated. Occasionally, these Witnesses and Judge can indicate a pregnancy, or the fertility of a project or new endeavor. It is favorable for all types of questions and situations, as long as communication lines and minds are kept open.

39. *Chalice Filled*: Lady of Life, Gateway

These Witnesses and Judge are among the best of all results to receive in geomantic divination. Abundance, love, happiness, and protection are all indicated by this combination. Success is likely to surpass your expectations. Proceed with your plans, and you cannot fail.

40. *Chalice Filled*: Gateway, Lady of Life

This is an extremely fortunate combination to receive. The Lady of Fortune is smiling on you and all that you do. Obstacles melt away, leaving the pathway to success clear before you.

41. *Chalice Filled*: Summerlands, Censer
Uncontrolled passions and emotions cause delay and disruption of plans, but as the Censer is a tool ruled by the element of fire, there is a full supply of energy here at your disposal. It only needs to be channeled in the right direction. Once this passion is taken under control, you will have greater success. Don't expend this energy on lust and petty traumas. Though it is likely that your objective will eventually be achieved, you must also exercise caution in using this energy; you do not want to overexert yourself, and lay yourself open to exhaustion or illness. Uncontrolled passions make this combination unfavorable for material affairs, since a clear head is needed to effectively deal with finances.

42. *Chalice Filled*: Censer, Summerlands
A situation starts out well, with confidence and enthusiasm. You aim high and have a solid vision for the future. However, things are heading for trouble, as emotions and passions erupt and disrupt your progress, leading to obstacles. The Censer is strong and hot; it can permanently warp the outcome of initial plans, making for an unfavorable result.

43. *Chalice Filled:* Underworld, Lord of Death
Energy, courage, and enthusiasm will allow you to make a good start in the situation, but you will have to deal with a minor disaster along the way. Even if you do gain what you desire, the goal will not seem as desirable as you once thought. The only thing this combination is favorable for is the ending of projects.

44. *Chalice Filled*: Lord of Death, Underworld
Strife, trouble, fighting, and conflict will abound. Everyone and everything may seem to be against you, and you will need to defend yourself at every turn. You may be partially victorious or have a semi-favorable outcome to the situation. However, the Underworld as Right Witness indicates loss. Thus, the Left Witness and Judge indicate that there will be partial restoration of what has been taken from you.

45. *Chalice Filled*: Pentacle, Knotted Cord

Any gain from the situation will be only partial. Restrictions, block-ages, and limitations stand in your way; you see opportunities passing you by because of your inability to take advantage of them. Now is the time to look deep within yourself and see if a lack of self-discipline has caused your present situation to manifest. Be firm with yourself, and you may still be able to record some good for your painstaking efforts.

46. *Chalice Filled*: Knotted Cord, Pentacle

You will achieve partial success in the situation. This is a time of iner-tia and limitations. The best road for you to take at this time is non-action. Allow things to develop on their own, because the result is likely to be better than if you bring your own energy to bear on the sit-uation. Sometimes favorable with regard to romance or relationships, as these figures can represent a steadying or consolidating influence.

47. *Chalice Filled*: Altar, Guardian

Inertia and limitations are stifling the expression of your desires. You may even find that these desires are perverted in their expression due to stagnating circumstances that seem to affect you beyond your control. This combination is unfavorable for all types of questions and situations.

48. *Chalice Filled*: Guardian, Altar

In order to succeed in the situation or bring about a favorable resolu-tion to your problem, you are going to have to use your powers of concentration to the utmost. This should not pose much of a problem to you at this time. You will meet obstacles along the way, but your wisdom and clear thoughts should allow you to overcome them. Gen-erally good for material endeavors, but less so for romantic relation-ships. Usually it indicates that a friendship is more viable than a romance with the particular person you have in mind.

49. *Chalice Emptied*: Coven, Chalice Emptied

Generally unfavorable for any situation or question. The general meaning of this combination is that you are looking for meaning and validation for your actions outside yourself to such an extent that your inner self is suffering. Self-image and self-esteem, as well as your view of your problem or situation, are based entirely on the opinions of others. You surround yourself with other people in order to avoid facing your own inner emptiness. Consider whether you are acting according to your own thoughts, or whether you are just trying to please others. If you are just trying to please others, it is not likely that you will meet with success.

50. *Chalice Emptied*: Chalice Emptied, Coven
This combination of figures is favorable for the successful resolution of almost all situations. It is particularly favorable if you are trying to make a new start in your life, and especially when you are working on eradicating some of your negative personality characteristics. The one area where loss may result is in personal relationships—whether in family, friendly, professional, or romantic relationships. You may isolate yourself emotionally from others, leading to strained relations.

51. *Chalice Emptied*: Knotted Cord, Cauldron
You will soon enjoy the gifts of bounty and success due to your hard work and organizational ability. The world will seem like your oyster, and nothing will seem to be able to stop you. However, beware that this expansive attitude does not lead you to do something that you will later regret. Everything in the universe strives toward equilibrium, and so too much of a good thing now will mean paying the price later.

52. *Chalice Emptied*: Cauldron, Knotted Cord
In order to attain success in this situation, you will have to use self-discipline and self-denial. You will really have to concentrate your efforts. When you finally attain to your goal, you will discover that it is not as wonderful as you thought. There will still be something missing, and you will feel somewhat emotionally empty.

53. *Chalice Emptied*: Censer, Gateway
All looks good at the outset of the situation, and the doors to opportunity are opening. However, these expansive emotions soon get out of balance, leading passion and excitement to spoil what would otherwise be a favorable outcome. All the good you will have had will be

lost, but take heart—it won't be irretrievable. It is just that your emotional attitude is not stable enough at this time to achieve success. Be wary if you are taking a journey; it will either be unprofitable or will not turn out as planned.

54. *Chalice Emptied*: Gateway, Censer

Passions and negative emotions such as anger, resentment, and indignation are ruling the situation now, and all will suffer from your lack of reason. The favorable outcome that might otherwise result in the situation will be clouded by your negative emotions. If you can make a change of heart, you may be partially successful in the situation. Otherwise, all is fairly well lost.

55. *Chalice Emptied*: Lord of Death, Guardian

Someone or something is blocking your way to success and the achievement of your goal. Inertia and self-imposed limitation will keep you fettered to outworn habits or routines. You need courage to break down these old habit patterns. You must literally fight for your freedom, and it is only a great onslaught of energy that will shatter your barriers. This will be followed by a period of physical and emotional emptiness as you seek to replace those old and useless constrictions. The upset will be stressful, but will be to your advantage in the long run. In the meantime, however, it is unlikely that you will achieve your goal. Unfavorable for almost all situations.

56. *Chalice Emptied*: Guardian, Lord of Death

The Lord of Death is the strong, all-conquering force of Mars, which will not tolerate anything standing in its way. However, there is something in the way—the Guardian. All of your enthusiasm and activity will run into a brick wall, and will be stopped dead. The Mars force here will not dissipate easily. Instead, it will collect and stagnate at the bottom of the wall. It will back up, build pressure, and may even turn on itself, creating a perversion of your original intent. In the end, the result will not be as you planned. There may be some partial success, however, in situations having to do with overcoming an enemy or competitor.

57. *Chalice Emptied*: Lady of Life, Summerlands

This combination is favorable for all types of situations and questions. Sometimes it can indicate the beginning of a new relationship of some type, a relationship that fills the void of loneliness or some other particular inner need.

58. *Chalice Emptied*: Summerlands, Lady of Life

You will attain partial success in your endeavors or the situation will work out partially to your advantage. Romantic relationships are not favored by this combination, however, since your head is too much in the clouds to form a secure attachment.

59. *Chalice Emptied*: Altar, Underworld

You will make a bad beginning. Fighting, strife, and disruption calls for communicating your emotions effectively to other people involved in the situation. Differences will be resolved and causes united, but enthusiasm and vigor will already have been somewhat deflated. The conflicts will have eaten up all the available energy. Regroup, refresh yourself, and begin again. Careful planning will make all the difference in the world the next time around.

60. *Chalice Emptied*: Underworld, Altar

The situation will start off well, but strife and arguments will soon turn your clear thoughts muddy. It is likely that someone has a hidden agenda that will prevent you from achieving your goal, usually by actions that threaten to disrupt your concentration. Keep your focus on your original purpose, formulate your plans clearly, and if hidden forces disrupt you, the loss will not be too bad.

61. *Chalice Emptied*: Great Rite, Pentacle

Loss of security will lead you to seek fulfillment either in the arms or under the protection of another person. Consider what the other person's view of the situation is, for a relationship built only on a quest for security is bound for disaster. If your mind is sharp and quick, you will be able to avoid all loss by careful planning.

62. *Chalice Emptied*: Pentacle, Great Rite

If the question relates to finances or material success, a partnership of some kind will lead to loss or an unfavorable result. In romantic questions, a partnership will lead to happiness, but only in the sense that your sensual needs will be met. In either case, there is shallowness and overconcern with superficial gain. The union is not formed for a greater common purpose, but personal and individual gain. This will lead to selfishness, which will cause all chances of success to collapse.

63. *Chalice Emptied*: Path, Chalice Filled

You will make an excellent beginning toward success, and will use your abundant resources wisely. However, your resources (material, emotional, or mental resources) and fortune will fluctuate somewhat, making for only partial success in the end.

64. *Chalice Emptied*: Chalice Filled, Path

You will start out on a journey toward your goal in fluctuating circumstances. Sometimes the tide will seem with you, buoying you up, and sometimes the tide will seem to be drowning you. Take heart during these initial ups and downs, as you will be partially successful in the end. Not all of your effort will be wasted. However, what you gain from the situation will only be a regaining of what you have previously lost.

65. *Coven*: Cauldron, Cauldron

This combination is usually favorable, as it indicates lucky breaks and much good fortune. The problem is that when opportunity arises, you don't take advantage of it. You don't have enough drive or motivation. Your energy level fluctuates, and the good fortune offered to you by other people passes you by. Be a little more aggressive and you will achieve greater success.

66. *Coven*: Coven, Coven

Favorable for questions involving women, groups, or the emotions. Unfavorable for everything else, however, since the situation or problem is almost completely out of your hands. This is the combination of fate or destiny. Other people and their decisions will influence the outcome of the situation more than your own thoughts and actions. Since other people involved are likely to have widely diverging opinions, the situation will be in almost a constant state of flux.

67. *Coven*: Gateway, Gateway

This combination is similar to a Judge resulting from the Cauldron and Cauldron as Witnesses (as in interpretation 65, above). There is a great deal of good fortune, happiness, and above all, opportunity, opportunity, opportunity! All you have to do is take advantage of it—no matter what the question—and the situation will have a favorable outcome. Usually good fortune will come from making connections and networking. This is a very expansive combination, extroverted and outgoing, indicating movement, growth, and progress.

68. *Coven*: Pentacle, Pentacle

This combination is unfavorable for all types of questions and situations. The situation starts out poorly and ends poorly, possibly with the result that you will break off a relationship with a person or group of people. Really, it is your own poor behavior that will get you into this sorry state of affairs. Try not to indulge in so much showmanship, ostentation, and other excessive behaviors to avoid repeating this pattern in the future. Also, save your money; even too much generosity can result in loss.

69. *Coven*: Summerlands, Summerlands

Achievement, success, and favorable outcomes are all that can come from this combination. You will have worked hard for it, and you will richly deserve all the bounty you gain.

70. *Coven*: Guardian, Guardian

Neither success nor a favorable outcome is likely to result from this combination. There is delay, frustration, and lack of progress at every turn. Your only hope is to abandon the situation and start anew, if you feel the work will be worth the goal.

71. *Coven*: Lady of Life, Lady of Life

This is an excellent combination of figures. The power of Venus is doubled here, indicating that your charm, grace, and diplomacy will earn you many admirers and people that will want to help you. These figures are particularly helpful in any questions or situations that involve creative endeavors and the public, such as theater, art, and music. If the question involves financial matters, the outcome will be favorable.

72. *Coven*: Underworld, Underworld

A terrible combination for every situation and question. No favorable outcome is possible, nor will success be achieved. If you cannot abandon the situation, your only possibility is to endure it until it works itself out. Whether you can see it or not, it is your own past actions that will have caused the situation to manifest so atrociously.

73. *Coven*: Altar, Altar

Success will be attained through communication, particularly by persuading other people of your point of view. However, your reasoning must be logical and airtight, or else your persuasive arguments may not work. This is a fabulous sign for material affairs, as it indicates that your reputation for clear thinking will have earned you the confidence of others. Thus, a group of people will come together to complete a project or figure out a solution to the problem. Also very favorable for travel.

74. *Coven*: Lord of Death, Lord of Death

This combination is not very favorable for any type of question or situation. There is too much male energy involved; too much enthusiasm and dynamic action can wreak havoc with a delicate situation. This is the situation of a bull in a china shop. Tact and diplomacy will be needed, and if not used, the situation will result in ruin. However, this combination can sometimes be partially favorable for questions involving the military, and other things traditionally associated with groups of men.

75. *Coven*: Chalice Filled, Chalice Filled

Good fortune, protection, security, confidence, and success will be yours for the taking. Your newfound abundance will allow you to be generous towards others, and may even gain you entrance to new social circles. Remember those who have helped you in the past, and return a good deed to them, if you are able.

76. *Coven*: Censer, Censer

Anger, strife, and conflict will soon characterize your situation or the matter involved in your question. These negative emotions will drive a wedge between the members of a group of people, leading to a most unfavorable outcome. If you are able to remove yourself from the situation, do so.

77. *Coven*: Chalice Emptied, Chalice Emptied

There will be many ups and downs in the situation before the matter finally comes to a partially successful conclusion. Favorable opportunities are open only for a brief period of time, so you must act quickly before your ability to take advantage of them passes. If the question or situation involves bringing a matter to a conclusion (such as signing a contract, sealing a deal, or finishing a project) the results are likely to be mediocre.

78. *Coven*: Path, Path

If your question involves starting a new project or becoming involved in a new situation, inertia is likely to cloud your initial progress. Your timing is off. It is better to wait to make the new beginning at a better time. If the question involves ending a project or bringing a matter to a successful conclusion, you are likely to encounter problems that will prevent you from bringing closure to the situation. Travel is somewhat favored by this combination, though any results coming from it will only be partially successful.

79. *Coven*: Great Rite, Great Rite

This is a good combination, favorable for all types of questions and situations. You will become acquainted with sparkling and witty new friends and associates. This combination is very good for any type of business transaction involving buying or selling. Your personality is showing at its best, and you can easily gain the confidence of others. This will turn the situation to your advantage, leading you to a successful conclusion of the matter.

80. *Coven*: Knotted Cord, Knotted Cord

There is restriction here on a grand scale. Nothing will move, and it will seem like nothing ever will, which indicates delay, frustration, and blocks to progress. You are only moving in circles. Occasionally this combination can be favorable for questions or situations involving the need to exercise self-discipline and restraint (such as directing or keeping on an exercise program).

81. *Path*: Path, Coven

You are torn between your inner and outer lives. Spiritual concerns and mundane responsibilities clash and create stress for you. This leads to an unfavorable result. You must do some careful introspective work, and decide whether you are determining your own path or allowing others to determine your path for you. There is a great deal of indecision indicated by this combination. The solution to the problem should be found through meditation and by listening to your intuition.

82. *Path*: Coven, Path

This combination will result in partial success in the situation asked about. Though you may feel lost and ungrounded in the near future, you will meet a person or several people that will point you in the direction of your goal. Consider getting advice from people who have travelled the route that you are contemplating. They will be able to give you some interesting insights.

83. *Path*: Cauldron, Pentacle

This is an excellent combination to receive. The possibility of loss will spurn you on toward greater heights and fulfillment (or perhaps it already has). The situation begins badly, but ends very successfully, allowing you to contemplate your next step and future goals.

84. *Path*: Pentacle, Cauldron

Negative outcomes and lack of success characterize this combination. Both the Jupiter-ruled Witness and the Venus-ruled Witness are poorly situated here. Abundant resources that you will have at the beginning of the situation will be squandered foolishly and carelessly. There will be too much waste. You may also take others for granted too much for too long, leaving you to walk this hard road alone. To help avoid this, try to be economical with both purse and heart.

85. *Path*: Gateway, Summerlands

These Witnesses and Judge indicate great success and good fortune with regard to your question or situation. Both the Summerlands and the Underworld can sometimes indicate karmic influences. So, the good fortune you will experience may not necessarily be the result of your hard work. Lucky breaks and fortunate coincidences will convince you that you are reaping a reward from planting a good harvest in a past incarnation. In the end, it doesn't matter where the good fortune comes from; just accept it, enjoy it, and go on your merry way.

86. *Path*: Summerlands, Gateway

A new opportunity will soon open up in the situation. You will have enough foresight to take advantage of it, and it will lead you on to great success. This is especially true if the question involves spiritual or non-material matters, as the influence of the Summerlands will tend to raise your eyes to the heavens instead of lower them to the Earth. Even if material benefits do result from the situation, know that these have come to you because of your proper implementation of spiritual principles.

87. *Path*: Guardian, Underworld

An unfavorable combination to receive unless the question or situation involves defeating enemies or rivals. If enemies or rivals are not involved, the situation will commence with strife and conflict. Even if these are worked through, you will encounter only further delay, obstacles, and frustrations blocking your path to success.

88. *Path*: Underworld, Guardian

Failure is almost certain even from the very inception of the situation or project. Even if you do manage to fight your way through delay, obstacles, and frustration, an unfavorable ending will be your only reward. Abandon the situation if you can. If not, endure.

89. *Path*: Lady of Life, Censer

The heat and friction of the sensual world will enfold you at the beginning of the situation, making your reasoning faculties muddled and confused. You need to clear your mind in order to work toward your goal. Seek out a woman who understands what you are going through, and she will be able to give you some good, practical advice. If the question involves romance, there is a strong possibility of sexual compatibility that will later blossom into emotional understanding, making for a good relationship.

90. *Path*: Censer, Lady of Life

This combination is unfavorable for almost all situations. Pleasure is allowed to get in the way of work, and this will bring an unfortunate ending to the matter. You may try to avoid this by being practical instead of pleasure-seeking. However, if the question involves romance, it can indicate the forming of a close bond. Be wary, however, that the relationship is not just based on sexual relations. If it is, there will soon be conflict in the relationship.

91. *Path*: Lord of Death, Altar

This combination is unfavorable for all situations and questions. You have charted your course too quickly, and have not taken possible problems into consideration. One source of conflict may come from a rash and inconsiderate man. You may try to win him over to your point of view before he causes too much trouble, but it is unlikely that you will be able to persuade him. Go back to the drawing board and plan out your actions more carefully and deliberately, or else failure is almost sure to result.

92. *Path*: Altar, Lord of Death

Even though you will be rash and impatient in working toward your heart's desire, your thinking is logical and your thought processes are clear. You may proceed without too much difficulty if you are contemplating a fresh course of action. You will achieve your goal if it is one to be completed in the short term. However, if you are asking about a long-term goal, the result will be less favorable. The energy that you will bring to the situation (because of the Lord of Death) will not be steady for long enough a period of time to counteract the fluctuations of the moon-ruled sign of the Path of the Seeker.

93. *Path*: Great Rite, Knotted Cord

This combination will bring a partially successful result to the situation. The beginning of the matter is fraught with hardship, delay, and frustration. However, your logical thinking, concentration, and careful planning should allow you to overcome these with only moderate difficulty. This will leave the path toward your goal open before you. However, only partial success is indicated because the previous hardship and delay will have reduced the value of what you are after.

94. *Path*: Knotted Cord, Great Rite

A partnership, marriage, business agreement, or other compromise imposes limitations on the people involved in the situation. These limitations will force you to develop greater self-discipline, and this creates pressure and stress for you. Oftentimes this combination will indicate that "emotional distance" has grown between two people, and while they may still be together in an outward sense, they are very much separated from each other inwardly—each is following his or her own ambitions and goals, instead of a common goal. For questions involving business or finance, however, partial success is indicated through the wise use of resources and the prudent implementation of limitations.

95. *Path*: Chalice Filled, Chalice Emptied
A period of ill fortune and lost opportunity will shortly be passing out of your life, leaving you to make a fresh start. This combination is an indication that you will achieve your final goal, but that you must be careful not to wreck your health and vitality level in the process. In any case, the outcome is favorable.

96. *Path*: Chalice Emptied, Chalice Filled
A good beginning that looks like it will lead to success will take a turn for the worse. If there are other people involved, there will be a loss of confidence. If material endeavors are involved, there will be some monetary loss. However, the outcome of the situation will still be partially favorable, just not as favorable as you expected it to be.

97. *Great Rite*: Great Rite, Coven
In questions or situations that deal with two or more people coming to a "meeting of minds" or common purpose, this combination will lead to a successful conclusion. In all other types of questions and situations, the results are usually less than hoped for, if any positive result is gained at all. If any positive result is achieved, it will not yield happiness for a greater time period than the short-term future.

98. *Great Rite*: Coven, Great Rite
You will be introduced to a group of people that will be favorably disposed toward you and your goal. There is strength in numbers. However, in any situation, success will only be fleeting if it is gained at all. The only exception to this is if the question deals with marketing, or selling a product or idea to a large group of people. In this situation, the success will be greater, but probably just as fleeting.

99. *Great Rite*: Cauldron, Chalice Filled
This combination indicates favorable results for all types of questions and situations. You will increase your material resources and strengthen your alliances, whether these are emotional or professional. You may proceed without difficulty or hazard.

100. *Great Rite*: Chalice Filled, Cauldron

Attainment, gain, and expansion of material possessions and emotional relationships are indicated by these two Witnesses and this Judge. You will be sitting on top of the world as king or queen. This will be the result of a new partnership, relationship, or inner harmonizing.

101. *Great Rite*: Pentacle, Chalice Emptied

Self-indulgent behavior, whether emotional or financial, will lead to loss and instability in the situation. You may have to lean on others for support and advice to get through the situation. You are not being at all practical, and the dreams and castles you have built in the air will come crashing down. The result will be unfavorable no matter what the situation or question.

102. *Great Rite*: Chalice Emptied, Pentacle

This is a bad time for financial gain, but a better time for love. The reason for this is that you are feeling vulnerable. This will put you in a position of material insecurity. Be cautious, and though you will not gain much materially, neither will you have any great losses. The combination of these two Witnesses in romantic matters will make you charming and attractive to others—perhaps your emotional vulnerability is attractive to them. In that case, beware of emotional predators that may be looking for a victim.

103. *Great Rite*: Gateway, Underworld

Results of this combination are favorable. Initial difficulties and perhaps even a minor disaster will yield to opportunity, laughter, joy, and progress. This combination is especially favorable for travelling and inner spiritual journeys designed to improve negative personality characteristics. If you do not meet with success despite the favorable testimony of these figures, you will not have to look far for the reason; the problem lies within you, not outside of you.

104. *Great Rite*: **Underworld, Gateway**

If the question deals with travel and communication, results will be partially favorable, but if the situation involves anything else—romance, business, solving a problem—the result will be disastrous. An opportunity will be taken advantage of, but it will not be all that you were led to believe. Someone may even by deliberately lying to you in order to induce certain actions on your part. If it sounds too good to be true, it isn't true. Journeys will end in disaster, and the purposes for which they are made will not be accomplished.

105. *Great Rite*: **Summerlands, Guardian**

This combination is very favorable for the resolution of all situations and questions. This is in spite of the fact that the beginning will be burdened by delays and indecision. The Summerlands figure indicates that spiritual forces will be brought to bear on the situation, no matter how mundane the area of concern, and will eventually lead you on to attainment and fulfillment.

106. *Great Rite*: **Guardian, Summerlands**

A positive result will not come from the situation, and the answer to your question is not what you want to hear. The beginning of the situation promises happiness and success in the end, but an obstacle will crop up, causing delay and indecision. It appears that the opportunity for a successful conclusion will be lost due to your hesitation.

107. *Great Rite*: **Lady of Life, Lord of Death**

This combination is favorable for all questions and situations, because it indicates desires with the necessary energy to manifest them. This is the consummation of the marriage between the God and the Goddess, Heaven and Earth. It can bring nothing but good. Occasionally it can indicate restlessness at the beginning of the situation. You know that you want something, but are not sure what. Once you focus on what it is that you desire, you will easily bring it into being.

108. *Great Rite*: Lord of Death, Lady of Life

This is similar to the previous combination insofar as that it indicates happiness, fruition of desires, and success. The difference, though, is that you know what you want right from the beginning of the situation, and that the means toward manifesting what you desire come a little bit later. Nevertheless, the result is very favorable.

109. *Great Rite*: Censer, Altar

The attainment of what you desire depends on coming to an agreement or compromise with another person. However, arguments and strife prevent this from occurring, leading to a negative outcome. Consider whether you are in the wrong, and whether you are being stubborn and intractable. If you can change your mind, you may be able to save the situation and reach a partially successful result. If not, your only choice is to agree to disagree with the other person and abandon the situation.

110. *Great Rite*: Altar, Censer

Success is indicated by this combination, but you will have to obtain the approval of another person before you can achieve what you desire. Logical persuasion should be successful once the initial emotional pressures are overcome. Occasionally this combination means that you will have to overcome your own base or sensual desires in order to think clearly about your situation or problem. Once you have done this, success will be assured.

111. *Great Rite*: Path, Knotted Cord

Personal relationships are somewhat stifling at this time, leading to sadness. There is a rocky road ahead if the question deals with romance. Some progress will be made, but the relationship will essentially remain as it is when the question is asked. This combination is more favorable for material or business endeavors or agreements, because it indicates you have narrowed down your goal to something achievable, and you have the discipline to pursue it to a partially successful conclusion.

112. *Great Rite*: Knotted Cord, Path

This combination of figures indicates that you have some new desire that you want to manifest or some new goal that you are going to set out to accomplish. You have no reason to believe that you cannot succeed at the beginning of the situation. However, circumstances will not permit you to achieve what you want. Emotional ties or lack of resources will restrict your endeavors. In the end you will realize that this is not something you want after all. In turn, this will lead you to fashion a more realistic, attainable goal that you really do want to achieve.

113. *Knotted Cord*: Knotted Cord, Coven

Your association with some particular group of people or some other affiliation leads to unhappiness. The affiliation is limiting you, holding you back, and dragging you down. Beware of the advice of others, as it will get you nowhere. This combination does not result in a favorable outcome for anything, unless you are asking about the ending of a situation. Endings will work out positively.

114. *Knotted Cord*: Coven, Knotted Cord

This combination is not favorable for any situation. The situation begins in an atmosphere of restriction and limitation. The opinions of other people further hinder you to the point where you feel confined and unable to act. Occasionally, for romantic questions, this combination can be favorable, as it indicates a solidifying of an emotional bond. Nonetheless, you may still feel like you are in an emotional rut.

115. *Knotted Cord*: Cauldron, Chalice Emptied

A period of ill fortune is just now ending in your life, so good things will soon be coming your way. You should take advantage of them. In the end you will be cheerful and content with your surroundings and what you have accomplished. These new gains should be consolidated as soon as possible.

116. *Knotted Cord*: Chalice Emptied, Cauldron

Good fortune and abundance are leaking away from your life like wine from a broken cup. A time for discipline is approaching, perhaps as a result of previous self-indulgence or taking undue advantage of the generosity of others. Tighten your belt and make no major moves. A time of austerity approaches.

117. *Knotted Cord*: Pentacle, Chalice Filled

Good fortune and happiness turn sour. You have been relying too much on your material possessions, and have taken your personal relationships for granted for too long. This leaves you feeling empty inside, sad, and melancholy. Your luck has run out. This combination is unfavorable for all situations except love and relationships. If your question concerns personal relationships, these will be strengthened and deepened.

118. *Knotted Cord*: Chalice Filled, Pentacle

This combination indicates that you will have a bad beginning to the situation; you may have to sacrifice something dear to you in order to serve a greater purpose or progress toward a greater goal. If you can make the sacrifice and not be too sad about it, you will achieve success in the end. It will be worth it. In emotional situations, other people are loyal and trustworthy.

119. *Knotted Cord*: Gateway, Guardian

A favorable result is indicated by this combination, as long as the question deals with material things, as opposed to emotions. In material endeavors, initial obstacles are overcome, leading the way to a solid success. In emotional matters, relationships become dry, stifling, and restricting; love may have passed out of the union.

120. *Knotted Cord*: Guardian, Gateway

You will be prevented from taking advantage of a favorable opportunity due to restricting outside circumstances. Even if you find yourself able to take advantage of the situation, you should not, for there are further obstacles ahead that will cause delay and frustration. The prize is not worth the price.

121. *Knotted Cord*: Lady of Life, Altar

This combination brings favorable results for all types of questions that have to do with love and pleasure. Material endeavors, however, are not favored. Possessions may end up too burdensome—it may take too much time to take care of them—so you will not enjoy them. New projects are also favored, as long as they have nothing to do with finances or material acquisitions. You can succeed as long as your concentration is not broken by being offered beautiful material things.

122. *Knotted Cord*: Altar, Lady of Life

The situation will begin harmoniously, but you must use your logical thinking abilities to keep things going your way. In the end, the situation is ruled by reason, not emotions. This combination of figures favors artistic endeavors of every kind. Where the situation involves a woman or women, beware. She does not really have your best interests at heart, and may be working toward her own ends.

123. *Knotted Cord*: Censer, Lord of Death

This is a very unfortunate combination for all types of questions and situations. You will begin the situation with much energy and enthusiasm. However, the situation requires careful planning and tact, not impatience and precipitous action. You will act passionately without thinking, and this will eventually end in conflict. Keep a cool head, and though you may not gain anything, you may prevent what would otherwise be losses.

124. *Knotted Cord*: Lord of Death, Censer

The result of this combination is unfavorable. You may be acting out of anger or misdirected passion and not common sense. Consider your own motivations and behaviors before you start blaming others. No matter how much energy you pour into this situation, it will not be enough. You will continue to be beset with delays, frustration, and obstacles. Abandon the situation if you can. If not, calm down, take no action, and let the situation resolve itself on its own.

125. *Knotted Cord*: Summerlands, Underworld
The situation begins badly, but ends favorably. You will be able to consolidate your well-earned gains. The exception is if your question involves personal relationships. You may gain what you desire, but the result will not be as favorable as you thought. Usually, there is too much restriction in the relationship for it to bring much happiness.

126. *Knotted Cord*: Underworld, Summerlands
The situation begins favorably, but ends very badly, no matter what the question is. You should not proceed with any new undertaking at this time, as your only "reward" will be loss.

127. *Knotted Cord*: Great Rite, Path
When these figures are received, you will attain your goal or whatever it is that you desire. However, the goal will not seem as fair once you have attained to it. Don't worry, though; success will be short-lived. Thus, while you will not gain anything in the end, you will not lose anything either. You will just be put back to the beginning of the path to start again.

128. *Knotted Cord*: Path, Great Rite
A meeting or other fortuitous circumstance will set you on the path toward a goal. Occasionally, this can represent becoming a student learning some new type of practice, craft, skills, or the like. It is likely, however, that you will abandon the situation in the end, as you do not have the requisite self-discipline to follow through with it. Usually unfavorable for all types of situations and questions.

MY ANSWER DOESN'T MAKE SENSE; WHAT NOW?

If your answer still seems unclear, you may form one final figure—the Reconciler. This is formed by adding together the heads, necks, bodies, and feet of figures XV (the Judge) and I (the first Mother). The resulting figure will help you answer your question. Refer to the general explanation of the figures as they are given on pages 112 through

117. You may also want to check the chart before the listing of the interpretations to determine whether the final outcome is favorable or unfavorable. If your answer is clear from the interpretation of the two Witnesses and the Judge, you should not fashion a Reconciler. It would be meaningless and likely to confuse or skew your interpretation.

If your answer is still not clear after fashioning the Reconciler, you have one final option. Note down the names of the Mothers—figures I through IV. The nature of figure I will show you how the matter involved in your question will begin. Figures II and III will show you how the matter will progress. Figure IV will show you how the matter will end. If necessary, refer to the general interpretations of the figures as given in this chapter.

If you are still unable to ascertain the answer to your question, take all of the information you have available—the two Witnesses, the Judge, the Reconciler, and the four Mothers—and meditate on them for half an hour each day for three days, remembering to do your "divination tune-up" exercises (as given in Chapter Three) before your meditation session. Note all thoughts that come to you during your meditations.

If this still yields no satisfactory results, the divination has failed. In the future, resolve to carry out your "tune-up" exercises more carefully since you did not make a good "inner connection" this time.

CONCLUSION

Geomancy may seem like a complicated practice, but once you get the hang of geomantic addition, and understand how the Mothers, Daughters, Nephews, Witnesses, Judge, and Reconciler are formed, you will be able to cast a chart quickly and efficiently, and obtain accurate results.

CHAPTER EIGHT

TALKING STONES

One of the easiest ways of making your own divination system is through the use of rune stones. We are not talking about the Norse runes—that is a separate system of divination unto itself, and one that I would class as one of the more complex, major systems of divination. Let's not use the word "rune" at all in our discussion. The word "rune," to my mind at least, has a "secretive" or "mysterious" connotation. Let's call this system of divination "talking stones." After all, we want them to "speak" to us, not glare at us, mute and mysterious.

The history of such talking stones is difficult to trace. Archaeologists and anthropologists tell us that certain primitive peoples used to cast knuckle bones of animals in order to foresee the future. This is probably the oldest known form of this type of divination. The Yoruba people of west Nigeria have a system of divination with cowrie shells, in their own language called *Ifá*. This is an ancient system, and one that is still practiced both in Nigeria and by practitioners of Santería and other African-based religious systems. The throwing of any type of object has generally become known as the "casting of lots." In French, this type of divination is known as "sortilege" coming from the French words "sorcier" and "sorcière" meaning male witch and female witch, respectively. All of these words, in turn, derive from the Latin word "sors," meaning "fate" or "destiny." The English language has adopted the word "sortilege" from the French, though it is rarely used nowadays, even amongst Witches. Eventually, someone had the great idea to carve or paint symbols on stones, and thus was born the art of lithomancy (from the Greek root word "lithos," meaning "stone").

Lithomancy, or the art of casting stones, is the art that you are going to learn here. Not only will you learn it, but you can re-create the system for yourself to fit your own particular needs. You may ask, will such a system work—a self-created one? In answer to such a question, I assure you that some of the best practitioners of divination that the world has known have created their own systems. Madame de Lenormand used a pack of thirty-two cards that she devised herself to predict Napoleon's marriage to Josephine and Napoleon's defeat at Waterloo. She was well known and highly sought after by the nobles of France and Europe. Another case is Nostradamus. No one is quite certain what method he used (though some have conjectured he used a combination of astrology, numerology, and Qabalistic teachings), but we can be certain that he created it himself. We need not comment on his accuracy.

GETTING STARTED: THE FIRST STEPS

The system that I am going to outline here is meant to be that—an outline. Feel free to tinker and tamper with it to coincide with your own particular needs as you see fit. Let's assume for the purpose of this exercise that your divination tool will be stones, rocks, or pebbles, though there is no reason you could not use small circular pieces of wood, a blank deck of index cards, or even popsicle sticks.

You can collect your stones at the beach, from the roots of a favorite tree, or just by foraging and digging through your backyard. You may want to collect your stones at a magical time, say on one of the eight Sabbats or during the night of the full moon. How many should you collect? How about thirteen—the Witch's number. They should be small enough to all fit in one hand or in both hands. Stones about the size of dice will be good, since they are going to be cast in a similar manner. What about the shade or natural coloring of the stones? This is up to you, but they should be light enough to be able to see a marked symbol on the top of them.

Now that you have your stones, let's decide what markings you are going to put on them. First of all, one stone should be set aside as the "Querent Stone." It will represent the person (presumably, most often, yourself) asking the question of the Talking Stones. You will place this stone at the center of your divination place before you ask your question. Then, when you have asked your question, you will throw your stones, and judge your answers from the stones that have fallen close to the "Querent Stone." So, what would be a good symbol to put on this stone? Well, we want to keep it within the range of the lowest artistic ability (that is, mine), so let's make the symbol for this stone an eye, something like this:

Doesn't that look intriguing? This is the stone that will represent the querent. What color should you make this stone? Whatever you like; you can even use several different colors, or make it very fancy and ornate with silver and gold pens, paints, or markers. Don't worry about artistic quality—you don't have to make it a work of art. Just make it recognizable.

If you don't like the symbol of the eye for the Querent Stone, consider using the symbol of your astrological sun sign. If you are not familiar with these zodiacal symbols, look yours up in one of the astrology books listed in the suggested reading section.

You might even decide to use an Egyptian hieroglyphic as the symbol for the Querent Stone. Below is the hieroglyph for the Egyptian words "I AM":

One stone down, twelve to go. Let's base our next seven stones on the seven planets known to the ancients—the Sun, the Moon, Mercury, Venus, Mars, Jupiter, and Saturn. We will decide on a symbol for each in turn. By the way, if you do not like a symbol that I have suggested, make up another one for yourself. After all, these are *your* Talking Stones. At the end of this chapter, we will go through all of the different meanings or interpretations that each stone can have in a reading.

The Sun Stone

The choice of symbol is quite obvious for this stone—the Sun. How about using the astrological symbol for the Sun, but making it with rays, like this:

The best color for this stone is probably gold or yellow. Of course, if you like, you can make your stones all the same color—black, red, or whatever. You can decide whether to use colored markers, paints, or another coloring medium.

The Moon Stone

Again, the choice here is obvious—some lunar symbol. I'll give you a couple options here—either a crescent moon by itself, or a symbol representing the three phases of the moon (which you may like better because it ties in with the Three Faces of the Goddess). Here are what the symbols might look like:

Choose whichever of the two you prefer, or make up a symbol yourself. The best color for this stone will probably be white or silver. Again, if you are using just one color for your stones, stick with that.

The Mercury Stone

Here the choice of symbol is not as obvious. We could use the astrological symbol of Mercury, or we could use one of the god Mercury's symbols, the caduceus. Have you ever tried to draw a caduceus? I've found it very difficult to get the intertwined snakes to look symmetrical, so let's leave off the bottom part of the caduceus and just have a circle with wings. Incidentally, a winged disk is a symbol for air in ancient Egyptian teachings, and Mercury and air correspond in most magical systems. Again, choose either these, or make up your own:

The best color for this stone is probably orange. Alternatively, Mercury has something of a changing, volatile nature, so you may want to make it several different colors—orange, yellow, red, green, and blue —or whatever you decide.

The Venus Stone

Ah, yes—the stone of love and friendship. Here you can use the astrological symbol for Venus, or come up with something else. You could use a heart. You could also use three interlocked rings. The number three is important to Venus, because that is the number of the Tarot card the Empress, which corresponds to Venus. Choose one of these symbols or make up your own:

The best colors for the Venus stone would depend on which symbol you choose. For the heart, pink would probably be best. Pink would be good for the other symbols, too. For the interlocked rings and the astrological symbol, green (the Empress' color) would also be a good choice. You could even have a green heart if you wanted. I've not mentioned red here, because that is the color that fits best for the Mars Stone, which is next.

The Mars Stone

Here you have a choice again. The astrological symbol for Mars would do, but since Mars is a war-like planet, we could come up with something reflecting that. How about a sword or a bundle of spears? Choose one of the following or make one up:

For the Mars Stone, you will probably want to use red, the color of war and anger. You'll notice that I've used five crossed spears. Five is the number of Mars. Mars in astrology, by the way, also rules sharp objects such as knives and swords.

The Jupiter Stone

We all know the astrological symbol for Jupiter. It looks like the numeral four. This is natural since the number related to Jupiter is four. Jupiter also implies abundance. You might choose a fish as a symbol here; the fish is the symbol of the astrological sign Pisces (which Jupiter co-rules with Neptune), and has long been considered a symbol for abundance. Plants and growing things are also considered symbols of abundance. You may come up with other symbols yourself.

The best color for the astrological symbol and fish would probably be blue. However, a blue plant may look mighty odd, so consider doing that in green, or green and gold. If you choose the fish, you could even put wavy lines behind it to indicate the sea.

The Saturn Stone

There are two different astrological symbols for Saturn. These are the first two symbols below. You will note that both of them look rather like scythes to indicate Saturn's connection to agriculture and the Grim Reaper. One of the astrological symbols looks like the letter "H," so you may just want to use that.

$$\mathfrak{H} \quad \hbar \quad \mathsf{H}$$

In keeping with Saturn's severe nature, the color black probably works best here.

That takes care of eight stones, leaving us to decide on five more. Really, these eight stones would work well together by themselves, since the seven planets can be correlated with anything in life. However, it would probably be best to use other stones in order to make our divinations more "topic specific." Therefore, I am going to suggest five more stones—the Life Stone, the Home Stone, the News Stone, the Magic Stone, and the Other Stone. If, after reading through the description of what these five stones mean later on, you decide that one really would not apply to your life, or that there is something more important in your life that deserves its own stone, omit one of these five stones and add one to represent your needs. Do this for as many stones as you feel necessary. For now, we'll stick with the five stones that I've listed.

The Life Stone

Here you are going to have to be more creative with both symbol and color. Any symbol that we give for this stone is going to be inadequate, for life is a comprehensive and weighty subject. The ankh, the Egyptian hieroglyph for life, is an obvious choice. We could also take the esoteric idea that when we become incarnate we enter the physical plane, and exit from the inner planes—entrance and exit. These things can be esoterically symbolized by the dragon's head and the dragon's tail, which are really the moon's nodes in astrology. Let's base our second symbol on the combination of two figures that represent these ideas in the art of geomancy. Alternatively, we could symbolize entrance and exit by two interlaced triangles, one pointing upwards, the other downward:

Red is the color of life, so consider using it for the ankh or geomancy figure. If you decide on the interlaced triangles, you may want to make each triangle a different color, say red for one and blue for the other, or gold and silver, or whatever combination appeals to you.

The Home Stone

Wait a minute, you may say—doesn't the moon, which rules the family, also cover the home? Technically, it does, in astrology, but remember, we are trying to make our stones as topic specific as possible, while still making the total number of stones used manageable. The Home Stone will refer to the home and the family environment; that way we can assign other meanings to our Moon Stone. Here are three designs from which to choose. One is a crude representation of a house, and the other is a crude representation of the members of a family. The third is based on a geomancy figure called "Carcer" in Latin, which you will recognize as the root for the word "incarceration." Carcer really just means an enclosed space, which a home or house certainly is. You can always make up your own design, however:

A good color for the Home Stone might be purple, which corresponds to the moon, and the moon rules the home in astrology.

The News Stone

A good symbol for this stone might be birds in flight; a stylized representation of this is our first symbol. One bird would also be a good symbol. Another might be a scroll with some writing on it:

You may want to use a couple of different colors for this stone—news can be good, bad, or even mixed. For instance, for the first symbol you may want to make one bird black, another white, and the third some other color like red, blue, or green. You could use a couple of different colors in drawing the second symbol as well. For the third symbol, you might want to make each of the wavy lines a different color.

The Magic Stone

The first symbol for this stone is an obvious choice—the pentagram, the great symbol of magic, of humankind's dominion over the elements, of mastery. Another good symbol for the Magic Stone might be the cauldron. While the cauldron is not the only magic tool that Witches use, it is probably the tool that the modern mind most associates with the archetype (or stereotype) of the Witch. You may come up with better symbols yourself:

The choice of color is wide open here, for there is no specific color of "magic." You may want to make the pentagram a gold or silver color, or use the colors of the elements (plus spirit) and paint each bar of the pentagram a different color—blue, green, yellow, red, and purple, with perhaps a silver or gold circle surrounding it. The cauldron can be any color you wish, but most are black.

The Other Stone

This stone is going to be used to represent other people who may be involved in a cast for the future, or to answer a specific question. The first symbol is a composite symbol of the letters O, T, and H. The second is derived from the geomancy symbol called "Populus," which is Latin for "people." Choose one of these or make your own:

The choice of color or colors I leave to your own devising.

An Alternative Set of Talking Stones

You have another option in making your own set of Talking Stones. Instead of choosing gray stones or pebbles and putting a symbol on each, you can use different types of what are commonly called gemstones or crystals. This way you need not put a symbol on the stone. For example, you could use a piece of pink quartz for the Love Stone, a piece of malachite for the Venus Stone, a moonstone for the Moon Stone, a piece of variegated or leopard-skin agate for the Mercury Stone, a turquoise for the Home Stone. What type of crystal you use to represent a particular Talking Stone is your own choice. You may want to coordinate the color of your crystals in accordance with the colors that have been suggested for each stone.

THE POUCH

You should also think about getting a pouch to keep your Talking Stones in when they are not in use. This will serve to keep them clean and free of dust, as well as insulate them against unwanted psychic vibrations. For the latter reason, silk is the best material to use, but any material of any color will do. You can embroider or decorate your pouch in any manner that you wish, perhaps with a magical symbol or a symbol of your magical name, if you have one. You may want to carry your pouch with you when you are in a magical Circle, so they are always on hand for a quick divination. If your pouch has drawstrings, it is fairly easy to loop them around a cord that you would wear with a robe.

CONSECRATION OF
YOUR TALKING STONES

As with any magical tool, your Talking Stones should be suitably consecrated before you use them. I give a small ritual here for this purpose, but you can make up your own ritual as well. The ritual is written for Talking Stones, so if you have made your divination device out of wood circles or some other material, you will have to adapt the ritual or write your own.

Consecration Ritual for Talking Stones

For this ritual, you will need the following items:

- A small table facing north to serve as an altar.
- A stick of incense (or granulated incense and a piece of charcoal upon which to burn it) set on the eastern side of the altar.
- A white candle set on the southern side of the altar.
- A bowl of water set on the western side of the altar.
- A small dish of salt or soil set on the northern side of the altar.
- Your completed set of Talking Stones and their pouch placed on the altar.

Before you begin the ritual, you should sit in front of the altar for several minutes to still your mind and meditate on the purpose of the ritual. When you feel composed, light the candle, and from the candle set your incense going. You may wish to cast a Circle for the consecration ritual, using your own method or the procedure given in the Appendix, but this is not strictly necessary. Raise your stones with both hands above the altar and speak the following incantation, which serves to state the purpose of your ritual:

> *Talking Stones, Telling Stones,*
> *Fashioned from the Mother's bones,*
> *Show the future in your cast,*
> *And answer questions that I ask.*
> *By the power of this Spell,*
> *Forever after Truth foretell.*

(Stones are the bones of Mother Earth, and this is the reference that is made here.)

Now place your stones on the altar. Take up one of the stones and pass it through the smoke of the incense, as you say:

> *By Earth of Air, and Air of Earth*
> *Receive the Breath of Life and Birth.*

Repeat this with the rest of the stones, one at a time.

Take up each stone and pass it through the flame of the candle, while saying:

> *By Earth of Fire, and Fire of Earth,*
> *Receive the Spirit of Life and Birth.*

Next, each stone will be anointed with a bit of the water from the bowl, but be careful not to smear or smudge the symbol on it. Do this one stone at a time, saying:

> *By Earth of Water, and Water of Earth,*
> *Receive the Blood of Life and Birth.*

Lastly, touch each stone in turn to the salt in the plate, saying:

> *By Earth of Earth, and Earth of Earth,*
> *Receive the Body of Life and Birth.*

Now, all of your Talking Stones are consecrated. You must still consecrate your pouch. Your stones have been blessed by the four elements. Your pouch will represent the fifth element of spirit. The element of spirit contains the four other elements within it, just as your pouch representing spirit will contain the stones blessed by the four elements. To bless your pouch, pass it over the incense, and the candle flame. Then anoint it with a bit of water, and touch it to the plate of salt. Hold it aloft over the center of the altar and say:

> *By One of Four, and Four in One,*
> *Thou art blessed! The Work is done!*

Place your stones in your pouch. Put out the candle flame, and leave the incense to burn until it goes out of its own accord. Then clean up.

Making Your Talking Stones Your Own

Now that you have a suitably consecrated set of Talking Stones, you are going to have to imbue them with your own energy. This can be done in several ways. A good way is to sleep with your stones underneath your pillow for a week or two (the stones should be in their pouch, of course). You can also imbue your stones with your essence by handling them frequently. For example, you may keep them in your hands or lap as you watch TV or read. After about a week of this type of activity, your stones should be ready for use.

If you go a long time without using or handling your stones, it is a good idea to set them underneath your pillow for a couple of nights in order to recharge them with your essence.

SOME GENERAL RULES IN USING THE TALKING STONES

- Keep to simple questions. Don't ask the stones a question to which you already know the answer.
- If you cast the stones, and no symbols show, do not cast them again for at least twenty-four hours.
- You can read the stones for another person. You set up the working place, but let them throw the stones. You then judge and interpret the stones.
- If you are casting the stones for someone not present, concentrate on his or her image and problem, and cast and judge the stones as if you were asking the question yourself.

- Do not lend your stones to another person, or allow people to handle them out of idle curiosity. Tradition says that if you do, the stones will no longer speak true. They will have to be re-consecrated, or you will have to make a new set.

CASTING THE TALKING STONES

You should have a piece of dark cloth upon which to cast your stones. It should be about three feet square. Next, procure a nine-foot cord. If you have a cord that you wear with your robe for magical rituals, you can use that. Arrange the cord in a circle on the cloth. A circle of two feet is about the right measurement. Place your Querent Stone in the center of the circle. Now take up your athame or wand (or if you do not have either of these, use the forefinger of your dominant hand), and trace three circles above your cord, each time saying:

Talking Stones, Telling Stones,
Fashioned from the Mother's bones,
By the power of this Spell,
Speak to me and Truth foretell.

Take up the stones and hold them in your hands. Think on any question that you have for them, or if you have no question, ask them to reveal the future to you in a general sense. When you feel that you are ready to cast the stones, say the following, which is an old Welsh divination charm:

ADA ADA IO ADA DIA
(pronounced: ah-da, ah-da, ee-o, ah-da, dee-ah)

Now toss the stones into the cord circle. Be careful not to throw them too forcefully. Some of the stones may fall outside of the cord circle. Remove these and set them aside. The stones that have fallen face down within the cord circle should also be removed. These are mute and will not tell you anything about your question or the future, since their symbols are not showing. The remaining stones that are face up are the only ones that are considered and will give you your answer or reveal your future.

JUDGMENT OF THE TALKING STONES

If you asked a specific question, the stones closest to the Querent Stone are judged to be the most important in the answer. The farther away the other stones are, the less important they are. If you asked about the future in general, the stones closest to the Querent Stone are the things that will happen closest in time, with the stones farther away representing more distant events, according to their distance. For this reason, if you ask for a general reading of the future, your question should carry with it a time limit—say three months. That way you will be better able to judge the time element.

Suggested Meanings of the Talking Stones

The Querent Stone
This has no interpretation in and of itself. It represents the person asking the question. It serves to provide a center against which the other stones in a cast react.

The Sun Stone
This is a favorable omen of success, especially when it is the stone closest to the Querent Stone. It represents honors, recognition from others, rewards, and happiness in general. It can also represent a man involved in the question or the vitality level of the querent.

The Moon Stone
As the opposite to the Sun Stone, the Moon Stone can represent a woman involved in the question. It also indicates that changes are on the horizon; things are in a state of flux. You can judge whether the coming changes will be favorable or not by looking at the stone closest to it. Because this is the Moon Stone, the changes will occur within twenty-eight days (a lunar month). This stone can also relate to childbirth, or the conception of other things, such as a new project or job. It can also represent the personality of the person asking the question.

The Mercury Stone

This stone represents short trips or travel over small distances. It can also represent children, or books, learning, communication, the intellect, or state of mind of the querent. Whether or not the state of mind is favorable or otherwise can be judged from the stone closest to the Mercury Stone.

The Venus Stone

This relates to all things pertaining to love and friendship. It can indicate the marriage of the querent or any close relationship you are involved in; it represents an emotional tie or bond.

The Mars Stone

This stone tells of angry words, strife, and quarrels. However, it can also represent a high energy level and strenuous activity.

The Jupiter Stone

This represents the culmination of some event, or expansion and growth in a situation. It is a fortunate stone and indicates a time of happiness, prosperity, and luck. It can also represent higher learning, wisdom, religion, philosophy, or travels of great distance.

The Saturn Stone

This is the unfortunate stone. It can represent an ending of something. It also represents loss, sorrow, misfortune, partings. It may represent learning through difficult experiences.

The Life Stone

This represents the querent's health, whether emotional, mental, or physical. You will have to look to the other stones close by in order to properly judge it.

The News Stone

This, of course, represents news coming to you. It differs from the Mercury Stone (which sometimes means communication) in that the News Stone generally represents news that you have not expected to receive, whether good or bad.

The Magic Stone

If your question concerned whether or not to perform a specific work of magic to aid in some situation, this stone will tell you whether or not it is favorable to do so, as judged from other stones near it. If your question did not concern this, this stone's appearance may suggest that you should consider performing some small magical act to help the situation.

The Home Stone

This stone represents the querent's home environment, and can also represent the family or living environment in general.

The Other Stone

This stone represents other people and their opinions, which may have some bearing on the question.

Combinations

It is, of course, not possible to list all of the interpretations for all combinations of the stones. However, there are certain combinations and things for which you should look. Below are some suggested interpretations. Pay attention only to those interpretations that relate to your question, or what you are concerned about generally in the future. When interpreting your cast, do not rely solely on the following interpretations. You should learn to judge the stones yourself. Just use these interpretations as guides.

"With" indicates directly next to or fairly near—two or more stones within an inch or two of each other.

The Querent Stone

The stone or stones that fall closest to the Querent Stone are generally the most important ones. The closest stone to the Querent Stone is called the Head Stone.

The Sun Stone

As the Head Stone — A very favorable outcome for the question. A bright future.

With the Moon Stone — Favorable changes within twenty-eight days. Success, honor, or recognition from women. A woman may be able to help you with your problem. Favorable for questions concerning women. A pleasant personality.

With the Mercury Stone — A pleasant or successful short trip. A book may shed some light on your question. A good attitude towards a problem. Favorable for communications with others, such as letters or phone calls. Good grades on tests. A male child.

With the Venus Stone — A successful, happy love affair or relationship; an engagement; a loving marriage. A good friend may be able to give you sound, helpful advice.

With the Mars Stone — Can indicate quarrels with a man, but because the Sun Stone is very fortunate, things will turn out well in the end. Alternatively, it indicates a high level of physical energy and vitality that can be used to deal with a problematic situation. A favorable time to take decisive action. If the querent is in the military, can mean a promotion.

With the Jupiter Stone — A very fortunate combination. Success and reaping of well-deserved rewards. Fortunate for higher learning, such as college or graduate work. A successful journey. Someone of great learning or wisdom can shed some light on your problem.

With the Saturn Stone — Any misfortune or problem that you are experiencing will turn out for the best, even though it may not seem so when the stones are cast. Parting may be for the best of all concerned.

With the Life Stone — An excellent omen for improved health and vitality if the question concerns physical illness. Your mental and emotional outlook will improve.

With the News Stone — Unexpected good news is on the way. A man may deliver this news, or it may be about a man. May deal with honors, success, or recognition.

With the Magic Stone — Any magical working you are considering will turn out favorably, especially if it concerns a man.

With the Home Stone — A happy home environment.

With the Other Stone — Others will be able to help you through any problem. Just ask. The opinions of others are favorable regarding the question. The opinion of a man—look to other stones to see if it is a favorable opinion or not.

The Moon Stone
Combinations covered above are not repeated (because the Moon Stone with the Sun Stone equals the Sun Stone with the Moon Stone).

As the Head Stone — Important changes that will affect the question or future within twenty-eight days. It is difficult to predict what will happen because things are in a state of constant change.

With the Mercury Stone — A short trip to see a woman to communicate with her, perhaps a female relative. An indecisive state of mind. A new project is taken up quickly. Expect changes within twenty-eight days—sooner rather than later, and quicker than expected. A female child.

With the Venus Stone — A woman may not be able to make up her mind. Changes in the status of a relationship—whether fortunate or not to be judged by stones closest to this combination. The beginning of a new relationship or friendship or other emotional tie. A woman with a pleasant personality.

With the Mars Stone — Quarrels with a woman. Unfortunate changes in your situation within twenty-eight days. Fluctuating energy level. An argumentative personality.

With the Jupiter Stone — A woman will somehow bring you good fortune. Very favorable for all questions regarding women. Favorable changes within twenty-eight days. A fortunate start to some new project.

With the Saturn Stone — Unfortunate changes within twenty-eight days. Misfortune, loss, sorrow connected with women. An unfortunate start to a new project. A despondent personality. An older woman may figure into your question or future.

With the Life Stone — Changing physical health, but sometimes emotional health. Look to stones close by to see whether the changes will be favorable or not.

With the News Stone — You may receive unexpected news that there have been changes in some plans. News about women or from women; look to other stones close by to see if it is favorable. You will receive some unexpected news within twenty-eight days; look to other stones to see if it is favorable. News about a pregnancy.

With the Magic Stone — It is probably best to wait a lunar month before considering any magical workings; things are in too much of a fluctuating state. If your cast does not seem to answer your question, try using some crystal gazing or other clairvoyant device to receive your answer.

With the Home Stone — Changes within the home environment within twenty-eight days. Could indicate childbirth, or the start of some new project related to the home. Family life may seem hectic. Change of residence.

With the Other Stone — Different people involved in the situation have different, perhaps conflicting opinions, or else they change their opinions constantly. A woman may be important to the resolution of a matter. The opinion of a woman—look to nearby stones to see if it is favorable or not.

The Mercury Stone
Combinations above are not repeated.

As the Head Stone — An important short trip. A book may change your life. It is important to communicate with others.

With the Venus Stone — A short trip to see a loved one may be in order. Good for communication in a relationship or marriage. A close friend may be able to give you good advice. Generally, a happy

state of mind. Communication with loved ones is favored. A love letter. Sometimes a marriage proposal or offer of friendship.

With the Mars Stone — Angry words and quarrels. Be careful not
to speak or act before you think things through.

With the Jupiter Stone — Highly favorable for all types of education or learning. Expanding one's mental horizons, such as reading
new things about philosophy, religion, science, or wisdom. A book
may hold the answer to your question, or a book will be influential
in your future. Highly favored for writing letters. Children do well
in school. Perhaps a trip to a foreign country.

With the Saturn Stone — Unfavorable time to communicate com-
plaints to others. A short trip may prove to be unfortunate. Be
careful when driving. Children may be troublesome or at the root
of a problem. A depressed state of mind.

With the Life Stone — An active, agile mind. A short trip or change
in environment may be what you need in order to improve physical
or mental health. This can also indicate books on health, nutrition,
et cetera. Could indicate a trip to the doctor. Look to nearby stones
to judge whether this combination is favorable or not.

With the News Stone — Unexpected news is on the way. News
about children, books, or learning. Perhaps someone makes a short
trip to see you.

With the Magic Stone — Favorable for small spells, amulets, talismans, and works of "low magic." May indicate travelling a short
distance to participate in some magical work.

With the Home Stone — Expect a visit from someone, most likely
a relative. Conversations in the home. A good time to curl up at
home with a good book. Children in the home—look to other
stones to see if they have a favorable or unfavorable influence.

With the Other Stone — Communicate with others and get their
opinions before you take any action. Do not assume you know
what another person is thinking. A visit from someone that needs
to communicate with you.

The Venus Stone

As the Head Stone — A speedy engagement, marriage, or successful and happy love affair.

With the Mars Stone — Quarrels with a loved one or a close friend. A rocky time in a relationship. Jealousy. Could indicate a break-up or separation. This combination may indicate a sexual experience of some sort, as well; look to other stones to see if something like this would really be in your best interests. Infrequently, represents the healing of a romantic quarrel.

With the Jupiter Stone — A very successful, and perhaps even profitable relationship—could be romantic or business. A widening of one's romantic horizons. An active social life. An engagement or a marriage may take place. A match "made in heaven."

With the Saturn Stone — A parting of the ways. Divorce, separation. Learning a hard lesson through a difficult relationship. Unfavorable for questions involving romance or finances.

With the Life Stone — A very active social life. If you are feeling blue, get out and do more things on a social level. You may need someone to look after you if you are physically ill. This combination can represent the health of loved ones; look to other stones to see if their health is good or not.

With the News Stone — News about a new relationship or a marriage or engagement, perhaps of or from a friend or close loved one.

With the Magic Stone — A close friend or loved one may request or need some magical work, but this is *not* an indication that you should be casting love spells on people!

With the Home Stone — A very favorable home environment. Pleasurable activities in the home, perhaps entertaining guests through social events, dinner parties, and the like. Could indicate a party held in your home.

With the Other Stone — Ask the opinions of close friends or loved ones. Could indicate that someone has a crush on you. May indicate the beginning of a new romantic relationship or friendship.

The Mars Stone

As the Head Stone — Strife and quarrels are imminent.

With the Jupiter Stone — The healing of a quarrel or rift, things work out amicably, unless the quarrel was about deeply-rooted ideas on philosophy, religion, and the like. Problems with a long journey. It may be that you are over-extending yourself, doing too many things at once. Look to surrounding stones to see if any stones are unfavorable regarding this.

With the Saturn Stone — A sad loss, perhaps through angry words or a quarrel. Low level of energy, so you may find it difficult to cope with problems. You may be on the losing side in a quarrel or debate, or perhaps you are just plain wrong. Look to surrounding stones to see if this is a favorable time to admit it, and try to set things aright. Usually an unfortunate combination.

With the Life Stone — Improved physical health. An excellent omen for someone that is ill. Generally, a swift recovery.

With the News Stone — This generally represents unfortunate, unexpected news. However, it can sometimes represent news that is learned in a flurry of activity. It can also represent news that comes to you when you are extremely busy, so you don't recognize its importance until later, so keep your ears open.

With the Magic Stone — If you have been in a quarrel or other type of strife, it is a good time to do some silent meditation to try to get at the root of the problem and try to resolve it. Generally unfavorable for other magical work, though.

With the Home Stone — Quarrels in the home or between family members. Could also represent stress in the home, or a great deal of activity in the home.

With the Other Stone — Someone is angry with you, and may be saying or thinking unfavorable things about you. Could indicate that an enemy is secretly at work against you. Someone's opinion of you is unfavorable.

The Jupiter Stone

As the Head Stone — Very fortunate for the question or future.

With the Saturn Stone — Any misfortune or problem you are experiencing is mitigated by this combination. It only seems like a problem, and will work out in your favor or in your best interests. A separation may be in your best interests. Could represent travel problems or delays. Also, serious study of serious subjects, such as philosophy, religion, and science.

With the Life Stone — An excellent omen for improved physical, mental, or emotional health.

With the News Stone — Favorable news is on the way, containing a message of prosperity or happiness. Could indicate that you will receive a gift of some sort.

With the Magic Stone — Magical workings are highly favored by this combination—not just simple spells, but elaborate rituals, too. A magical working will be able to turn the tide in your favor if you are in a troublesome situation.

With the Home Stone — Prosperity in the home. Could indicate home improvement or expansion projects.

With the Other Stone — Other people have very favorable opinions of you. You are held in high regard. Sometimes means promotions at work. You can get some excellent advice from other people, and it should be taken.

The Saturn Stone

As the Head Stone — Unfortunate for the question or future.

With the Life Stone — Illness. A death. Mental or emotional stress that affects physical health.

With the News Stone — Sorrowful or unfortunate news is on the way. News of parting or loss.

With the Magic Stone — Magical workings are not favored by this position. Silent meditation, however, may prove beneficial to your situation and help you see things more clearly.

With the Home Stone — Loss, sorrow, or partings in the home. Could represent an older woman or matriarch figure that "rules the roost."

With the Other Stone — Someone has an unfavorable opinion about you or what you are doing.

The Life Stone

As the Head Stone — The question may be about physical, mental, emotional health. Look to surrounding stones to determine whether the answer is favorable or not.

With the News Stone — News about someone's health. Look to surrounding stones to see if it is favorable news or not.

With the Magic Stone — A spell or work of magic involving healing may be in order.

With the Home Stone — The cast is trying to tell you something about the health of someone in your home, that is, a family member. Generally a favorable combination, but look to other surrounding stones to judge whether it is good or bad.

With the Other Stone — May indicate a trip to the doctor. Look to surrounding stones to see if the results of the trip are favorable or not.

The News Stone

As the Head Stone — Unexpected news that is very important or could change your life in a major way.

With the Magic Stone — News about a magical working. Could represent an important realization that you receive unexpectedly during meditation or a ritual. A discarnate entity or other spirit or inner plane being may be trying to communicate with you.

With the Home Stone — A family member brings you unexpected news. News about the home, either your own home, or the home of someone close to you; that is, a relative.

With the Other Stone — Someone communicates his or her opinion to you. Look to surrounding stones to see if it is favorable or not.

The Magic Stone

As the Head Stone — Magic will figure prominently in the question or the future. See surrounding stones to judge favorability.

With the Home Stone — A work of magic performed in your home. Could indicate a group of people in a Circle or coven.

With the Other Stone — Ask other people to help you in performing some magical work. Alternatively, ask another practitioner for advice as to whether magical work should be done.

The Home Stone

As the Leading Stone — The question may concern the home or family. The home will figure prominently in the future.

With the Other Stone — Represents the home or family of another person involved in the question. A new baby, perhaps.

The Other Stone

As the Head Stone — The situation is out of your control. Others will decide how the situation will turn out, and there is little you can do. Could represent karma, destiny, or fate.

Whenever a particular combination indicates something neutral—for example, news about someone's health or the opinions of others—look to surrounding stones to judge if these things are favorable or unfortunate. Often three or four stones will fall together. To interpret these, look at how they can be variously combined. If two stones fall one on top of the other, both showing a symbol, these two will contain the answer to your question, or will be the most important indicator of future events, regardless of whether they are closest to the Querent Stone.

ASKING "YES OR NO" QUESTIONS

Sometimes you will just need a quick yes or no answer to a specific question. For these, you should prepare your working cloth and cord as usual. Use only two stones—the Jupiter Stone and the Saturn Stone. Ask your question using the usual procedure. Throw the stones. If Jupiter is closer to the Querent Stone, the answer is yes. If Saturn is the closer stone, the answer is no. If you need more information about why a question was answered yes or no, ask the same question, but do a full cast. Judge the reasoning behind your yes or no answer from this second cast.

CONCLUSION

That, in a fairly large nutshell, is the art of lithomancy, the art of the Talking Stones. As you continue to use the stones, you will become better at interpreting them. Don't limit yourself to the interpretations and combinations that are given here. Any cast and any stone will have to be judged in light of the question that is asked and the circumstances that exist at the time the cast is made. Additionally, the seven "planet stones" can be interpreted through use of books on astrology (see the suggested reading list at the back of this book).

CHAPTER NINE

THE DRUID'S WAND

This form of divination is somewhat unusual. You do not use this method to ask questions. It is used when you have no specific question in mind, but want some idea of what is coming up in the next lunar month or twenty-eight days. Many forms of divination allow the diviner to find out about past, present, and future influences. This system is limited strictly to the future, so if you need to know about a past or present influence, you should consult another of the divination systems in this book.

You may be familiar with other Druidic wands used in divination. Often these are small sticks corresponding to the trees of the Ogham Tree alphabet. Sometimes they are just sticks of wood marked with the letters of the Ogham alphabet. Usually, these sticks are thrown or several of them are randomly chosen from a pouch and their meanings interpreted. There are already several books that describe this type of divination (you can consult the suggested reading list at the end of the book for references), so I will not describe it here.

The wand is an excellent tool for divination, because it is (amongst other things) a symbol of measurement to the subconscious mind. Measurement is exactly what one does in any form of divination; the diviner seeks to measure the inner and outer plane forces acting upon a given situation. However, this form of divination literally entails measurement—measurement between two heavenly bodies in the sky.

Through the principle "As above, so below; as below, so above" we can take a measurement of celestial bodies and thereby find a

183

"measure" that will help us determine some future event. The branch of astrology known as horary astrology, which seeks to answer questions from a chart calculated for the time when a question is were asked, operates on roughly the same principle.

The Druids were extremely interested in the measurement of celestial bodies. Many scholars have put forth the theory (now generally accepted) that Stonehenge was actually a type of astronomical observatory, as it measured the risings and settings of the sun and moon on Druidic holy days. Other stone circles in Great Britain and Europe undoubtedly served a similar purpose.

In the eighteenth century, the Druid scholar William Stukeley made an interesting discovery. He found that there was a "base unit" used in the construction of Stonehenge. The measurement of twenty and four-fifths inches was repeated throughout all of the construction of the stone circle. Research showed that twenty and four-fifths inches was important for some other stone circles as well. Thus, twenty and four-fifths inches came to be known as the **Druid cubit**. You will be using the Druid cubit to construct your Druid's Wand.

CONSTRUCTING THE DRUID'S WAND

Making a Druid's Wand is simple. First you need to choose what type of tree from which you would like to make your wand. Any type of wood will do, though you may want to choose one that has magical significance. For instance, in the Druidic tradition, alder, hazel, and apple all have particular connections with Otherworldly wisdom. You may choose a wood that has significance for divination, such as almond or maple. You might choose a wood that has lunar significance, such as willow. Failing that, you could choose a wood that has general magical significance—oak, ash, rowan. The choice is yours.

You should cut the wand directly from the tree, so you should choose a branch that is straight and of fairly even thickness (half an inch to an inch thick will serve well), and one out of which you can make a wand at least twenty and four-fifths inches long. In taking your branch from the tree, observe the following procedures:

Beginning on the day of the full moon, water your chosen tree with a mixture of eleven parts water, one part milk, and one part honey. Water it again with the same mixture on the day of the half moon (it will be a waning half), the day of the new moon, and the following day of the half moon (the waxing half).

Then, on the next night of the full moon (that is, the full moon following the full moon when you first started watering the tree), approach the tree with your cutting instrument (which may be a consecrated white-handled knife, if you own one, or just a regular knife or saw if you don't) and nine silver coins (such as nickels, dimes, quarters). Walk around the tree nine times clockwise, saying the following incantation for as long as it takes you to complete your circuits:

> *Tree of Wisdom, Tree of Life,*
> *Forgive the cutting of my knife.*
> *A single branch I'll take from thee*
> *That I may hence the future see.*

When you are finished with your circling, cut your branch, again asking aloud the tree's forgiveness and giving it your thanks. When you have your branch, bury your nine silver coins at the roots of the tree, saying:

> *May the Forest Lord and Earth Goddess*
> *Bless thee for thy service, Creature of Earth!*

Now take your wand home and clean it—peel off the bark, use some sanding paper on the rough spots. You should also cut the branch down to its required length—twenty and four-fifths inches.

Your next step will be to draw the proper symbols on your wand.

The Coelbren of the Bards

The symbols that you will use are from a variant of one of the Druidic alphabets, known as the **Coelbren of the Bards**. The variants of the Coelbren alphabet number anywhere from twenty to twenty-five letters. You will be using a twenty-letter variant, which is shown in the chart on the next page. Each Coelbren symbol represents a Druidic Triad, which figures into the interpretations. The word "coelbren"

THE COELBREN OF THE BARDS

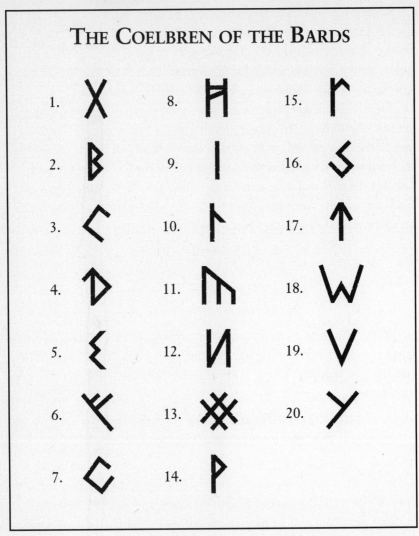

Table 9

actually comes from the Welsh word for the tablets of wood upon which these letters were first written. The English translation would be "the wood of credibility." The Druids considered the letters of the Coelbren alphabet to be the root structure of the Universe, each representing a particular vibration or force from which the Gods created all things. Hence, the Druids considered it a magical alphabet.

Taking your Druid's Wand, and using a ruler, mark off two-fifths of an inch on either end. One of these ends you will color black, and the other red. You can use either wood paints or suitable colored markers. This now leaves twenty inches of the wand blank. Again, using your ruler, divide these into twenty one-inch spaces making nineteen small circles around the circumference of the wand. Use either black paint or a black marker.

Your next task is to fill in the letters of the Coelbren along the wand with black paint or black marker. Start with the red end of the wand and the figure labeled with number one in the chart on the opposite page. Continue drawing the figures onto the wand in numerical order, going up toward the black end of the wand. You may choose to write the figures either horizontally or vertically along the wand, as you wish. It doesn't matter, so do what looks best to you (see figure 9a).

When all of the figures are filled in, your wand is finished. You can apply a coat of sealing agent to the wand, if you wish, or you can leave it natural. You will now have to consecrate your completed wand before it can be used. Since you will have to wait until before the next full moon to do this, you should wrap your wand in a piece of clean white linen or cloth until that time.

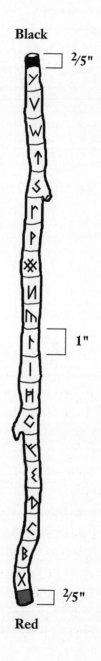

Figure 9a:
The Druid's Wand.

Black

2/5"

1"

2/5"

Red

CONSECRATION OF THE DRUID'S WAND

Two days before the day on which the full moon falls, take your wand from its keeping place, but keep it wrapped in its cloth. Obtain a plastic bag in which your wand will fit (a small kitchen garbage bag will work fine). Take your bundled wand to the top of a hill and bury it in the ground. It is best to bury it horizontally, since it would take you a much longer time to dig a hole that would fit the wand placed vertically. Don't bury it too deep—three to five inches will suffice. Also make sure that the wand is completely secure in the plastic bag, as you don't want it getting wet if it rains. When the hole is dug, place the wand within it. Before you cover it back up again with the soil, repeat the following incantation three times:

> *Made to measure Star and Moon,*
> *From earthly wood thy form was hewn.*
> *I lay thee to thy peaceful rest*
> *That Sun and Earth shall make thee blessed!*

Now replace the soil atop the wand and cover the spot with some rocks and leaves. Leave it buried there.

Sometime during the day that follows the day of full moon, go back to the hilltop and dig out your wand. Be sure to replace the soil after you have taken your wand. (You wouldn't want to leave a hole in the ground for someone to trip in.) Take the wand home and take it out of the plastic bag. You should keep your newly consecrated wand wrapped up in its white cloth until you are ready to use it.

USING THE DRUID'S WAND

As I mentioned previously, the Druid's Wand cannot be used to answer a specific question. Rather, it is used to "measure" the inner plane forces that surround you at a given time—inner plane forces that will ripen into a specific occurrence in your life within the next twenty-eight days (a lunar month). Because you are measuring these forces for the next twenty-eight days, you may only use the Druid's Wand once during this period.

This is how the wand is to be used. You must go outside on a clear night, when both the moon and the stars are visible. Try to stand in a spot where you will not be disturbed by passers-by. When you have found your place, relax and close your eyes. Take some deep and rhythmic breaths. With your eyes still closed, concentrate on the movement of air around you. Even if it is a very still night, there will be some movement of air around you, even if it is the tiniest of breezes. When you feel some movement of air, note what general direction it comes from: east, south, north, or west. If from the east or south, you will be measuring from the red end of the wand. If from the west or north, you will be measuring from the black end of the wand.

Having noted this, raise your wand up to the sky. Place the end of the wand that you are using flush with the outer curve of the moon. If it is a waxing moon, the outer curve will be on your right. If it is a waning moon, the outer curve will be on your left. If the moon is full, or so near to full that you cannot tell if it is still in a waxing or waning phase, you will measure from the right-side curve of the moon.

Using this point on the moon as your pivot, maneuver the wand so that it touches Polaris, the pole star. (If you are unfamiliar with the location of this star in the sky, you can buy a star guide in any book-store that will help you locate it.) Note upon which section and symbol of the wand that Polaris falls (figure 9b). This symbol represents

Figure 9b: Using the Druid's Wand.

an influence that will be coming into your life during the next lunar month. You may consult the list of interpretations for the symbol that represents this triad.

Now it may be that, because of the location of the moon in the sky at the time you begin to measure, the wand will not reach to Polaris. If this is so, you must abandon the divination and try again on another day.

When you are finished with your measurement, remember to wrap your wand up in its cloth and to put it away for safekeeping.

You may also wonder exactly when it would be appropriate for you to take the wand out to perform a measurement. The answer is anytime you like, provided that the moon and Polaris are visible, and provided that you have not performed a measurement within the last twenty-eight days. This is the same principle that is used in horary astrology, which was mentioned before. The principle of "As above, so below" holds true at all times, since it is a universal law.

INTERPRETATIONS OF THE COELBREN

The Druid's Wand will not give you information regarding a specific event. The interpretation of each letter is keyed to a Druidic Triad, sometimes known collectively as the Welsh or Bardic Triads. These statements (there are thousands of them; the Druid's Wand uses only twenty), which always involve the description of three related things, are written in general terms. They describe principles, not events, and contain the bulk of the wisdom teachings of the Druids. The triad form of listing things was very common in every aspect of Celtic society. Many of the laws and legal principles of the Celtic peoples were recorded in triad form. Much theology and many customs were also embodied thus.

LIST OF INTERPRETATIONS

The list of interpretations follows below, listed in order of the symbols of the wand. After giving the triad, I have made a short commentary on each.

Three Reasons to Keep Silent:

Against saying something you should not, against speaking in a way you should not, and against speaking in a place where you should not.

This triad cautions you to hold your tongue about any projects that you are working on, whether starting a new romance, charting a new career direction, or even beginning some magical project. When this symbol is received, the lesson you need to learn is that silence is power. Take pride in your work, but feel it internally and don't go bragging about things to others. If you do not heed this rule, you may find that by speaking about a hopeful future occurrence to others you lessen its chances of manifesting.

Three Things that Patience Brings:

Love, peace, and help from others.

This is a very good symbol to receive as it indicates the beginning of some new adventure within the next lunar month. It indicates that something grand will come from a small beginning. Usually this will be in terms of relationships or the endings of conflicts, and does not usually indicate financial matters. Be on the watch for someone that may assist you in this endeavor. That person may be the key to your success.

Three Things that Bring Strength to Face the World:

Seeing the beauty and quality of truth, seeing behind the veil of falsehoods, and seeing to what ends truth and falsity come.

Usually this figure indicates that you will uncover a secret influence regarding a problem that you have been having. It indicates that you will soon understand how and why the trouble arose, and you will also be mentally inspired with the means of correcting it. This is the symbol of wisdom, and the very substance of wisdom is in knowing what is truth and what is not. It sometimes indicates that someone is deliberately deceiving you. If this is so, the deception will be uncovered during the next twenty-eight days.

Three Persons Loved by the Gods:
Those in whom strength and justice meet, those in whom bravery and mercy meet, and those in whom generosity and satisfaction meet.

Receiving this symbol is an indication that you will be encountering obstacles and difficulties within the next lunar month. However, you do have the will power and inner strength to get through this time period. If you allow these obstacles to frustrate you, to make you moody or edgy, snapping at everyone that comes within your orbit, the obstacles will be harder to surmount, and their effects will last longer. If you meet them with strength and bravery, and can maintain a pleasant disposition toward all involved, you will more easily prevail. You should find this attitude easy to maintain, since the symbol clearly indicates that you have the strength to triumph over these difficulties. Remain confident, but calm.

 ### Three Persons Who Never Meet with Success:
He who marries by the counsel of his flesh, he who eats by the counsel of his hunger, and he who fights by the counsel of his anger.

When this symbol appears, it is a sign that you will have an important decision to make within the next lunar month. It may not seem like a weighty decision at the time, but it may have much greater consequences than you realize. Two phrases of the triad speak of the sensual nature (flesh and hunger), and one phrase mentions the emotional nature (anger). If you follow your physical or sensual impulses in making your decision, it will come out badly. The same will happen if you follow your emotional nature. Your mind is clouded, and you will need to use your full mental and reasoning capabilities to make the right decision. The druids taught that intuition was born out of reason. So, if you have a hunch or strong spiritual impulse one way or the other, follow it.

Three Things that Must be Done in Order to Learn:

Listen intently, contemplate intently, and be continually silent.

When Polaris touches this symbol, any difficulties or decisions to be made during the next lunar month should be dealt with in meditation. It may be that this problem is currently vexing you, and the appearance of this symbol could indicate that it will be solved within the next lunar month.

In this one triad, the Druids tell us the secret to successfully accessing the wisdom of the Higher Self through meditation. During the first part of your meditation, contemplate the problem—think of how it arose, who is involved, what possible solutions to which you might have recourse. Then silence yourself, both body and mind. Make sure you are relaxed and are breathing easily. Mentally state your problem again briefly, just one time. Then still your thoughts completely. Forget about all of the people involved, how the problem arose, and forget about possible solutions. Your attitude should be one of complete willingness to learn, as if you knew nothing about the problem and knew no way of solving it. Then listen. Adopt a listening attitude, but not a passive one. You must listen actively, as if you were about to hear a far-off sound. Maintain this for no longer than ten minutes.

After your meditation, note any impressions that came to you. You may have to do this process several times in order to get the hang of it. Base how you deal with the situation on information or impressions that you receive during these meditations. Following this inner advice, the whole problem will be cleared up in twenty-eight days.

Three Things that Always Lead to Deception:

The love of a person too strong in sensuality, the good will of one's superiors, and the promises of one cursed with ill-luck.

With this symbol, stormy times are ahead for you during the next lunar month, usually because you have misplaced your reliance in someone that you believe to be loyal and telling the truth to you. Do not place your faith in those that are working toward their own ends and not yours, or you will be severely disappointed and will be pessimistic in all of your future dealings with this person. It is not that someone is deliberately or maliciously deceiving you. It is that the person is promising things that he or she is not sure can be delivered. Cultivate your own independence in whatever matter is at hand, and you will end the month without too much difficulty. Beware of fair-weather friends.

 Three Things to Commend a Lover:
A virtuous face, discretion in speech, and kindness in manners.

This is a very good symbol to receive if you are currently in a relationship, or are romantically inclined and available. It usually indicates the commencement of a new relationship (perhaps you will just meet the person during this lunar month, and things will develop in their own time) or the deepening of a commitment in an old one. However, beware of the lover whose lies to you are written in his or her face, who gossips, or who is unkind in how he or she treats you.

 Three Things that May Not be Conquered:
Nature, fate, and change.

During this lunar month, you will find yourself in a situation that you will not be able to control, either with words or deeds. You must accept the occurrence, which usually manifests as an ending of some kind. If you fight against it, you will only be opening yourself up to disappointment and pain. Learn the lesson from the situation, and move on. You will be powerless to do anything else.

 Three Blessings of the Home:
An honest guard, a cautious hearth-keeper, and an astute messenger.

The "home" mentioned in this triad is obviously a symbol of protection. The home is the place where you hoard up on your reserves of strength. If you encounter obstacles or difficulties in some situation that is important to you, remember to spend some time at home relaxing, sorting out your priorities. The appearance of this symbol sometimes indicates some project to be undertaken in the home or some purchase to be made for the home, after due consideration that it is needful. All types of creative work can be undertaken in the home when this symbol appears. Also, if there is someone who is ill in the family, he or she will recover within the lunar month.

 ### Three Things that the Diligent Will Attain:
Honor, success, and the compliments of sages.

This is a very good symbol to receive, as it indicates that you have labored long and hard in some endeavor, whether it be in forming a relationship, closing a business deal, or improving yourself in some way. Within the lunar month you will begin to reap the benefit of your labors.

 ### Three Times When a Sage Must Speak:
To instruct against ignorance, to advise against strife,
and to tell the truth against an evil lie.

This symbol and triad have much to do with communication. The interpretation of this symbol can be in one of two ways. Within the next lunar month you will be called upon to instruct someone in some matter, to advise someone to keep the peace, or to set some false matter aright by telling the truth. You should be happy if this is what happens, as the other alternative is much less pleasing—someone will instruct you out of your foolishness, someone will advise you that your anger is inappropriate, or someone will still your gossiping tongue. Though less pleasing, it will still be a blessing, though you may not realize this at first.

 ### Three Things that Bring Great Opportunities:
Speaking little (and then always with circumspection), quiet
humor without superficiality, and behaving without vanity.

The appearance of this symbol suggests that within the next lunar month you will be presented with a new opportunity. Usually this will be in terms of work, money, or other business matters. You will undoubtedly have pleased someone in a superior position to yourself by virtue of your personality or demeanor. Therefore, this person would like to help you or be associated with you in some way. As long as you beware of being too talkative, too superficial, or too vain, all should go well.

Three Things that Bring Health:
Moderation in eating, moderation in work,
and moderation in merry-making.

When this symbol appears, be prepared to cut back on some of your professional and social engagements in the coming lunar month. You may extend yourself too far and spread yourself too thin, so that everything you do is done poorly or half-heartedly. Ignoring the counsel of this symbol may leave you mentally and physically exhausted by the end of the month. Since your body would be low on defense, a minor illness may result.

Three Persons from Whom You Should Keep Yourself:
He who praises you too much for easy deeds, he who speaks against you for his own benefit, and he who boasts of deeds never done.

Though this triad speaks volumes of wisdom, it is not so easy to keep oneself away from the flatterer, slanderer, and braggadocio in the modern world. You must try, though, for one or the other of these will come within your orbit within the next lunar month. All three types are working for their own ends and, most likely, deliberately against your own goals. See that none influences your reasoning abilities in decision making and remember that truth will eventually conquer all flattery, slander, and bragging.

Three Gifts from the Gods to Seek during One's Lifetime:
Hope, love, and joy.

The measuring of the wand to this symbol is a very fortunate happening. Nothing but good can come from it. Most often it indicates the beginning of a new emotional relationship. However, sometimes it can indicate the emergence of new talents. These in turn may lead on to more material benefits. Experience has also shown that in some circumstances, it can indicate a change of job or home or some other beneficial change in the life. As this is a feminine symbol, it can also indicate physical births or conceptions.

 **There are Three Things:
Wisdom, Loss, and Remorse.**
He who does not have the first will have the other two.

Make no mistake about it—trials, tests, and obstacles are coming your way during the next lunar month. However, the bright side (always look for the silver lining) is that these obstacles will force you to develop yourself and become more aware of your environment. These tests and trials can come from any area of your life. The most effective way of dealing with them is personal sacrifice of some type. If you are called on to give up something that is dear to you, do so. You will be better off in the end.

 Three Things that Never End Well:
A lie, envy, and deception.

When the wand reaches this symbol, you must take care to guard your own moral character during the coming lunar month. You will be put into a compromising situation and will be tempted to take the easy way out. Have the courage of your moral convictions, and remember that truth is the watchword of the wise. What makes receiving this symbol difficult is that sometimes the lie and deception is perpetrated on yourself—turning your head away from some evil you know to be present in your environment, burying your head in the sand, refusing to face facts. This feigned ignorance will make the situation worse than it might otherwise be. Take heart and take action.

Three Things that Are the Reward of the Sincere Person:
The favor of friends, the respect of the wise, and success.

This is a very positive symbol for the Pole Star to fall upon. It indicates the culmination of events into personal success, prosperity, happiness, and well-being. The harvest is ready to be brought in within the next lunar month.

 Three Virtues of the Sage:
To remain calm when others cannot, to remain quiet when others are not, and to remember the Gods when others do not.

During the coming lunar month, you will find yourself in a somewhat threatening situation, most likely in the company of other persons. Keep your wits about you, and you may save the day for you and all of your companions. Others may spend their time prattling about how to cope with the situation, but taking no action. They may allow frustration to cause them to treat others unkindly. Do not follow their example. Remain calm, take quiet action, and remember that the Gods will return unkindness to you for unkindness to others.

AFTER THE INTERPRETATION

Once you have measured your future for the coming lunar month, and have received your symbol and read its triad, do not simply go blithely on your way into the world. While you need not actively meditate on the message that your particular triad has given to you, you should keep it in mind during the whole of the lunar month. A good idea might be to write the triad on a slip of paper and then tape it to your bathroom mirror or keep it by your bedside. That way, you will be forced to look at it at least once a day. Don't just look at it. Think about it. Think of how you could have benefitted in past situations by adhering to the advice or message of the particular triad. This time, however, you will be forewarned and prepared, and will not need to make another mistake in order to learn the lesson of the triad.

PART IV

TRANCE ORACLES AND DIVINATION

CHAPTER TEN

THE DANCE OF THE LAME GOD

Up to this point, we have been dealing with divination systems that do not necessarily involve altered states of consciousness. Certainly, those with natural clairvoyant abilities may "slip in" to such states (either consciously or accidentally) when interpreting the Talking Stones or the figures of geomancy, for example. However, there are systems of divination more directly based on altered states of consciousness. The first of these we will discuss is the Dance of the Lame God, a dance that culminates in a trance state.

It should first be noted that this form of divination is best practiced with a group. An absolute minimum of three people is recommended, preferably more. There are several reasons for this. First of all, the dance is a circle dance, with the participants linking hands. Three people is the absolute minimum one can have to form a comfortable dance circle. Second, when trance does result in one of the participants, one of the other Witches should attend to him or her to ask questions or deal with any trouble that may arise during the trance. The duty of a third Witch would be to record responses to questions or any other information that is received.

Another reason for working with a group is that not all Witches possess the ability to enter a deep trance state. Some are born with this ability; others cultivate it through varying degrees of training. The more people involved in the dance, the more likely it is that one of them will have the requisite ability to enter the inner planes. A final reason for performing the dance with a group is that the dance involves

201

chanting. A greater number of chanting participants will usually translate into greater power raised by the dance, and thus, greater success in having someone achieve the requisite trance state.

This form of divination would be classified as rather advanced, requiring at least some participants that are skilled in trance workings. Groups of complete beginners should probably experiment with this form with caution. Preferably, at least one or two more experienced Witches should be present.

SOME MYTHOLOGICAL BACKGROUND

The Dance of the Lame God is related to the god Haphaestus of Greek mythology, a god of fire and the forge. Of the varying accounts of the birth of Haphaestus, one tells us that he was the son of Zeus and Hera. When Haphaestus was born, Zeus saw that the child-god was so ugly and deformed that he began blaming and berating Hera. Haphaestus quickly came to his mother's defense. Haphaestus then became the object of mighty Zeus' wrath, and Zeus physically cast him out of Olympus. The island of Lemnos broke both Haphaestus' fall and his left leg. The god was thereafter lame, and always walked with a limp.

A legitimate question to be asked is: "What on earth does Haphaestus, a god of fire, have to do with divination and altered states of consciousness?" To answer this question we must ask what Haphaestus' particular attributes meant in the ancient mysteries.

Fire has long been seen as a symbol of divine presence throughout the ancient mysteries. For instance, the Bible relates the story of Moses and the burning bush. The visions of Ezekiel and St. John also identify fire with divine presence. The Chaldean Oracles relate that when a mystic achieves divine consciousness, he or she will experience a vision of a cloud of fire turning in upon itself. Even the Tarot card Judgement, which in some occult systems is attributed to the element fire, bears out this relationship. The Qabalistic tradition assigns a specific state of consciousness to Judgement—the Perpetual Intelligence. What is intimated here is that those who achieve this state of consciousness are continually aware of the presence of deity. Additionally, Paul Foster Case notes in his book *The Tarot* that the scene in Judgement takes place on the astral plane, not the physical plane. When the Dance of the Lame God culminates in trance, it is the astral plane on which the trance subject operates.

Haphaestus' limp is also significant. In astrology, the zodiacal sign Pisces is most associated with trance states, mediumship, the astral plane, occultism, spirituality, and divine guidance. In older systems of astrology, Jupiter was the sole ruler of Pisces (today it is co-ruled by Neptune). In systems of occult anatomy, Pisces rules the feet. Jupiter also rules Sagittarius, assigned to the legs in occult anatomy. The legs and feet both indicate the lame god's limp. Thus, the fire god's attributes are not so tenuously connected to divination as they might seem at first.

PURPOSES OF THE DANCE

Patricia Crowther, in her book *Lid off the Cauldron*, notes that success in the Dance of the Lame God depends on the purpose for which it is used. Of course, the dance should not be used for frivolous purposes, or in a frivolous state of mind. The dance can basically be used for two purposes: to answer questions framed by the participants, or to contact the shades of the dead. If approaching the dance with the seriousness it is due, one would never perform the dance to answer questions concerning frivolous subjects or to contact the dead out of idle curiosity, "just to see if it works." It is a religious rite and should be treated as such.

Therefore, the group must first determine that there is a need to perform the dance. That need might stem from the fact that other systems of divination have been used, but no satisfactory or clear answer has been obtained. Also, when there is only one person that can answer a question, and that person is deceased on the physical plane, the group might try to use the dance to contact the departed shade and query him or her. Neither contact with the dead nor the use of trance states should be undertaken lightly.

There are two other reasons one might use the Dance of the Lame God to contact departed shades. (Strictly speaking, however, these do not fall under the heading of divination.) One reason is that those persons that die suddenly or in a violent manner may be confused on the inner planes, not realizing that they have "dropped" their physical bodies. Contact with such a shade may be undertaken to explain the actual state of events to him or her. This type of work is best undertaken by Witches that have had specific training in this area, and the novice and intermediate-level Witch would do well to leave it alone for the time being. (Those that are interested in the risks, benefits, and mechanics of this phenomenon should consult Dion Fortune's *Through the Gates of Death* for greater understanding.)

The second reason the dance might be used to contact the dead is that one of the dance participants had such a strong bond of love to the departed shade that he or she must have contact with the shade one more time. While the teachings of reincarnation and the Summerlands do much to assuage the feelings of grief of those Witches that ascribe to these beliefs, even Witches are occasionally overcome with such devastating grief that they find themselves unable to "pick up the pieces" of their lives and continue living after what many would consider a "reasonable grieving period" (if such a thing exists). In such situations, contact with the departed shade is permissible. Surely such contact would benefit the grieving person, and it is almost certainly true that the departed shade would like to see the grieving person return to a normal lifestyle. However, the dance should be used for this purpose only once. Repeated contact with the shade will actually hinder the work that the shade must do in the Summerlands, and will prevent the person "left behind" from returning to a healthy emotional and psychological state.

Sometimes, however, a shade will come unbidden to the trance subject. In these instances, the shade should not be turned away in favor of some other purpose of the dance. The trance subject should ask the shade why it has come, and listen to what the shade has to say. This might occur especially if the dance is performed as part of a Samhain or Hallows celebration. Only the deliberate summoning of specific shades when there is no real need should be avoided.

To summarize, the group should determine that there is a need to perform the Dance of the Lame God for one of the following reasons:

- To induce a trance state in one of the participants so that questions answered insufficiently by other forms of divination may be asked of him or her.

- To induce a trance state in one of the participants so that contact may be made with a departed shade who is the only entity able to answer a question.

- To contact a shade for the benefit of a grieving individual (to be used rarely).

If the group decides to answer a question or questions through the dance, those questions should be written down, and each of the group should memorize them. For this reason, the questions should be limited in number, with three as the maximum. Each member of the group should be familiar with the questions because the group does not know beforehand which one of their members will actually fall into the trance state. However, if through long use of the dance, the group learns that one or two among them are consistently overcome by the trance state, those Witches should obviously be most familiar with the questions. Nonetheless, each member of the group should know the questions as a precautionary measure, since only one person is allowed to enter the trance state. There is a first for everything, and one of the members might fall into the trance state before one of the more "experienced" Witches does.

If a shade is to be contacted, either for the purpose of divination or comfort for a grieving Witch, a picture of that person should be studied by every member of the group. Each participant should be able to visualize the person to be contacted. Usually, one of the group will be a family member or friend of the shade to be contacted, and will be able to relate to the others of the group the personality, mannerisms, and idiosyncrasies of the person as he or she was on the physical plane. Almost without exception, shades retain their personality characteristics after they pass over to the other side. They do not automatically become wise, high, and lofty beings by virtue of dropping the physical body. Keep this in mind when the advice or answer of the shade is being evaluated. If the person was a scatterbrained gad-about that always gave bad advice to family and friends, his or her advice or answers should be evaluated in light of this.

TIMES TO PERFORM THE DANCE OF THE LAME GOD

As the Craft traditionally teaches, the Sabbats of Hallows (October 31) and Beltane (April 30) are the times of the year when the veil between the worlds is at its thinnest. These times are excellent for all types of divination. Hallows is particularly appropriate for two reasons. First, it is considered by some as the start of the Witches' New Year, this having come down to the Craft through the Celtic tradition. In addition, Hallows is the traditional Feast of the Dead, so the dance might be performed to contact shades at this time.

Nights of the full moon are also suitable for the performance of the dance, and covens or other groups should find it easy to work the dance into their ritual framework. The full moon is the time when psychic power is at its peak in most individuals, and access to the astral plane may more easily be gained.

If a specific departed shade is to be contacted, the group might decide that it is best to perform the dance on a date that had some earthly significance to the shade, such as a birthday, a wedding anniversary, handfasting, or the date of physical death. While time is a muddled concept on the astral plane, the group's thoughts will serve to notify the shade of the significance of the date, and those thoughts may serve as a "gateway" to contact with the shade.

Of course, since *need* is the watchword of this form of divination, the dance can be used at any other time when there is urgent need. The group may decide that it cannot wait until the next full moon to perform the dance if an answer is needed immediately. However, in those instances when the dance does not induce a trance state in a participant, the group may decide to perform the dance again at a more "psychically advantageous" time to increase the chances of success.

For this reason, a record should be kept of the time and date when the dance is performed.

In any of these cases, night time performance of the dance is to be preferred to day.

PREPARATION FOR AND PERFORMANCE OF THE DANCE

As I said before, all those participating should be familiar with the questions and/or the picture and mannerisms of the shade to be contacted. It is probably best that the dance be performed within a properly cast Circle even if the dance is not performed as a part of the group's or coven's regular magical activities. This performs two functions paralleling the usual functions of a magical Circle; the Circle will keep out any harmful or disruptive external astral influences, as well as help contain the power that is raised during the dance. The group's usual Circle-casting is fine for this purpose. (Though I caution groups of beginners not to perform the dance until they have training and/or experience in trance states, I well know that my advice may be ignored. Though the school of experience is the most costly one, many Witches consider it a valuable education. Thus, for beginners unfamiliar with the procedure of casting a Circle, please refer to a good beginner's guide such as Scott Cunningham's *Wicca: A Guide for the Solitary Practitioner*, or Doreen Valiente's *Witchcraft for Tomorrow*, both of which are listed in the suggested reading section. Both books contain basic, though excellent, Books of Shadows including methods for casting a suitable Circle. A basic Circle casting is also given in the Appendix of this book.)

No special equipment is needed to perform the dance. There should be at least one candle burning within the Circle (to represent fire), but such would usually be present anyway for lighting purposes. If the dance is to be performed outside, the group may decide a small bonfire would better serve as a symbol for fire, with the dance taking place around it. If a bonfire is used, however, the participants must be extremely careful that when one of the group drops into trance, he or she doesn't drop into the bonfire as well. In such instances, it would be a good idea to appoint someone to watch the dancers, immediately coming to the aid of a trance subject, and aiding the trance subject in lying on the ground instead of just falling.

A list of the questions and any pictures of a departed shade (if necessary) should be placed in the center of the altar.

The group may decide to have a person accompany the dance and chant with a slow drum beat. That person does not participate in the dance, but stands facing south within the circle of dancers. Past performances of the dance have shown that the drum is an excellent accompaniment and helps to induce the requisite trance state in a participant. The lower the "note" of the drum, the better. However, the group may decide that the sound of the drum is more hindering than helpful, or that there are not enough participants for one to perform the drumming duties.

When the leader of the group decides it is appropriate to start the dance, the dancing participants form a circle. The drummer should take his or her place in the center of the circle, or if there is an outside fire, the drummer should stand in the north near the outermost edge of the circle, facing south. The leader begins the dance with the following incantation and statement of purpose:

Join we now the Lame God's dance,
To call Him forth by stride (or "by drum") and chant,
To hear what answers He will grant,
By Shades of Death or Fallen Trance!

To know by symbol, word or deed
An answer that will serve our need!
His hammer strikes! Now slowly speed!
The Lame God comes! The dance proceeds!

The dancing Witches now join themselves for the dance by crossing their arms and linking hands. Then they begin circling clockwise very slowly while dragging the left foot. Forward steps are taken only with the right foot. If the group decides that it is difficult to keep their balance in this position, they may join themselves together by simply placing their right hands on the left shoulder of the person before them. The right foot is still the dominant foot, and the left foot is still dragged. While they are circling, the Witches slowly chant:

IO

The chant is to be pronounced EEEEEEEE-O, with the "I" accented and drawn out, and the "O" a shorter, more abrupt sound. Additionally, the "O" could be a note lower than the "I." If there is a drummer, that person should play a suitable beat at medium volume to accompany the chant. The drum beat should not drown out the sound of the chant.

The dancers continue in this manner for a period of time. Twenty to thirty minutes is about as long as the group can probably perform the dance and maintain their concentration. If the dance does not result in trance within this time period, the group should end it. At any rate, the group should decide how long they will dance before beginning.

The full-blown trance state will commence with a feeling of coldness or tingling in the left or "lame" foot. This sensation will slowly overtake the entire body. When it reaches the head, a trance will result. Usually, the affected participant will fall to the floor or earth. At this point, the dancers end their circling and unlink their bodies. The drummer should stop drumming. A previously appointed Witch (the attendant) should attend to the trance subject, and another Witch should stand by ready with pen and paper to record any messages or answers (the recorder).

The next step will be governed by the purpose of the dance. If the object is to answer questions for the group, but not to contact a departed shade to answer them, the attendant should call the trance subject by his or her regular or magical name to see if the person is lucid and capable of answering questions. If the subject is lucid, the attendant may softly ask the three questions and listen to the responses. The subject may very well be in contact with the astral plane. This is similar to crystal-gazing, but the trance subject perceives entities, symbols, scenes, et cetera directly, with no external aid, as, indeed, sometimes occurs with the use of a crystal ball or black mirror. In response to the questions from the attendant, symbols, words, or scenes will arise before the subject's mind. In fact, the subject is "scrying in the astral." The subject should softly communicate these and any other impressions received, to be later interpreted by the group as a whole. If the subject is not capable of verbal communication with the attendant, the group will just have to trust the subject to remember the questions and to ask them mentally, and to remember what impressions arise in response to the queries. These impressions should be recorded immediately after the subject comes out of the trance state.

If the group is contacting a departed shade, as soon as the trance subject falls, all other participants should mentally focus on the image of the shade and his or her personality and mannerisms, silently calling the shade by name to communicate with it. The shade may come in either one of two ways. If the trance subject has mediumistic ability, the shade may use the trance subject's vocal cords to communicate directly with the group. Questions may then be asked of the shade directly. In rare cases, the shade may use the astral-etheric substance from the trance subject's body to physically manifest some type of form—a head, a mouth, or, very rarely, even a full physical body. Alternatively, the trance-subject may "mentally" meet with the astral form of the shade. In this case, the trance subject may serve as a relay between the shade and group (a psychic telephone line, of sorts), relaying questions and answers. Again, the trance subject may not be capable of verbal communication at all, and in this case, the group will just have to trust the subject to meet with the shade and ask the questions. If the shade is contacted to allay the grief of a Witch participant, that Witch may serve as the attendant.

There are few hard and fast rules that can be given to fit every situation. This is why it is important to have on hand a Witch experienced in these matters to make judgement calls.

The trance should be allowed to last for only five to ten minutes, and no more. This is ample time for the trance subject to have the three questions answered or to meet with the departed shade. If the shade does not come at the end of ten minutes, the trance should be ended.

While the subject is in trance, all but the attendant and recorder should stay well away from that person's body. The trance subject's body should not be touched unless the attendant is arousing him or her from the trance. Otherwise, the trance may be ended before the questions are answered or before the shade is met.

If the attendant notices any signs of emotional or physical discomfort on the part of the trance subject—either by movements of the body or facial expressions—the trance should be ended at once. The attendant should gently rub the subject's hands and feet and softly call the subject by his or her magical name. If the trance subject is lucid, or when he or she becomes so by the rubbing of the hands and feet and the calling of the name, the attendant should advise the person to visualize the feet. This will swiftly return the trance subject to the physical body.

If a shade has assisted in the answering of questions, he or she should be thanked for the advice before the trance is ended. To waken the trance subject to normal consciousness, the attendant should rub the subject's feet and hands, calling the person by his or her magical name, and advising the subject to visualize the feet when he or she is lucid.

The subject may still be a bit groggy after awakening to normal consciousness. This is perfectly normal. Some food—crackers, juice, bread, water, cookies, tea—should be on hand for the subject to eat. Eating a small snack will fully close down the psychic centers that opened during the dance.

The leader should formally close the dance by giving thanks to any departed shade that has assisted, and of course, giving thanks to the Lame God in any suitable words.

The Circle should be closed or the rituals continued, as appropriate. After the Circle is closed, all other participants should eat a light meal to make sure that their psychic centers are closed down as well.

INTERPRETATIONS

Answers to questions may be given quite explicitly, leaving little need for interpretation. However, if the subject receives answers to questions through symbols, phrases, or scenes, the entire group should talk over the likely interpretation given the nature of the question and the images received. First impressions, as in all forms of divination, are very valuable. Especially consider the first impressions of the person who formulated the question and upon whom the answer directly bears.

Some groups will experience success with the dance the first time it is tried. Otherwise, it may take several trials before one of the group finally falls in trance. Do not be discouraged by this. Oftentimes, the group will need to become comfortable in performing the dance together. Sometimes the time chosen is dictated by need, and not by when psychic currents are running high on the astral plane. When the dance is successful, a careful and complete record should be made of the entire proceeding so that the group will begin to understand what elements account for success in the dance. Likewise, failures should be recorded so that the group can isolate elements that do not seem to help induce the trance state.

CHAPTER ELEVEN

THE SWORD TRANCE

This form of divination is best used when you have to make a decision between two courses of action or a choice between two things. As with all three forms of divination in this section, this type of divination is rather "free form." There are no set rules for interpretation. Of course, this is as it should be since the Sword Trance entails receiving symbols while in a dream state, and there are no better interpreters of dream symbols than dreamers themselves.

THE TEMPLE SLEEP

Many Witches and Pagans, as part of their magical training, learn how to keep a record of their dreams and how to interpret the symbols that appear in them. Most often a notebook is kept beside the bedside, and any dreams recorded in it upon waking, with interpretation and analysis of the dream done as soon as possible thereafter. Nightly dreams can give you insight into your character, realizations about daily events, inform you of the contents of your subconscious mind, and can even clue you in on future happenings. In more specialized magical training, Witches and Pagans may be taught how to dream "with a purpose." Usually, one simply goes to sleep without searching for an answer to a particular question, letting the subconscious mind determine what the contents and messages of one's dreams will be. Yet learning how to "dream with purpose" can prove an invaluable divination tool.

Psychology and magical theory agree that dreams are mental images arising from the subconscious mind. However, magical theory goes further by saying that the subconscious mind of every individual is linked to the Universal Subconscious Mind, which holds all the memories, knowledge, and experience of every being that has ever lived. It is as if every individual subconscious mind is a little bay of water opening up into a vast ocean that is the Universal Subconscious. Since we all have this inherent link with a storehouse of limitless knowledge and experience, it is possible to draw upon this fund of wisdom through our dreams, which, we've noted, arise from the subconscious mind. This is the theory behind "dreaming with purpose."

Almost all magical traditions throughout the ages have taught some form of "dreaming with purpose." Perhaps the most well-known example comes from the Greek tradition and the cult of Aesculapius (es-ku-lay'-pee-us), the Greek god of healing and medicine. Aesculapius was the son of Apollo (the god of the sun, also associated with healing and medicine) and a Thessalian maiden named Coronis. Aesculapius married Epione, and fathered two mortal sons—Machaon and Podalirius, both famous physicians—and two divine daughters—Hygeia and Panacea, both goddesses of health.

For hundreds of years, the sick, maimed, and blind sought the healing aid of Aesculapius. They would travel to his temples (the most famous one was at the city of Epidauros) where they would pray and make offerings to his image. When night drew near, they would crowd around beneath his image and the votive offerings to go to sleep and dream. In their dreams, Aesculapius would come to them, telling them what must be done to be rid of their ailing conditions. Upon awakening, the priests of Aesculapius would interpret the words and symbols that the god had presented to the supplicants. Thousands of sick people believed that they were cured through the god's intervention.

Additionally, snakes were allowed to roam throughout the temple since they were seen as the divine servants of Aesculapius. Snakes have long been seen as symbols of wisdom and truth. They were also associated with Aesculapius' father, Apollo, who had once killed the serpent-monster Python at Delphi. Apollo later founded the Delphic Oracle, and the priestess of Apollo there was known as the Pythia or Pythoness.

Apollo was also the god of truth and prophecy, so it is natural that Greeks would seek out his son, a god of healing, for advice.

Of course, the divination method presented here is not used to gain medical advice. You should see a licensed physician or health professional for that purpose. We can, however, make use of some of the imagery associated with Aesculapius, particularly the serpent-wisdom symbol.

However, our primary imagery will come from another Greek deity—Hecate (hek'-uh-tee), the Dark Lady of the Crossroads. Hecate is seen as a Crone figure by some. Here, she is considered a dark Mother figure. She is a goddess of night, Witchcraft, the Under-world, and the dark of the Moon. The Greeks sometimes called her Hecate Antea (ann-tee'-ah), with the epithet "Antea" indicating that she is the sender of night visions. Thus, she is perfect for invoking in this form of divination.

BACKGROUND TO THE SWORD TRANCE

The Sword Trance is not a complicated ritual, but does require some preparation. Since you are opening yourself up to the deeper levels of your subconscious mind and the Universal Subconscious, the ritual will take place in a properly cast and purified Circle, with the appropriate forces invoked. This serves two functions, as all magical Circles do: it protects you from encountering interference from mischievous astral entities, and it helps you contain the power that you will raise by your working.

The sword is obviously a central emblem of the ritual. The sword is a symbol of having to make a decision, because it is double-edged and can cut both ways. Cut in the right direction and you will be victorious. Cut in the wrong direction, and you might chop off your foot.

Some traditions assign the sword to the element air, and some to the element fire. If you assign the sword to air, the sword is a symbol of the intellect, the reasoning faculty, and the mind. Reasoning, like a sword, always comes to a point. So the sword in this instance would be a symbol of using your intellect to make a decision. If you assign the sword to fire, you might think of it as a symbol of action, resolve, and courage. In this instance the sword would be a symbol of making a decision so that you may act upon it decisively. In the end, it does not matter which attribution you prefer, since both fit with the intention of the ritual.

After you have prepared your Circle, you will lie down in its center in the pentagram position (stretch your arms out fully to your sides, and spread your feet apart, so that you will be forming a five-pointed star with your body). You will then place your sword on your chest, so that the "cross" formed by the sword hilt and crossbar covers your heart. The blade of the sword will run between your legs to point toward your feet.

Not everyone has a ritual sword or access to one. You may use an athame or other ritual knife, as long as it is double-edged. If you have only recently procured one, and it is not yet blessed, you may give it a simple consecration by the elements after you have cast your Circle. Simply pass the knife over the altar candle flame three times (fire), pass it through the smoke of the incense three times (air), then anoint it three times with a bit of consecrated saltwater (earth and water). You may say appropriate words of blessing for each element, such as "Athame, be thou blessed by the element fire." Though you may wish to give it a more appropriate consecration later on, this simple rite of blessing will serve your purposes for the Sword Trance. As a last resort, you can visualize a sword placed on your chest. As long as you build up a good image of the sword, the effect should be the same.

Once you are in this position, you will prepare to enter the trance through a vision journey. If you are performing the ritual without the assistance of others, you will have to memorize the images of the vision journey before you start the ritual. This should not be difficult since the journey is relatively simple. Alternatively, you could tape-record the journey beforehand and play it back to yourself at the appropriate point in the ritual. Your third option is to have someone assist you by reading it to you, then leaving the ritual area while you prepare to sleep. Even though this is called the Sword Trance, technically, you will not be in a trance state for the duration of the ritual. Your intention is to pass into the sleeping state where you can dream and discover your answer.

The placing of the "cross" of the sword over your heart is symbolic. The heart region (and its chakra, which is a power point on the etheric body) is attributed to the sun. Esoteric tradition tells us that power from the Universe enters our solar system through the sun, and that the sun then "distributes" it to the rest of the planets, each one receiving the type of energy that accords with its nature. Since magical tradition regards man as a miniature universe, it deduces that the sun/heart region is also the area where people receive energy from the Universe. By placing the sword "cross" over your heart, you are symbolically affirming to your subconscious mind that your ritual intention is to receive information in guiding a decision or choice. All power that enters your body from that point will "pass through" the sword, continually re-affirming your intention, even while you sleep and dream.

The best time to perform the Sword Trance is the night of the full moon, or failing that, during the time of the waxing moon.

PERFORMING THE SWORD TRANCE

The Sword Trance requires few materials. All you need are the materials required to cast a Circle, a sword, and perhaps a blanket, and a small pillow or two. Also place a notebook and a pen under the altar. You should also have a small basket of fruit and bread beside the altar to serve as an offering to Hecate Antea.

Your first step is to cast the Circle in your ritual area. You may do this according to your own tradition and teachings, or use the ceremony given in the Appendix. After you have invoked the Guardians of the Quarters, and the God and Goddess, you will move to the north edge of your Circle, and face south. You will now make a triple-invocation to the Triple Hecate. Before you make the invocation, you must form a solid mental image of this goddess. This image will take form on the astral plane, and the power you invoke with your invocation will ensoul it for the duration of the ritual. Hecate should be visualized standing in the south, facing north, as follows:

She has a triple form and should be visualized as three women standing with their backs forming a triangle. All three are in black robes, with the cowls pulled over the heads, such that you cannot see the facial features of the goddess. Nevertheless, there is a distinctly powerful feminine aura about the figure. One form is facing you head on. She carries a torch in each hand. The second form is behind the first form, facing roughly towards the southeast. Though you cannot see very much of her, you see that she carries a black-handled, double-edged knife in each hand. The third figure is also behind the first form, though roughly facing to the southwest. Again, you cannot see much of her, but see that she carries a writhing serpent in each hand. Take a least five full minutes to build up this image in the south.

When the image is solid in your mind (which will indicate its solidity on the astral plane), you may commence your invocation. You will be concentrating on a different aspect of the goddess with each part of the invocation. With the first part, you will concentrate on the "Knife-Bearer." With the second part, you will be addressing the "Torch-Bearer." With the third, the "Serpent-Bearer." Be sure that you are addressing the appropriate form of the goddess with each part of the invocation. You are still standing in the north. Raise your arms up in a gesture of supplication, and say in a powerful voice:

Hecate Antea,
Giver of Visions in the Night,
Dark Lady of the Three Ways,
I call upon Thee in Thy form as Knife-Bearer!
Remove all obstacles hindering me,
So that all Ways will be clear before me!
Guide my feet,
That I may choose my Path with Discrimination!

Hecate Antea,
Giver of Visions in the Night,
Dark Lady of the Three Ways,
I call upon Thee in Thy form as Torch-Bearer!
Raise Thy Torch on high
That I may see the end and consequences
Of all Ways that lie before me!
Give me courage
To choose my proper Path!

Hecate Antea,
Giver of Visions in the Night,
Dark Lady of the Three Ways,
I call upon Thee in Thy form as Serpent-Bearer!
Send your serpent-servants
To accompany me on my Inner Journey
That Thou mayest guide me
With Thy Wisdom!

When your invocation is completed, feel the presence of the Dark Lady enter the Circle. Spend a few minutes experiencing her aura of wisdom and strength. When you are ready, write down your exact question on a piece of paper in the notebook.

Now you should extinguish any candles or incense that you have used to cast your Circle. You will be going to sleep in the Circle, and would not want to wake up with your house around you in flames because the cat knocked a candle off the altar.

Take your sword (or athame or other magical knife) from the altar and lie down in the center of the Circle, with your head pointing south and your feet to the north. You may want to have a couple of small pillows to support your head and the small of your back. Place the sword "cross" hilt over your heart region. The sword should be in its sheath, if you have one for it. If not, wrap the blade in a piece of dark, thick material such as felt. You don't want to cut yourself in your sleep. You may then cover yourself with a blanket, if you wish. If you use a blanket, it must be placed over the sword. Now you will assume the pentagram position.

Begin breathing deeply and rhythmically, relaxing all parts of your body, starting with your feet and working upward. Spend at least five minutes in becoming as relaxed as possible.

It is now time for you to commence your inner journey to the cave of Hecate. If you have memorized the images, you can begin immediately. Otherwise, start your tape-recording of the journey, or signal to a helper (if you have one) to begin reading the Inner Journey to you slowly, pausing after every sentence to allow you to build the images.

The Inner Journey

Visualize that your whole body is enveloped in a thick, warm, soothing, gray mist. You feel completely safe and secure within this mist and are completely relaxed. You see nothing and know nothing but this warm, gray mist. After a few moments, you begin to feel that you are standing upright in the mist. You notice that the mist is clearing in front of you, thinning and thinning and thinning.

As the last of the mist clears, you see that you are standing on a beach. It is just after nightfall. You can see the full moon rising in the indigo sky above a shallow bay. The night is chilly, so you pull your dark cloak closer around you for warmth. In one of your hands you carry a small pouch of fruit and grain—offerings for Hecate. Behind you is a thick forest, and you can see nothing within it, though you can hear the sounds of the night woodland creatures that live there. Before you, floating at the edge of the bay, is a small boat made entirely of glass. In it stands a robed and hooded figure. This entity silently gestures you forward into the boat. Here is your way to reach the cave of Hecate. You step in the boat, and your guide begins to push out into the bay. Once you have cleared the land, you begin to move toward the mouth of the bay, out to the vast and open sea.

You draw farther and farther away from the coast. The only things you are aware of are yourself, the sky, the moon, and the open sea—and, of course, your silent guide. Onward and onward you paddle, growing somewhat weary of the rocking of the boat on the sea.

Suddenly, your guide stops the boat. Following his line of vision, you see an island off in the watery distance. The hooded being proceeds to guide the boat toward it—closer and closer and closer you draw. Your guide finally leads the boat to the shore of the island.

It is a small island with a rocky shore. There is very little vegetation, except for the cypress trees that cover the island. In the center of the island stands a large, rocky hill, with a path winding up like a serpent. On the very top of the hill you see two small fires burning. Your guide points out a large black dog standing on the shore; it will be your guide and guard on the rest of your journey.

You step out of the glass boat onto the rocky shore, and make your way toward the dog. As you approach, the dog runs off toward the start of the path up the rocky hill. You can easily see the path by moonlight, and steadily make your way forward. Upward and around you make your way, the dog just staying within your field of vision ahead. Finally, you reach the top of the rocky hill. At the summit, you see what you thought were two fires. Actually, they are two large, blazing torches illuminating the entrance to a small cave. The dog barks once and runs into the cave. You follow.

The inside of the cave is not large; it has curved walls and ceiling with a dirt floor perhaps twenty feet long and wide. It is illuminated by torches set into the walls. At the back of the cave you see a large granite statue of Hecate, appearing exactly as you envisioned her when you invoked her in your Circle. You note that there is a pile of rough blankets before the statue. The dog, your guide and guardian on this part of your journey, stands to the side of it. You approach the statue silently, in a reverent manner, and place your offerings of fruit and grain from your pouch in front of it. Now, ask your question of Hecate, phrasing it as you wrote it down in your notebook, and directing your words to her statue image.

Now it is time for you to sleep in front of the statue. You arrange the rough blankets into a suitable bed, and close your eyes to sleep and dream, in order that Hecate may show you the proper path to take in your mundane life.

(At this point, your journey ends for the time being. You will start your Temple Sleep in the Circle. Your assistant, if you have one, should stop reading now and leave you in peace, making sure all candles and incense are extinguished, if they haven't been cared for previously. If you tape-recorded your journey, you should stop the tape at this point.)

If you are having difficulty falling asleep, repeat the following charm over and over until you do so:

SOMINA

OMINAS

MINASO

INASOM

NASOMI

ASOMIN

During the night, Hecate will send you dreams and visions advising you what you should do, and how your decision is to be made. If you awaken during the night, and remember your dreams, you should get up and slowly move to the altar, light a candle, and record your dreams in your notebook under the altar. If you feel that you have received your advice from Hecate because the dream is so clear, you may end the ritual at this point, or go back and assume your position in hopes of having more dreams and getting more advice.

If you awaken during the night, but do not remember any dreams, just go back to sleep, using the previous sleep charm if needed.

If you sleep through the night, and awaken in the morning, record your dreams in your notebook immediately upon awakening. When you have done so, you will begin to end the ritual.

The first thing you must do is make sure you are fully back from your night journey to the cave of Hecate. This is fairly simple to do. Lie down again in the center of the Circle (though there is no need to use the sword, now), and imagine the cave of Hecate building up around you. The dog and statue are still there, but outside you can see that the sun is shining. You pile the blankets back up in front of the statue and prepare to leave. The dog guides you out of the cave and back down to the rocky shoreline where your other guide awaits you in the glass boat. After you have climbed into the boat, the guide begins to push out into the open sea. The journey back to land seems much shorter now, and in no time at all, you are heading into the confines of the shallow bay where you started.

When you reach the shoreline, the guide beckons you out of the boat. You step out, and note that there is a dark gray mist just at the edge of the forest. You make your way toward it and step inside it. Again, you feel the warm, comforting mist envelope you. Gradually, it thins, and you find yourself once again in the safe confines of your Circle.

When you are fully awake in your normal consciousness, it is time to busy yourself in closing down the Circle.

Your first task will be thanking Hecate Antea for her aid. Stand in the north, facing south, and once again bring to mind your mental image of her. Speak the following or words from your heart:

Hecate Antea,
Giver of Visions in the Night,
Dark Lady of the Three Ways,
Triple Goddess of Magic,
I give Thee thanks for Thy aid and blessing!
I shall always sing Thy praises!
Depart to Thy proper place
And may there ever be Peace between us!

Imagine your image of Hecate slowly fading from your mind, and feel her presence slowly fading from the Circle. You should take a couple of minutes to do this.

Now banish the Circle you cast the night before, thanking the God and Goddess, dismissing the quarters, and so on, using your accustomed ritual, or the ceremony given in the Appendix. Note that you will not need to extinguish the candles and incense as the Appendix ceremony directs, since these will have been extinguished the night before.

Interpreting Your Dream Symbols and Visions

As mentioned before, the best interpreter of dream symbols is the dreamer. If your dreams and dream symbols do not immediately indicate to you what your decision or path should be, you should use the following technique, which has been found to be extremely effective. Make sure your dream notes are as full as possible, and that you have written everything down.

Call up or visit a friend, having your dream notes handy. Describe your dream and symbols to your friend. Your friend, however, must pretend that he or she is from another planet, and does not understand what any of the images are. For instance, if you say, "In my dream, I was walking along a sunny country lane, when all of a sudden I saw an elephant butting its head against a tree." Your friend would then ask, "What's an elephant and what does it represent to you?" You might respond, "It's a large, gray, fat creature from India or Africa. It has a long snout and tusks." Your friend continues, "What is India and what does it represent for you?" You describe what you know of India. Your friend might ask what a tree is, and you would describe this as best as you could. Continue in this manner until you have described all of your dream images to your friend, with your friend asking questions all the while, being as thorough as possible. At the end of the exchange, you should be able to interpret the images fairly easily and know what course you must take in making your decision. Your descriptions of what the images represent are your interpretation.

If, even after this, you do not know what decision to make, you may repeat the process with another friend. If this still brings no enlightenment, take your dream symbols, one a day, and spend fifteen minutes meditating on them. Write down all you can think of about the symbol—what is it, what does it represent, how do you feel about it, and so on. When you have done this with all of your images, read back over all of your notes. By this time, your decision should be fairly clear to you.

As a last resort, you may consult a popular "dream dictionary," but be aware that the interpretations given in such books are substandard to interpretations that you can come up with yourself.

In the rare circumstance that you do not understand your dream after all these measures have been taken, you must resign yourself to the fact that the divination has failed. Don't be too discouraged, though. Even the most skilled practitioners of divination among Witches and Pagans have their off days.

WHAT TO DO IF YOU DON'T REMEMBER THE DREAMS

Obviously, if you don't remember any dreams upon waking, you must consider the divination as failing, but don't make this judgement until at least forty-eight hours have gone by after the completion of the ritual. Sometimes when we wake, we cannot immediately remember our dreams, but then during the day, something triggers our memory of the dream, and it comes flooding back into consciousness. If this happens to you, immediately write down the dream images, or you will once again forget them.

If you want to guard against the untoward possibility that you will not remember any dreams upon waking after the ritual, you may want to take some precautions. Every night for two weeks prior to the ritual, before you go to bed, mentally affirm to yourself that you will dream during the night, and that upon waking, you will remember your dreams. Keep a notebook and writing instrument by the bed so that you may record your dreams upon waking. This two-week "training period" will help you remember your dreams. By the end of the two weeks, you should have no trouble performing the divination ritual. If at the end of two weeks you are still not remembering your dreams, keep going with the exercise for two-week periods until you have success at it.

CONCLUSION

There may be a few people who will skip over this chapter, saying "I never dream, so I'm not going to bother with this form of divination." However, psychologists and sleep scientists tell us that we dream every night for most of the night. It isn't that you are not dreaming, it's that you are not remembering your dreams. Try the two-week training exercise and you may surprise yourself at how much you really do dream, and how much you will be able to recall upon waking.

There is one other thing you should be aware of about the Sword Trance. Prolonged and continued use of it may develop clairvoyance in its practitioner. After many years, you may find that when you are confronted with a decision or choice, symbols will immediately flow up from the Universal Subconscious. All you will have to do is interpret them and you will have your guiding advice. By that time, you should be an expert in the Sword Trance.

CHAPTER TWELVE

THE OMEN WALK

Our last form of divination, the Omen Walk, is the least structured of all the divination systems in this book. Therefore, you will have a lot of room to tailor it to your own needs and according to your own creative impulses.

Briefly, the Omen Walk entails mapping out a Nature walk for yourself, putting yourself in a light state of trance, and then taking the walk in order to look for specific omens to answer your question. Ultimately, it will be up to you to fashion your own system of omens, though I will mention several ideas you can use.

Divination by omens occurring in nature has long been a part of the Western magical tradition. Druids performed divinations by judging weather conditions, such as the shape of clouds, the sound of thunder, and a strike of lightning. Also, specific birds were related to each letter of the Ogham alphabet, the script of the Druids. Each letter had a specific divination meaning, and if a Druid seeking omens saw a certain bird, he or she would relate it to its letter and consult the letter for the meaning of the omen. The priests of ancient Rome were particularly adept at the practice of augury, a term sometimes used to refer to divination in general, but which often entails judging the future of a situation by examining the flight patterns, numbers, and other information from specific birds. The priests of Zeus in ancient Greece would seek the will of their patron deity in his oak groves, the most famous of which was located at Dodona.

FIRST STEPS: PLANNING YOUR SYSTEM

Fashioning your own system of omens is quite easy. There are really no particular requirements, other than that if you are going to go on a nature walk, your system will include animals, birds, trees, clouds, storms, and other things that occur in Nature. As we have mentioned previously, the magical theory behind divination is based largely on the contents and patterns that you hold in your subconscious mind. Though your personal subconscious mind is filled with images and patterns that you have inherited by virtue of being a member of the human race (and if you subscribe to a belief in evolutionary reincarnation, of animal and plant life as well), it is possible to train your subconscious mind to give meaning to personally chosen symbols.

For instance, suppose you have a list of twenty natural manifestations that you wish to form into a divination system for your Omen Walk. For instance, you may associate thunder with anger or an unfavorable outcome to your question, lightning with disasters or perhaps spiritual enlightenment, robins with new and favorable beginnings, roses with love and friendship, hummingbirds with speedy messages, squirrels with money, and so on. No matter what interpretations you have given to each object, they will work for you, provided, however, that you study your list so thoroughly that they pass into your subconscious mind and become a permanent part of your subconscious knowledge.

You may ask, "How on earth will I know when my symbols have passed into my subconscious mind? How will I know when I can begin using the symbols for divination by omen?" We find our answer, once again, in basic magical theory. You are already familiar with the fact that the subconscious mind is symbolized by the Moon in most magical traditions, just as the Sun (and sometimes Mercury, as we have seen) symbolizes the self-conscious mind and your normal waking consciousness. The moon is also a symbol of our emotional natures. This fact is used by astrologers to judge the basic emotional nature of a person in a horoscope. Thus, if the moon represents the subconscious, and the moon also represents the emotions, we can deduce that the subconscious mind must also be closely linked with our emotional natures.

We also know from dream specialists and psychologists that our basic image-making faculties are linked to our subconscious minds. This is why we dream in images and pictures and rarely (if ever) in words. When the self-conscious mind is stilled in slumber, the subconscious mind has free reign to throw its images into our field of awareness, causing dreams. Qabalistic tradition also confirms the connection between images and the subconscious mind. The seat of the subconscious in Qabalah is termed "Yesod." Yesod, as a center of awareness, corresponds to the Moon. What is even more interesting is that Qabalists often call Yesod "the Treasure House of Images." The images referred to in this phrase are the personal images of your subconscious mind, as well as the images that we are continually creating on the astral plane by virtue of being thinking and feeling creatures.

If you are new to magical theory and magical religions, all of this can seem a bit daunting. However, all you need to realize at this stage is that your subconscious mind is inextricably bound up with the images that you feed it. We can make use of this fact in training ourselves in a personal omen system.

The first thing you must do is decide on a system of symbols, either by creating your own or adopting one outlined in this chapter. Twenty symbols is probably the fewest that you can get by with. Forty symbols would probably be a good maximum at this stage, unless you have a very good memory and have been trained in transferring emotionally charged images to your subconscious mind such that you can do it quickly and efficiently.

Once you have decided on your symbols, your next step is to take one symbol and meditate on it for at least three days. For example, say you have chosen thunder as a symbol for anger, war, dissension, and conflict. Sit in an upright chair, making sure you will not be interrupted. Compose yourself by relaxing your whole body and breathing deeply and rhythmically. When you are relaxed, begin thinking of your symbol. Imagine that you are walking outside. Storm clouds cover the sky, and you begin to hear thunder. Keep hearing the thunder sounding out over and over.

When you have attained some facility in hearing the thunder, you can proceed to the next stage. While still imagining the thunder sounding out periodically, begin to reflect on the ideas of anger, dissension, and conflict. You can remember past events where you were angry with someone or at some situation, or you can remember seeing images of others in conflict. In any event, try to arouse the emotion of anger in yourself. Call this up as vividly as you can. Persist in this exercise for no more than ten minutes. Remember to keep hearing the thunder, for only then will your subconscious mind begin to associate thunder with anger. Keep to the exercise for three days.

At the end of the three days, you will begin to notice a change in your thought patterns. Every time you see others in conflict or begin to experience anger yourself, you will think of thunder. Likewise, every time you hear thunder outside, it will remind you of anger. When this starts occurring—when one symbol immediately and effortlessly throws the other symbol into your mind—you will know that this particular symbol and its association has passed into your subconscious mind. Then you will be ready to use it for your Omen Walk.

Let's take another example. Suppose you have chosen the squirrel as a symbol for theft, dishonesty, or swindling. During your three-day work on this symbol, you will call up images of squirrels, perhaps stealing nuts and hiding them away somewhere. When you have gained facility in imagining this, you will begin to think of theft, dishonesty, and swindling. Think back on times when something was stolen from you, times when others have been dishonest with you, or incidents of swindling and cheating. If you have no such situations in your past, think of situations that you have read in books or seen in movies or on television. Continue to link the squirrel with these ideas. At the end of your three days, you should begin to think of theft, dishonesty, and related ideas whenever you see a squirrel. The converse is also true; when you hear of or see incidents of theft or dishonesty, you will think of squirrels. When one image calls forth the other, you can be certain that the association is firmly ensconced in your subconscious mind.

You will proceed with the rest of your list of symbols in the same manner, keeping in mind that it is the emotional charge that you give to these symbols that will transfer them to your subconscious mind.

Link a picture or image ("image" refers not just to visual images, but also to all perceptions of the senses—sounds, tastes, and the like) to a specific interpretation. If you ever want to add another omen to your list, you would follow the same procedure. It is imperative to keep a record of your symbols, just in case you forget an interpretation or two. This might be quite possible if you have a lengthy list. If you ever do forget a symbol and its interpretation, you should take another three days to go over it again, just to make sure you have it in your subconscious mind.

Now it doesn't mean that, for instance, if you have linked squirrels with theft, every time you see a squirrel in daily life someone is going to steal something from you. These interpretations are meant to hold true only during your Omen Walk. After all, squirrels are quite common in most places, and it simply wouldn't be fitting for you to walk around in a continual state of paranoia just because you live in an area with a high squirrel population.

You would be well advised to compile your own system of symbols and interpretations for the same reason you should interpret your own dreams (see the previous chapter on the Sword Trance for an explanation of this). Greater personalization of symbols and interpretations often leads to greater accuracy.

However, something is to be said for using symbols that are commonly used in other magical practices. Many of these "prepared" symbol systems already exist in your subconscious mind by virtue of the fact that you are human. Magical theory informs us that our own individualized subconscious minds are linked to a greater, vaster body of knowledge held in the Universal Subconscious Mind.

This is a difficult concept for some to grapple with, but you can think of it in this way. Imagine that your personal subconscious mind is represented by a river that leads out into a great ocean. Every other person on Earth also has a river leading into this ocean. Now while you may have your own particular field of awareness (your river), the water that flows through you is exactly the same as the water in the great ocean and in everyone else's river.

Suppose you have a particular thought about a symbol. This thought we can liken to a fishing-float that you have placed in your river. Eventually the currents of your personal river will drive the float out into the ocean. That is, your thought will eventually add to the Universal Subconscious Mind. Likewise, suppose another person has placed a fishing float in his or her river, and it eventually makes its way into the ocean and then into your personal river. This fishing float (or thought) has now come into your field of awareness, and you can make use of it.

Imagine now that one thousand people have placed an identical thought into their subconscious minds. The fact that a larger number of people are thinking the same thought increases the potency of the thought in the Universal Subconscious. Eventually this thought will make its way to your individual subconscious mind. You may not be immediately aware of it (since none of us is ever fully aware of all the contents of our subconscious minds), but it is still subsisting below the surface of your normal waking consciousness to be used when needed.

Now let's intensify the example. Imagine that thousands of people over the course of hundreds of years are all putting the same thought out into the Universal Subconscious. As an example, let's say that the thought is one linking the Norse rune Beorc to ideas of fertility, birth, and new beginnings. Even though you may not be consciously aware of the interpretation of this rune, by virtue of the fact that others have, over the course of many years, linked this rune to these meanings, you are already subconsciously aware of the meaning.

Such potent symbols as the runes need very little work to make them a part of your subconscious knowledge. In fact, the knowledge is already there; you just have to consciously realize it. Those that have gone before you in this field have done much of the work already. This is true of other symbols as well, such as numbers, the Tarot symbols, planets, and zodiac signs.

So, in the end, it doesn't matter if you adopt a system of well-prepared symbols or develop your own. Each has its advantages.

THE NORSE RUNES

Since I mentioned the Norse rune Beorc in the above example, we will take it as a starting point for our first possible system of omens.

The Norse runes are also called the Futhark runes, a name taken from the first six letters of the runic alphabet. There are two variations of the Futhark runes, called the Elder Futhark (which has twenty-four characters and was probably more common) and the Younger Futhark (which has sixteen characters). Since we want to have at least a minimum of twenty characters to start our omen system, we examine the Elder Futhark here. If you are interested in learning more about these Norse alphabets, you may profitably read *A Practical Guide to the Runes*, by Lisa Peschel, or *Northern Magic*, by Edred Thorsson (both cited in the suggested reading list).

For the time being, however, all you need to do is familiarize yourself with the chart given on pages 234 and 235. The names of the Elder Futhark are given, their shapes, and a brief interpretation of each. If you are going to choose this system for your Omen Walk, you will probably want to acquaint yourself with the runes in a little more depth after you have mastered the simple interpretations given here. The above two recommended books and their bibliographies will provide you with ample material.

After you have learned all the runes and have linked them with their appropriate associations and meditated on each for three (or even more) days, you will be ready to use them in your Omen Walk. While on your walk you will be in a light state of trance. You will see one or more images of the runes occurring in the patterns of Nature—in tree branches, cracks in the ground, in the shapes of plants, or even in the clouds.

THE OGHAM ALPHABET

Another system that you could profitably use involves the Ogham alphabet. The symbols of this alphabet appear on pages 236 and 237. You will work with them exactly as you would work with the Norse runes. Meditate on each figure for three days, building up associations to them and charging them with emotion. On your Omen Walk you will endeavor to see these figures occurring in nature, just as you would with the Norse runes.

The Elder Futhark

Fehu—Prosperity, fulfillment, hopeful beginnings.

Uruz—Strength, either physical or emotional; men; changes, often for the better.

Thurisaz—Protection; good fortune, but obstacles will be overcome only if you're careful; sometimes opposition.

Ansuz—Take the advice of those wiser than you; help offered; eloquence and persuasion.

Raidho—Pleasant journeys; spiritual progress; move ahead; sometimes indecision.

Kenaz—Protection; leaving worries behind; energy; creativity; strength; power.

Gifu—Excellent outcome; gifts; good fortune; problems over; happiness, peace.

Wunjo—Joy; happiness; success; positive results.

Hagall—Limitations; problems; delay; disruption; conflict; someone working against you.

Nied—Delay; patience needed; bad health; forces against you; trials and tribulations; failure; do not begin anything new.

Isa—Delay; frustration; dishonesty; passions cooled; little done.

Jera—Rewards; repayment; justice; as you sow, so will you reap; tempting fate.

Lagaz—Heed intuition; psychism; protection from higher powers; women; success through imagination.

Ing—Successful endings; relaxation and relief; end of the old, beginning of the new.

Daeg—Increase, growth; prosperity; success; victory, but may have to surmount minor obstacles.

Otbel—Possessions, material things, money; hold fast to what you believe is right.

Tir—Victory, success in competition; motivation; increase in material things; recovery.

Beorc—Birth; beginnings; family; home; fertile new ideas.

Ebwaz—Slow but steady progress; change for the better; physical movements; journeys.

Mannaz—Help, aid, advice offered that will help solve a problem; proceed with plans dealing with others people.

Eihwaz—Obstacles, but protection; change for the better, but delay; need foresight and tenacity.

Perdhro—Secrets; mystery; occult power; finding things; new opportunity; surprises; the unexpected.

Eolh—Protection from friends; new positive influences; good fortune; protection from misfortune.

Sigel—Victory; great power, vitality; good health.

Table 12a

The Celtic Ogham Alphabet

Beth/Birch— New beginnings, growth, positive changes.

Luis/Rowan—Forces against you mean you need to keep control of things. Protection in the face of difficulties or obstacles.

Nion/Ash—Decisions made or actions taken at this time will have far-reaching consequences. You need to examine things from a larger point of view. Study the situation.

Fearn/Alder—The gods are trying to speak to you through your intuition. Follow your instincts, and you will achieve the correct result.

Saille/Willow—Women, fertility. Follow your heart, not your head. New feelings about the situation.

Muin/Vine—A time of endings. Enjoy the fruits of your past labors. If you do not see success by now, you may never see it.

Gort/Ivy—Difficult experiences and ordeals will lead to understanding whether you succeed or not. Running in circles. Chasing impossible dreams.

Ngetal/Reed—Time to let things go. If you cling to things, they will be taken from you forcibly by fate. Destruction of an old way of life. Courage needed.

Straif/Black Thorn—The only course of action is unpleasant. Difficulty, struggle, a breaking down of a way of life. Live through it, and you will be reborn anew.

Ruis/Elder—Difficult experiences. You must adapt to changes. A growth process, but not painful. The caterpillar becomes a butterfly.

Ailim/Silver Fir—Plan for the future, but keep your plans to yourself. Power in silence. Progress will be made if you keep quiet.

Obn/Furze—Gather strength to reach your goal. A successful end is near. Prosperity and increase.

Ur/Heather—Healing, success, positive results.

Eadba/Aspen—Fears, doubts; the odds are against you. Spiritual guidance and great wisdom are necessary if you are to succeed at all. Pressure from daily life makes you indecisive.

Iodbo/Yew—Learn from your past experiences; they hold the key to your future. You will not be able to avoid the destiny you have created for yourself.

Huatb/Hawtborn—Waiting, patience, keep to yourself. Get your priorities straight before you take action. Not a time to start new things.

Duir/Oak—Strength, resolve, willpower. Changes are coming, but will require sacrifice. Persevere and you will come out on top.

Tinne/Holly—Tests, trials, conflict, strife, obstacles. Sacrifice necessary. Fear will bring failure.

Coll/Hazel—Seek your answer in quiet meditation. Follow your intuition. Wisdom and care are necessary. Be cautious. The Otherworld may inspire you.

Quert/Apple—Beauty, women. Trials and difficulties coming to an end. Rest, relaxation, healing.

Table 12b

You can also extend this system by using other correspondences to the Ogham letters. As mentioned before, each letter has a bird associated with it. By correlating the birds to the letters, you can easily double your number of omens. If you are interested in doing this, you can consult any book on Celtic magic or magical alphabets to learn the correspondences. Be sure, however, if you are going to add new symbols, that you meditate on each one for three days to build up the proper subconscious associations.

BIRDS, ANIMALS, AND OTHER NATURAL PHENOMENA

This is another set of symbols that you can use by itself or in conjunction with other omen symbols. Think of all the common animals and birds of your geographic region—squirrels, deer, hedgehogs, bees, robins, starlings—and assign a meaning to each of them. Don't worry about what meanings others assign to them in books or other sources. Go with your own personal meaning for each. For instance, if you find dogs frightening or distasteful, you obviously wouldn't assign the meaning of friendship to them based on the idea of "man's best friend." Meditate on your symbols and meanings, and use them in your Omen Walk.

You can also use other natural phenomena—fog, rain, thunder, lightning, mist, hail, snow, winds and breezes from each of the four directions (which would give you four different meanings), or the sun suddenly coming out from behind a cloud. Use your imagination and creativity to make your own personal system.

NUMBER SYMBOLISM

You can also expand your omen repertoire by incorporating number symbolism into your methods. For example, say you are using the rune method on the Omen Walk. You see the figure Beorc, not once, but three times. If you have assigned an interpretation to the number three, you can fine-tune your interpretation of Beorc, combining it with the meaning of "three." For example, say you have assigned a meaning to the appearance of crows. On your omen walk you encounter two crows fighting in a tree. What you have here is really three symbols: the crow, the fact that there are two of them, and the fact that they are fighting. Assigning an interpretation to the number two will help you fine-tune what this omen means to you.

Any basic book on numerology can give you the meanings of the numbers one through ten. Books may differ on the interpretations of the numbers, so choose one set of interpretations and stick with it. A brief list of common meanings might look like this:

1: Attainment, success, leadership.

2: Love, companionship, cooperation, peace.

3: Communication, self-expression, artistic things, creativity.

4: Work, effort, difficulties.

5: Change, freedom, travel, progress.

6: Responsibility, the home, family, marriage.

7: Solitude, philosophy, spirituality, dreams, science.

8: Power, authority, money, success.

9: Understanding, intuition, sacrifice, endings.

10: New beginnings follow endings, readjustment, new goals.

If you are going to work with numbers in your search for omens, it is probably best if you work only with the numbers one through ten. Numbers higher than that can be reduced to their component parts. For instance, suppose you see a small flock of twelve geese flying south in an arrow. You have an interpretation for geese, and you reduce the twelve to its component parts—ten and two. You now have three symbols to combine and interpret: geese, ten, and two. You may also have assigned an interpretation to the arrow pattern.

The number twelve would reduce to ten and two (as opposed to five and seven, three and nine, et cetera) because the numerical system is based on the number ten. Also, the number represents the ending of a cycle and the beginning of a new one, so ten is a natural point of division in reducing larger numbers to component parts.

Here is another example: Say you have assigned to the starling the meaning of a bright, happy message. You see fourteen starlings on your Omen Walk. Breaking this down, you have a bright, happy message (the starling), new goals (ten), and work (four). If your question concerned employment, you might interpret this omen to mean that you will soon take a new, challenging job, or perhaps earn a promotion with new responsibilities.

Whichever system you choose, or however you make up your own, just remember that the important part in training to read omens is in fixing your symbols and associations in your subconscious mind. Again, try not to go too far above forty symbols when you are beginning. However, you may also include the ten numbers beyond this number of symbols, giving you a total of fifty symbols with which to work. That is plenty to try to remember.

CHARTING YOUR PATH

After your symbols are firmly fixed in your subconscious mind, you can start thinking about where you would like to perform your Omen Walk. If you are fortunate enough to live near a wooded area, you can chart a course through the woods to look for your omens. If you live in an urban area, consider charting your walk through a park, or taking a morning or afternoon trip into some familiar countryside. If these are not options for you, you may consider, as a last resort, sitting in your backyard for a certain period of time, letting your omens come from your immediate surroundings.

If you are going to walk through the woods, in the countryside, or through a park, you must plan a beginning point and ending point for your walk and stick to them. You should plan to walk for about fifteen minutes. In the woods or countryside, you can pick your starting and ending points out from natural landmarks—starting at a certain tree then turning around at a certain boulder and heading back to your starting point, for instance. If you are in a small park, you may want to walk around the perimeter several times, or plan that you will walk around it twice and then criss-cross through it once. Whatever method you choose, just make sure you are walking for about fifteen minutes. You can even draw yourself a small map of the area and diagram your walk.

You may use different areas for your Omen Walks on different occasions, or you may prefer to stick to just one area and one charted course for a long period of time. Either way is fine, but you may find that keeping to the same course for every Omen Walk will build up a rapport between you and the Nature spirits of the area, intensifying your experience.

Once your walk is planned, you can proceed to put yourself into a trance state.

ENTERING THE TRANCE STATE

If possible, it is best to be at your starting place for your Omen Walk when you put yourself into trance. Otherwise you might come out of the trance state while moving from one place to another. Just find a comfortable spot to sit near your starting place. You can even lean against the trunk of a tree. Also, make sure that you take a small notepad and a writing instrument with you. When you are comfortably seated, begin to relax your body. Breathe deeply and rhythmically for about five minutes.

At the end of this time, ask your question aloud (or mentally, if you are likely to be overheard), framing it in words similar to these: "Lady of the Moon and Lord of the Winds, through the symbols of your Web of Nature, I ask that you show me an omen regarding the following question [state your question]?" Your question can be phrased any way that you like, though you should probably avoid questions like "Should I [do this] or [that]?" It is better to ask, "What will happen if I [do this]?" or, "Will I benefit from [whatever it is]?" or even, "Will I [specify some future event—marry John, take a new job offer]?"

Next, close your eyes, and bring to your mind's eye the Lovers card that you used for your exercise in Chapter Three. Spend another five minutes going over its details in your mind and thinking on its meaning. Continue to be relaxed, breathing deeply and rhythmically. After the five minutes are up, let the Lovers image fade from your mind.

Your next step is to run through the colors of the rainbow in order to relax your consciousness. Imagine your entire body enveloped in an oval of red light energy. Breathe this energy into your body, letting it color every cell of your being. Spend a minute or so doing this. Then repeat the procedure with orange, yellow, green, blue, indigo, and violet, in that order. Spend a minute on each color. Each time you pass down to the next color, feel your body become more relaxed and your mind more calm. When you have finished with the violet phase of the exercise, you will be in a light state of trance. (This state may be very easy for you to achieve, or it may take several attempts. Each time you do this rainbow exercise, however, you will find it easier to reach this light trance state. In fact, it will take you much less than a minute to go through each color after you have attained some proficiency in the exercise.)

Allow the violet oval to fade from your mind. Once again, ask your question: "Lady of the Moon and Lord of the Winds...." Now pick up your notepad, move to your starting point and begin your Omen Walk.

DURING THE OMEN WALK

The important thing to do now is to keep your eyes open. Walk slowly and deliberately. Anytime you see one of your omen symbols, write it down. If you see many omen symbols, write them down in the order that you see them. Those that you see first will be closer in time to the present; those seen later will be further away from the present. If your system involves the runes or Ogham letters, look at the trees around you—don't just stare at the ground. If you have birds in your system, look in the sky for them. Use your common sense in where to look.

When you have reached the end of your walk and your ending point (or if you have to just sit in your backyard, after fifteen minutes have elapsed), sit down for a few minutes and bring yourself to your normal waking consciousness. If you find this difficult, go through the colors of the rainbow as before, but in reverse order: violet, indigo, blue, green, yellow, orange, red. This will bring you out of the light trance state fairly easily.

You may also want to have some tea and crackers on hand to drink and eat in order to fully close down your psychic centers.

INTERPRETATION

You may see only one or two omen symbols, you may see many, or you may see none. If the latter is true, the divination has failed, and you will have to do another Omen Walk in not more than twenty-four hours. If you have only one or two omen symbols, they should be fairly easy to interpret in light of your question. If you do not understand the meaning of the symbol in reference to your question, you must meditate on the question and the symbols received until the meaning dawns on you. It will also help you to perform the exercises given in Chapter Three. The meaning will reveal itself, if you persist.

If you received many omen symbols, interpret them in the order in which you saw them; those seen first will manifest as events first, those seen later will manifest as events later. Write out the symbols and interpretations if you have to, then make a story of your interpretations in reference to your question. You will thus have your answer.

It is likely that during your Omen Walk you will see many interesting things. However, do not take any notice of symbols that you have not programmed your subconscious mind to understand, no matter how significant they may seem to be. If you see a fox hunting through the woods and the fox is not one of your symbols, take no notice of it. (Unless, of course, it is hunting you, in which case, run like mad!) Do not write the fox down on your note pad. If, at the end of the Omen Walk, you find that you have written down some symbols that you have not worked with in meditation, simply cross them off the list.

Also, if you see one of your symbols either before you reach your starting point or after you have reached your ending point, do not write it down. It will have no meaning in your divination, no matter how significant it may seem.

CONCLUSION

The Omen Walk is a form of divination that can be great fun, especially when you become practiced in it. It really helps to intensify the feeling that the Universe really is an orderly place. Furthermore, you will begin to marvel at the power of your subconscious mind.

BASIC CIRCLE CASTING AND BANISHING

Here is a basic Circle opening and closing that you can use in conjunction with any of the forms of divination given in the preceding pages. Most Witches and Pagans are already acquainted with similar procedures from their own traditions and practices. The following is given for beginners to the Craft.

NECESSARY MATERIALS

First of all, you are going to need a ritual space. This need not be the traditional nine-foot Circle. It can be as small or as large as your needs dictate. If you are merely doing a divination at your altar, you may wish to construct only a five-foot or seven-foot Circle—just large enough for what you want to do. The altar should either occupy a central position or be placed in the north. You will need the following:

- A small dish of salt placed on the north side of the altar.
- A small bowl of water placed on the west side of the altar.
- A candle placed in the center of the altar.
- A small pot of earth set on the east side of the altar.
- A stick of incense, or a charcoal block with granulated incense in the pot of earth.
- A staff, wand, sword, or athame. If you have acquired none of these yet, use the index finger of your dominant hand.

- Any other materials that create an atmosphere for you—
  images of the God or Goddess, crystals, important magical
  possessions, or anything you consider special or magical.
- Any materials that you will need for your divination or
  spell work.

You may also place any magical tools that you own in their appropriate quarters, either on the floor or on or around your altar.

PREPARATION

As before any type of magical undertaking, you should make sure that you are clean and calm. A ritual bath beforehand may help in this. Add a handful of sea salt to a warm bath and say some appropriate words such as "Water, be thou cleansed and made holy by the power of the God and Goddess. May I be cleansed and made holy through thee." When you are finished, dry yourself with a rough towel. You may either be robed or skyclad in your work, as you wish.

When all is set, commence the Circle casting ritual.

THE CIRCLE CASTING

Light the central candle, and from it set your incense going. Take up your staff, wand, sword, or athame (or use the index finger of your dominant hand), and move to the east. Point your instrument to the floor and begin drawing a circle around your area. See a flame of bluish violet light emanating from the instrument, leaving a boundary of light as you recite the following words:

> *Be this my Circle,*
> *A Sphere of Protection,*
> *A Womb of the Goddess,*
> *A Boundary of Light.*

Stop when you reach the east again. Now draw another circle, about thigh level, commencing in the east again, visualizing the bluish violet light, and reciting the above incantation. When the second is completed, cast a third circle at chest level using the same procedure. Return your instrument to the altar.

Next, take up the bowl of water with both hands and hold it above the altar. As you say the following words, imagine that the water is glowing with the power of your blessing. Visualize this as the bluish violet light:

> *Creature of Water,*
> *Thou art blessed and made holy*
> *By the power of the God and Goddess.*

Replace the bowl on the altar and take up the bowl of salt. Again, hold it up and recite the following words, visualizing the bluish violet light emanating from it:

> *Creature of Earth,*
> *Thou art blessed and made holy*
> *By the power of the God and Goddess.*

Take three pinches of the salt and place them in the water. Stir it three times with the index finger of your dominant hand. Next, take up the candle from the center of the altar. Move to the east, raise the candle in a gesture of blessing, and say:

> *Fire, make thou holy*
> *The Quarter of East.*

Continue to the south, west, and north, substituting the appropriate direction each time you say the blessing. Make a full circle by returning to the east, and holding up the candle again in a gesture of blessing, silently. Return to the altar and take up the pot of earth with the incense. Move to the east, and raise it in a gesture of blessing, saying:

> *Air, make thou holy*
> *The Quarter of East.*

Continue to the south, west, and north, substituting the appropriate direction each time you say the blessing. Make a full circle by returning to the east, and holding up the incense again in a gesture of blessing, silently. Return to the altar and take up bowl of consecrated saltwater. Move to the east, and raise it in a gesture of blessing, saying:

Salt and Water, make thou holy
The Quarter of East.

Sprinkle a bit of the saltwater in the quarter. Continue to the south, west, and north, substituting the appropriate direction each time you say the blessing. Make a full circle by returning to the east, and holding up the bowl again in a gesture of blessing, silently. Return to the altar and replace the bowl.

Move to the center of the Circle facing north (if your altar is in the center, just stand before it facing north). Now raise your arms and say:

Sphere, thou art blessed,
A fit place for man,
A fit place for Gods,
Where Many are One.

Now move to the east and stand in the pentagram position (legs spread, arms out to sides at shoulder level, head erect). Call on the powers of air by saying:

I summon, stir, and call ye up,
Ye Mighty Ones of the East!
Spirits of Air, attend!

When you are finished reciting this, imagine a fierce wind blowing at you from the east in response to your call. Feel the wind blowing on your body. Hear its roar. Spend at least a minute doing this.

Move to the south, and stand in the pentagram position. Call on the powers of fire by saying:

I summon, stir, and call ye up,
Ye Mighty Ones of the South!
Spirits of Fire, attend!

When you are finished reciting this, imagine a raging fire springing up just outside the Circle boundary in response to your call. Feel the heat of the fire, hear it crackle, see its yellow, red, orange, and blue flames. Spend at least a minute doing this.

Move to the west, and stand in the pentagram position. Call on the powers of water by saying:

> *I summon, stir, and call ye up,*
> *Ye Mighty Ones of the West!*
> *Spirits of Water, attend!*

When you are finished reciting this, imagine the ground opening up just outside the Circle boundary in response to your call. It uncovers a blue-green sea. See the waves crashing just outside the circle. Hear the roar of the waves. Feel the spray of foam at your feet. Spend at least a minute doing this.

Move to the north, and assume the pentagram position. Call on the powers of earth by saying:

> *I summon, stir and call ye up,*
> *Ye Mighty Ones of the North!*
> *Spirits of Earth, attend!*

When you are finished reciting this, again imagine the ground opening up just outside the Circle boundary in response to your call. Out from it arises a snow-capped mountain. Feel the Earth tremble and shake as the mountain rises. Feel the coldness from the snow atop it. Hear the call of the woodland creatures that live there. Spend at least a minute doing this.

Now you will invoke the God and the Goddess. This should be done even if you are invoking another entity as a part of your divination (for example, invoking Hecate in the Sword Trance).

Face south, and call upon the God with the following incantation:

> *By burning fire at forest's edge,*
> *By cloven hooves on trampled hedge,*
> *By Oak and Ash that sift and sigh,*
> *By bay of hound and wolven cry,*
> *By flash of horn, by gleam of knife,*
> *By powers of Love, by powers of Strife,*
> *I call upon the Hornéd Lord*
> *To guard and guide me in my work!*

Spend a minute feeling the presence of the God entering the Circle. When you are finished, face north, and call upon the Goddess with the following incantation:

> *By fulsome Moon that rides the sky,*
> *By shadowed trees that sift and sigh,*
> *By hallowed land and sacred well,*
> *By charm and rune and magic spell,*
> *By fields of grain and fertile earth,*
> *By the holy womb that gave me birth,*
> *I call upon the Great Goddess*
> *To guard and guide me in my work!*

Spend a minute feeling the presence of the Goddess entering the Circle. When you are finished, proceed with the work for which you have cast the Circle.

THE CIRCLE BANISHING

When you have completed your work, and are ready to close down the Circle, move to the center of the Circle and give thanks to the God and Goddess with the following, or with words spoken from your heart:

> *Great Goddess and Hornéd Lord,*
> *I give thanks to you for your presence.*
> *Return to Sun and Forest, Moon and Sea,*
> *And may there ever be Peace between us.*

Now you must banish the forces you have previously summoned in the quarters. Move to the east and stand there with your arms open wide at shoulder level and your legs together. Say the following:

> *Powers and potencies of the East and Air,*
> *I give thanks to you for your presence.*
> *Return to your proper places*
> *And come again when you are called.*

Now bring your hands together in front of you, making a gesture as if you were closing curtains. Repeat this procedure in the south (substituting "south" and "fire" for "east" and "air"), west (substituting "west" and "water"), and the north (substituting "north" and "earth").

Now take up your Circle-casting instrument again (or use your finger). Move to the east. See the first glowing circle that you drew, the one closest to the floor. Point your instrument at it, and move widdershins (counter-clockwise), drawing up the flame back into the instrument. When you reach the east again, stop. Next, draw up the second circle you drew by the same procedure, again moving widdershins. Finally, draw up the third outermost circle by the same procedure.

When you are finished, place your instrument back on the altar. Put out the altar candle. Your Circle is now completely banished.

GLOSSARY OF
TERMS AND NAMES

Aesculapius—Greek god of medicine and healing. Son of Apollo (cf.) and the nymph Coronis. His cult was associated with caves, sleep, dreams, and serpents. See Chapter Eleven for additional information.

Agrippa, Henry Cornelius—Magician born in the city of Cologne in 1486. His most famous works are the *Three Books of Occult Philosophy*, a veritable gold mine of magical information. (A compendium of the *Three Books* is available from Llewellyn Publications, translated by James Freake, and masterfully annotated by Donald Tyson.)

aleuromancy—Divination by interpreting the patterns revealed after casting or scattering flour or meal. Interpretations are done as in tea-leaf reading—looking for symbols or shapes that are significant.

Apollo—Greek god of the sun, music, poetry. One of the twelve Olympians, a son of Zeus and Leto, and twin brother to the Moon goddess Artemis. Also a god of medicine and prophecy.

augury—The modern meaning of this word is associated with general divination or "fortune telling." More specifically, however, it refers to divination based on the manifestation of natural phenomenon. Vocabulary purists might even assign a more specific definition: divination based on flight patterns of birds.

Avalon—The magical Isle of Apples, associated with the Celtic Otherworld. Said to be the place whither King Arthur was carried by the three mystical queens who collected him after his death at the hands of his son, Mordred.

Awen—A Druidic term that refers to divine inspiration or enlightenment.

black mirror—A scrying device used to induce clairvoyant or prophetic visions. Also occasionally used in the invocation of spirits or other discarnate entities. It often takes the form of a concave piece of glass, painted black on one side, and mounted in a frame.

bodhran—A specific type of Celtic drum.

caduceus—Symbol of the god Hermes/Mercury. An emblem of wisdom and medicine. A knobbed and winged staff with two serpents twined around it.

Cassandra—Princess of ancient Troy, daughter of King Priam and Queen Hecuba. Apollo fell in love with her, and promised to grant her any wish she desired if she would be his lover. She asked for the gift of prophecy. He granted the gift, but she would not make good on her part of the bargain. Because he could not withdraw his gift, Apollo punished her by placing a curse on her that no one would ever believe what she prophesied. Many years later, Cassandra foresaw the fall of Troy, and wandered through the streets of that city trying to warn its inhabitants, but no one believed her, to their later dismay. The moral of the story is: keep your bargains with the gods.

Cernunnos—(cf. Herne) Ancient Celtic god of the forests and woodlands. Remains of his worship have been found throughout Europe and the British Isles. He is sometimes known as the Lord of Revelry or Misrule, and is associated with the Wild Hunt (cf.).

Coelbren—An ancient magical Druidic alphabet. Comes from a Welsh word for the tablets of wood upon which the letters of the alphabet were engraved or drawn. See Chapter Nine on the Druid's Wand for more details.

Cumaen Sybil—The most famous human prophetess of the ancient world. Apollo granted her the gift of prophecy and a thousand years of life, but she forgot to ask for eternal youth as well. She eventually became so shrivelled and ghastly looking from such extreme old age that she begged Apollo to release her from her fleshly prison. He did so by turning her into a grasshopper. For this reason, you might consider using the chirping of a grasshopper as one of your omens in your Omen Walk (see Chapter Twelve).

Daughters—The secondary figures calculated in a geomancy reading. Daughters are derived from the Mothers.

divination—The practice of measuring and weighing inner plane forces to discern how they will manifest in a given situation on the physical plane. More generally, the practice of discerning future events or contemporaneous events taking place at a distance.

dowsing—*See* water witching.

Druid cubit—A measurement of twenty and four-fifths inches, which the scholar William Stukeley discovered was the "base measure" for the construction of Stonehenge and other stone circles.

Futhark—Also known as the Norse runes or the Futhark runes, this is the term for various Norse alphabets. Two important ones are the Elder Futhark (which has twenty-four runes), and the Younger Futhark (which has sixteen runes). The Norse god Odin was said to have sacrificed himself on the World Tree in order to obtain them, and are considered to embody great wisdom and teaching. (See the suggested reading list for books on the subject.)

geomancy—Literally, "divination by means of earth," though you may occasionally see this term also used to refer to the study of ley lines or various power centers and tracks running over the Earth's surface. More widely used to refer to a divination system involving chance production of four divination figures from which other figures are derived, then interpreted. *See also* Daughters, Judge, Mothers, Nephews, Reconciler, Witnesses.

Haphaestus—Greek god of smithcraft and fire. Son of Zeus and Hera. See Chapter Ten on the Dance of the Lame God for the story of his birth and disabling fall.

Haruspex—A practitioner of the ancient Roman divination method using entrails (often the liver) of certain sacrificial animals. The practice is known as haruspicy. This form of divination is still with us, though in a modified form using the yolks and whites of eggs.

Hecate Antea—Greek goddess of Witchcraft, crossroads, and the night, named here with her epithet "Antea," meaning "giver of night visions." See Chapter Eleven on the Sword Trance for additional information.

Hermanubis—Greco-Egyptian composite of the Greek god Hermes and the Egyptian god Anubis, associated with divination and the guiding of souls. You can see a depiction of this jackal-like god in most Tarot decks on the Wheel of Fortune card.

Herne—Celtic god associated with Cernunnos (cf.). Master of the Wild Hunt. See Chapter Four on Herne's Head for additional information.

I Ching—An ancient Chinese system of divination using yarrow stalks or coins.

Ifá—Another ancient method of divination using nuts or shells, originating with the Yoruba people of Northern Africa.

imbas forosna—A Druidic method of inducing the enlightened state of mind necessary for the practice of divination or prophecy. Involves seclusion in a dark place for a period of time, followed by an abrupt entrance into a brightly lit environment.

Judge—The final figure of geomancy information that serves as a primary source as an answer to the divination question.

lithomancy—Divination by means of stones. Can take many forms, one of which is presented in Chapter Eight, "Talking Stones."

lunar mansions—A system of dividing the sphere of the heavens into twenty-eight equal compartments, with divination meanings assigned to each division. Known in many ancient cultures such as the Arabic, Greek, Roman cultures.

macrocosm—The "greater world," the Universe.

microcosm—The "lesser world," often used to refer to the Universe within every person.

Mothers—The initial figures of a geomancy reading.

Nephews—The tertiary figures of a geomancy reading, calculated from the Mothers and Daughters.

nuts of wisdom—In Celtic lore, these are usually hazelnuts—the fruit of the hazel tree. They are said to drop into a sacred well underneath a tree, where they are consumed by salmon, which are also associated with wisdom and knowledge in Celtic lore.

Ogham—A term for any number of magical Celtic alphabets. There are Oghams based on trees, animals, flowers, et cetera.

omen—A thing or happening, usually unexpected, that reveals a future event.

planetary intelligences—In geomancy readings, any question can be assigned to a planet, according to the nature of the question. Each planet has an "intelligence," or guiding entity that is invoked prior to the geomancy divination so that the mind of the person performing the divination is properly attuned to receive and correctly interpret the divination answer. See Chapter Seven, "A Witch's Geomancy" for more information.

psychism—Sensitivity to forces beyond the physical or "sense-based" world.

psychometry—The practice of picking up psychic impressions about a person or place from objects associated with the person or place (or that were once in contact with them).

querent—A questioner or person asking the question during a divination. May be the actual diviner.

Reconciler—A geomancy figure formed from the first Mother and the Judge. Only calculated when previous interpretations of the Witnesses and Judge are unclear.

scry—To gaze, most often referring to a crystal ball, a black mirror, or any other reflective surface that may induce a clairvoyant state. Also occasionally used to refer to seeing astral visions.

skyclad—Nude. A preferred method of worshipping and doing magic and divination by some Witches and Pagans.

triads—Also known as the Welsh Triads or the Bardic Triads. Very often these are wisdom-sayings that involve three different things or situations, showing a single underlying connection between them. Laws were also codified in triads. They embody spiritual, moral, and legal precepts.

water witching—Also known as dowsing. The practice of searching out a material or substance by means of a forked stick, pendulum, or similar devices. Commonly used in rural areas to seek out underground wells. The technique may also be used to search for lost items, minerals, et cetera. During World War II and the Vietnam and Korean Wars, some military personnel were trained to seek out enemy vessels or traps by this method.

Wild Hunt—A pack of ghostly or Otherworldly dogs led over the English countryside by their master, who is identified with Herne and Cernunnos. Sometimes said to be a presaging sign of disaster, storms, et cetera. though also said to be the means by which the spirits of the newly deceased are collected and ushered to the Otherworld.

Witnesses, Right and Left—Two geomancy figures derived from the Nephews. The Witnesses are important in a geomancy divination as influences on the question or situation by themselves, and also as the figures from which the final Judge is derived.

xylomancy—Divination involving the rustling of leaves or trees, or by symbols marked on wood. ("Xylon" is Greek for "wood.")

BIBLIOGRAPHY AND SUGGESTED READING

Throughout my ten years in the Craft, I've found information and inspiration in many different books and authors. The divination systems described in this book draw upon these sources and their information.Below is a list of recommended books, organized by general subject. A short commentary follows each, indicating the usefulness of the book in studying divination. I have included books covering standard forms of divination as well as Tarot, astrology, and geomancy.

WICCA

Buckland, Raymond. *Complete Book of Witchcraft*. St. Paul, MN: Llewellyn Publications, 1988.

A very good introduction to Wicca, set in a series of lessons through which the reader can progress. Includes a good chapter on divination.

Crowther, Patricia, *Lid off the Cauldron*. York Beach, ME: Samuel Weiser, Inc., 1985.

This book contains a system of divination using stones.

Cunningham, Scott. *Wicca: A Guide for the Solitary Practitioner*. St. Paul, MN: Llewellyn Publications, 1988.

An excellent introduction to Wicca. A Book of Shadows comprises the last part of the book. Divination is also covered.

Huson, Paul. *Mastering Witchcraft*. New York: G. P. Putnam's Sons, 1970).

An excellent beginner's guide with a full chapter on divination.

Valiente, Doreen. *ABCs of Witchcraft: Past and Present*. Custer, WA: Phoenix Publishing, Inc., 1973.

A good general introduction to Witchcraft set in encyclopedia format. Many good entries of different divination topics: scrying, Tarot, et cetera.

—————. *Witchcraft for Tomorrow*. Custer, WA: Phoenix Publishing, Inc., 1978.

This book is of particular interest in that it mentions a system of divination by stones, similar to the Talking Stones system presented in this book. Also covers scrying. The last part of the book contains a simplified, but excellent, Book of Shadows.

MAGIC AND MAGICAL THEORY

Agrippa, Henry Cornelius. *Three Books of Occult Philosophy Written by Henry Cornelius Agrippa of Nettesheim*. Translated by James Freake. Edited and Annotated by Donald Tyson. St. Paul, MN: Llewellyn Publications, 1993.

Butler, W. Ernest. *The Magician: His Training and Work*. North Hollywood, CA: Wilshire Book Co., 1969.

Though the author does not explicitly discuss divination, he presents magical theory very well and presents much information on the power and training of the subconscious mind.

Fortune, Dion, *Practical Occultism in Daily Life*. Wellingborough, England: Aquarian Press, 1985.

This book is of interest for its short chapter on divination. While the author uses the Tarot as her primary example, many of the principles she mentions are applicable to other divination systems.

—————. *Through the Gates of Death*. Wellingborough, Northamptionshire, U.K.: Aquarian Press, 1987).

A good book to read in conjunction with Chapter Ten, "The Dance of the Lame God."

Kraig, Donald M. *Modern Magick*. St. Paul, MN: Llewellyn Publications, 1988.

A very good introduction to both "low" and "high" magic, presented in lesson format. This book also contains good information on how the subconscious mind works.

TAROT

Abraham, Sylvia. *How to Read the Tarot: The Keyword System*. St. Paul, MN: Llewellyn Publications, 1994.

This book presents the Tarot in an easy-to-read format, and is a good introduction to practical Tarot divination.

Ashcroft-Nowicki, Dolores. *Inner Landscapes*. Wellingborough, England: Aquarian Press, 1989.

Not a book about Tarot divination per se, but a series of pathworkings designed to acquaint the reader with the esoteric meanings of the Major Arcana. Helpful in that the spiritual principles embodied in each pathworking can help the reader to more fully understand the cards in divination.

Compton, Madonna. *Archetypes on the Tree of Life: Tarot as Pathwork*. St. Paul, MN: Llewellyn Publications, 1991.

Another good book involving learning the deeper meanings of the Major Arcana through pathworking.

Gray, Eden. *Complete Guide to the Tarot*. New York City: Bantam Books, 1972.

A mass-produced paperback that you can find in almost any bookstore. It is a very good introduction to the Tarot as a system of divination.

Peach, Emily. *The Tarot Workbook*. Wellingborough, England: Aquarian Press, 1984.

—————. *Tarot for Tomorrow*. Wellingborough, England: Aquarian Press, 1988.

Both of these books are excellent. The first is something of a primer for the second. Both of them present Tarot in terms of Qabalah.

ASTROLOGY

George, Llewellyn. *The New A to Z Horoscope Maker and Delineator*. St. Paul, MN: Llewellyn Publications, 1981.

A good introduction to astrology, taking the reader all the way from mathematical calculations to interpretation of the natal chart, progressions, and transits. A classic text.

Hewitt, William. *Astrology for Beginners*. St. Paul, MN: Llewellyn Publications, 1992.

A very good introductory text.

Lewi, Grant. *Astrology for the Millions*. St. Paul, MN: Llewellyn Publications, 1990.

—————. *Heaven Knows What*. St. Paul, MN: Llewellyn Publications, 1990.

Both of these books are classics in their field. They present astrology as a "ready-to-use" system.

Paterson, Helena. *The Handbook of Celtic Astrology*. St. Paul, MN: Llewellyn Publications, 1994.

A skillful combination of astrology and teachings on the Celtic Tree Calendar.

Volguine, Alexander. *Lunar Astrology*. New York: ASI Publishers Inc., 1974.

An excellent introduction to the twenty-eight lunar mansions for both beginning and advanced students of astrology.

Ryneveld, Edna. *Transits in Reverse*. St. Paul, MN: Llewellyn Publications, 1988.

A comprehensive view of transits and how they can be used to predict future trends.

SCRYING AND CLAIRVOYANCE

Butler, W. Ernest. *How to Develop Clairvoyance*. Wellingborough, England: Aquarian Press, 1979.

An easy-to-read introduction to developing clairvoyance.

Tyson, Donald. *How to Make and Use a Magic Mirror*. St. Paul, MN: Llewellyn Publications, 1990.

An excellent and affordable introduction to clairvoyance through mirror gazing.

NUMEROLOGY

Coates, Austin. *Numerology: The Meaning of Numbers*. New York: Carol Publishing Group, 1991.

An excellent guide in the analysis of numerology charts.

Goodwin, Matthew Oliver. *Numerology: The Complete Guide* (two volumes). North Hollywood, CA: Newcastle Publishing Company, Inc., 1981.

A comprehensive guide to all facets of number symbolism and interpretation, including how to forecast future life trends with numerology.

NORSE RUNES

Gundarsson, Kveldulf. *Teutonic Magic: The Magical and Spiritual Practices of the Germanic Peoples*. St. Paul, MN: Llewellyn Publications, 1990.

Focuses on the Elder Futhark alphabet in divination, ritual, and talismanic magic contexts.

Peschel, Lisa. *Practical Guide to the Runes*. St. Paul, MN: Llewellyn Publications, 1990.

Presents a Norse form of divination using twenty-five runes. Very thorough interpretations are given for each rune, including various combinations of runes falling together in a reading. Also includes a large section on using the Norse runes in magic—making amulets, talismans, et cetera.

Thorsson, Edred. *Northern Magic*. St. Paul, MN: Llewellyn Publications, 1992.

A good introduction to the religious practices of the Northern traditions. Includes information on the runes.

CELTIC LORE

Glass-Koentop, Patti. *Year of Moons, Season of Trees*. St. Paul, MN: Llewellyn Publications, 1991.

Gives much information on the trees associated with the Celtic Ogham letters. Also includes various rites and rituals using the symbolism and teachings of different trees throughout the year.

Thorsson, Edred. *The Book of Ogham: The Celtic Tree Oracle*. St. Paul, MN: Llewellyn Publications, 1992.

A gold mine of information about the Celtic Ogham letters and their use in divination.

GOLDEN DAWN

Cicero, Chic and Sandra Tabatha. *The Golden Dawn Journal, Book One: Divination*. St. Paul, MN: Llewellyn Publications, 1994.

A fine compendium of several divination systems, including Tarot, geomancy, augury, et cetera.

Zalewski, Christine. *Enochian Chess of the Golden Dawn*. St. Paul, MN: Llewellyn Publications, 1994.

The Enochian chess game can be used as a divination system in conjunction with meanings derived from the Enochian tablets and astrology. Though Enochian chess was played by members of the Golden Dawn earlier this century, this book is the first comprehensive view of this fascinating system.

HISTORY AND MYTHOLOGY

Frazer, James George. *The Golden Bough*. London: Oxford University Press, 1994.

Originally a multi-volume work, though several abridgements are now available.

Hamilton, Edith. *Mythology*. New York: Penguin Books, 1989.

Mythology for story tellers and story lovers.

Morford, Mark P. O., and Robert J. Lenardon. *Classical Mythology*. White Plains, NY: Longman, Inc., 1985.

A wonderful presentation of mythology in a semi-historical context.

Rolleston, T. W. *Celtic Myths and Legends*. New York: Dover Publications, Inc., 1990.

An excellent resource.

Spence, Lewis. *The Mysteries of Britain*. London: Bracken Books, 1993.

This book mentions the Coelbren of the Bards, as well as a source for it—a Welsh manuscript called *The Barddas*.

Squire, Charles. *Celtic Myths and Legends*. New York: Grammercy Books, 1994.

An excellent resource.

Zimmerman, J. E. *Dictionary of Classical Mythology*. New York: Bantam Books, 1996.

An excellent basic resource work.

MISCELLANEOUS

Cunningham, Scott. *The Complete Book of Incense, Oils and Brews*. St. Paul, MN: Llewellyn Publications, 1991.

This book will be of interest to the practitioner of divination since it presents several recipes for incenses, perfumes, and teas that help enhance psychic awareness.

INDEX

A

Aesculapius, 214–215
Agrippa, Henry Cornelius, 101
Antea, see Hecate Antea
Apollo, 3, 214–215
apple, 57–58, 75–76, 78, 80–81,
    84–85, 93, 184, 237
apple seeds, 37, 58, 75–76, 78, 81,
    83–87, 89–98
Aquarius, 49
Aries, 44
Arthur, 32
astral plane, 4, 6, 28, 203, 206, 209,
    212, 217–218, 229
attendant, 209–211
Avalon, 75
Awen, 34, 37, 41–42

B

Bartzabel, 108
Beltane, 78–80, 82, 96–97, 206
bird, 11, 22, 34, 37, 40, 50, 80, 163,
    227–228, 238, 242
bodhran, 76
bodies (of a geomancy figure),
    13–14, 110–112, 153, 183–184,
    204, 209

C

Cancer, 45
Candlemas, 79–80, 94–95, 97, 103
Capricorn, 49
Case, Paul Foster, 203
Cassandra, 3
Cernunnos, 31
chalice, 34, 37, 41–42, 80–82,
    112–114, 117, 120–123, 127,
    130–138, 141, 146–147, 150–151
Chasmodai, 108
Circle, casting and banishing, 36,
    66, 81, 83, 165, 207, 211,
    216–217, 222–223, 245–251
Coelbren of the Bards, 185–187,
    190
consecration, 36, 38, 66–67, 81, 83,
    103–105, 165, 188, 216
crossbar, 34, 37, 54, 216
crown, 20, 65, 70, 80
Crowther, Patricia, 203
cubit, see Druid cubit
Cunningham, Scott, 207

D

dance, 201–209, 211–212
Daughters, 106, 110–111, 154

dream notebook, 213, 217, 219,
    221–222, 225
dreams
    interpreting, 223–224
Druid cubit, 184
Druidic Triads, 7, 190–198
Druids, 7, 24, 184–186, 190,
    192–193, 227
drums, 3, 7, 13, 75–79, 81–82, see
    also Witch's Drum

E
eight-pointed star, 34, 37, 43, 75, 79
Elder Futhark, see Futhark, Elder
equinox
    autumn, xiii, 79–80, 95–96
    spring, 79–80, 95
eye (symbol), 34, 51, 65, 67, 70, 157

F
feet (of a geomancy figure), 106,
    110–112, 153
Fludd, Robert, 101
Fortune, Dion, 204
free will, 26
Futhark (Elder), 233–235

G
Gemini, 45
geomancy
    A Witch's geomancy chart (dia-
        gram), 106
    figures
            table, 113
            how to form, 109–112
            explanations, 112–117

H
Hallows, 78–79, 81–82, 84, 94, 96,
    204, 206
Haphaestus, 202–203

heads (of a geomancy figure),
    110–112, 153, 217
Hecate Antea, 5, 215, 217–223, 249
Hermanubis, 32
Hermes, 32
Herne, 7, 31–32, 60
Herne's Head (diagram and sym-
    bols), 34–37
High Priestess (Tarot card), 15,
    19–21, 24
hilt, 34, 37, 40, 55, 216, 219
Hismael, 108
House of the Goddess (diagram and
    symbols), 63–65
Huson, Paul, 75

I
I Ching, 8, 102
Ifá, 155
imbas forosna, 24
incense, 19–20, 22, 36, 38, 66–67,
    81–83, 104–105, 115, 165–167,
    216, 219, 221, 223, 245–247
intelligences, planetary, 108

J
Judge, 102, 105–106, 112, 117–119,
    123–124, 126, 129–133, 139, 143,
    147, 153–154
Judgement (Tarot card), 202–203
Jupiter, 107–108, 113, 115–117,
    157, 160, 170, 172–173, 175–178,
    181, 203

K
Kedemel, 108

L
labrys, 63, 69
Lammas, 79–80, 94–95
Law of Correspondences, 10, 12, 18

Leo, 46, 65, 70
Libra, 47
Light Stone, 33, 38–40, 59–60
lightning, 65, 70, 227–228, 238
lithomancy, 156, 181
Lord of the Winds, 20, 241–242
Lovers (Tarot card), 15, 21–23, 241–242
lunar mansions, 61, 63

M
Mabinogion, 31–32
macrocosm, 12
Magician (Tarot card), 15, 20, 27
Mars, 80, 107–108, 113–116, 136, 157, 159–160, 170, 172–173, 175–177
Master of the Wild Hunt, 32
maze, 34, 37, 58
Mercury, 20–24, 27, 32, 107–108, 113, 115–116, 157–159, 164, 170, 172–174, 228
microcosm, 12
mistletoe, 34, 37, 40, 80
moon
    full moon, 32, 36, 66, 80–81, 103–104, 156, 185, 187–189, 206, 217, 220
    waning, 43, 65, 73, 80, 185, 189
    waxing, 47, 66, 80, 185, 189
moonstone, 61-62, 66-68, 72, 164
Mothers, 106, 110–111, 154

N
necks (of a geomancy figure), 106, 110–112, 153
Nephews, 106, 111–112, 154
Norse runes, see runes
Nostradamus, 3, 156
number symbolism, 238
nuts, 34, 230

O
ocean, 214, 231–232
Odin, 5, 20
Ogham alphabet, 183, 227, 233, 236–238, 242
Owain, 31–32

P
Pan, 27
pentagram, 76, 78, 108–109, 163, 216, 219, 248–249
Peschel, Lisa, 233
Pisces, 50, 160, 203
pituitary gland, 34
planetary intelligences, see intelligences, planetary
pouch, 105, 164–167, 183
purification, 27–28, 80, 107
prophecy, 3, 7, 15, 17, 21, 23, 215, see also Voice of Prophecy

Q
Qabalah, 6, 14, 156, 202, 229

R
Reconciler, 153–154
runes (Norse), xii, 232–233, 242–243

S
Sagittarius, 48, 203
Saturn, 34, 65, 72, 107–108, 113, 115–116, 157, 161, 170, 172, 174–178, 181
Scorpio, 48, 65, 71
scrying, xi–xii, 6–7, 210
scythe, 65
serpent, 34, 37, 40, 58–59, 65, 72, 80, 218, 220
shades (of the dead), 203–206, 208
Shadow Stone, 33, 38–40, 59–60
sickle, 65, 80

sigils (of the planetary spirits), 108–109

sleep, 24, 44, 58, 167, 213–214, 216–217, 219, 221–222, 225

sleeping charm, 221–222

solstice
summer, 79–80, 95
winter, 79–80, 94

Sorath, 108

sortilege, 155

spears, 63, 69, 160

Stukeley, William, 184

sword, 20, 34, 37, 39–40, 53–54, 63, 69, 80, 114, 160, 215–217, 219, 222, 245–246

subconscious mind, xii, 11–12, 15, 17, 19, 21–22, 24, 27, 41, 183, 213–215, 217, 228–232, 238, 240, 243–244, see also Universal Subconcious Mind

sun, 12, 14-15, 34, 37, 56, 67, 80, 103, 105, 107-109, 113, 157-158, 169, 171-173, 184, 188, 214, 217, 222, 228, 238, 250

T

Talking Stones (suggested symbols)
Home Stone, 162
Jupiter Stone, 160
Life Stone, 161–162
Magic Stone, 163
Mars Stone, 160
Mercury Stone, 158–159
Moon Stone, 158
News Stone, 163
Other Stone, 164
Querent Stone, 157
Saturn Stone, 160
Sun Stone, 158
Venus Stone, 159
Taphthartharath, 108

Tarot, xi–xii, 5, 7, 14–15, 18–19, 27, 159, 202–203, 232

Taurus, 44, 80, 115

Thorsson, Edred, 233

triads, see Druidic Triads

triangle, 34, 37, 51–53, 65, 71–72, 116, 162, 217

U

Universal Subconscious Mind, 214, 231–232, see also subconcious mind

V

Valiente, Doreen, 207

Venus, 65, 69, 80, 107–108, 113–115, 117, 140, 157, 159, 164, 170, 172–174, 176

Virgo, 46

Voice of Prophecy, 3, 15, 21, 23
see also prophecy

W

wand, 5, 7, 20, 101, 168, 183–185, 187–190, 196–197, 245–246

water witches, 4

Wicca, 4–6, 10, 12, 28, 207

Wild Hunt, 32

winged disk, 65, 71, 159

Witch's Drum (diagram), 79

Witch Stone, 103–105, 109–110

Witnesses, 102, 105, 112, 117–119, 124, 126, 129–133, 139, 143, 147, 154

Y

"yes or no" questions, 68, 181

Yesod, 6, 229

Yoruba, 155

Z

Zazel, 108

STAY IN TOUCH. . .

Llewellyn publishes hundreds of books on your favorite subjects.

On the following pages you will find listed some books now available on related subjects. Your local bookstore stocks most of these and will stock new Llewellyn titles as they become available. We urge your patronage.

Order by Phone

Call toll-free within the U.S. and Canada, 1-800-THE MOON.
In Minnesota, call (612) 291-1970.
We accept Visa, MasterCard, and American Express.

Order by Mail

Send the full price of your order (MN residents add 7% sales tax) in U.S. funds to:

    Llewellyn Worldwide
    P.O. Box 64383, Dept. K054-X
    St. Paul, MN 55164–0383, U.S.A.

Postage and Handling

- $4.00 for orders $15.00 and under.
- $5.00 for orders over $15.00.
- No charge for orders over $100.00.

We ship UPS in the continental United States. We cannot ship to P.O. boxes. Orders shipped to Alaska, Hawaii, Canada, Mexico, and Puerto Rico will be sent first-class mail.

International orders: Airmail—add freight equal to price of each book to the total price of order, plus $5.00 for each non-book item (audiotapes, etc.). Surface mail—Add $1.00 per item.

Allow 4 to 6 weeks delivery on all orders. Postage and handling rates subject to change.

Group Discounts

We offer a 20% quantity discount to group leaders or agents. You must order a minimum of 5 copies of the same book to get our special quantity price.

FREE CATALOG

Get a free copy of our color catalog, *New Worlds of Mind and Spirit*. Subscribe for just $10.00 in the United States and Canada ($20.00 overseas, first class mail). Many bookstores carry *New Worlds*—ask for it!

Buckland's Complete Book of Witchcraft
Raymond Buckland

Here is the most complete resource to the study and practice of modern, non-denominational Wicca. This is a lavishly illustrated, self-study course for the solitary or group. Included are rituals; exercises for developing psychic talents; information on all major "sects" of the Craft; sections on tools, beliefs, dreams, meditations, divination, herbal lore, healing, ritual clothing and much, much more. This book unites theory and practice into a comprehensive course designed to help you develop into a practicing Witch, one of the "Wise Ones." It is written by Ray Buckland, a very famous and respected authority on Witchcraft who first came public with the Old Religion in the United States. Large format with workbook-type exercises, profusely illustrated and full of music and chants. Takes you from A to Z in the study of Witchcraft.

Never before has so much information on the Craft of the Wise been collected in one place. Traditionally, there are three degrees of advancement in most Wiccan traditions. When you have completed studying this book, you will be the equivalent of a Third-Degree Witch. Even those who have practiced Wicca for years find useful information in this book, and many covens are using this for their textbook. If you want to become a Witch, or if you merely want to find out what Witchcraft is really about, you will find no better book than this.

0-87542-050-8, 272 pp., 8½ x 11, illus., softcover   **$14.95**

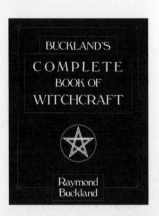

Wicca
A Guide for the Solitary Practitioner

Scott Cunningham

Wicca is a book of life, and how to live magically, spiritually, and wholly attuned with Nature. It is a book of sense and common sense, not only about Magick, but about religion and one of the most critical issues of today: how to achieve the much needed and wholesome relationship with out Earth. Cunningham presents Wicca as it is today: a gentle, Earth-oriented religion dedicated to the Goddess and God. This book fulfills a need for a practical guide to solitary Wicca—a need which no previous book has fulfilled.

Here is a positive, practical introduction to the religion of Wicca, designed so that any interested person can learn to practice the religion alone, anywhere in the world. It presents Wicca honestly and clearly, without the pseudo-history that permeates other books. It shows that Wicca is a vital, satisfying part of twentieth century life.

This book presents the theory and practice of Wicca from an individual's perspective. The section on the Standing Stones Book of Shadows contains solitary rituals for the Esbats and Sabbats. This book, based on the author's nearly two decades of Wiccan practice, presents an eclectic picture of various aspects of this religion. Exercises designed to develop magical proficiency, a self-dedication ritual, herb, crystal and rune magic, recipes for Sabbat feasts, are included in this excellent book.

0-87542-118-0, 240 pp., 6 x 9, illus., softcover   **$9.95**

Prices subject to change without notice
To order, call 1-800-THE MOON

The Three Books of Occult Philosophy
Completely Annotated, with Modern Commentary— The Foundation Book of Western Occultism
Henry Cornelius Agrippa
edited and annotated by Donald Tyson

Agrippa's *Three Books of Occult Philosophy* is the single most important text in the history of Western occultism. Occultists have drawn upon it for five centuries, although they rarely give it credit. First published in Latin in 1531 and translated into English in 1651, it has never been reprinted in its entirety since. Photocopies are hard to find and very expensive. Now, for the first time in 500 years, *Three Books of Occult Philosophy* will be presented as Agrippa intended. There were many errors in the original translation, but occult author Donald Tyson has made the corrections and has clarified the more obscure material with copious notes.

This is a necessary reference tool not only for all magicians, but also for scholars of the Renaissance, Neoplatonism, the Western Kabbalah, the history of ideas and sciences and the occult tradition. It is as practical today as it was 500 years ago.

0-87542-832-0, 1,024 pp., 7 x 10, softcover   **$39.95**

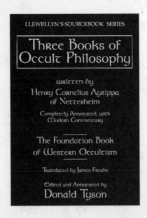